REVOLUTION IN BANKING

Second Edition

New Fed Policies, New Technologies, Legislative/de Facto Deregulation, and Powerful Market Forces Bring the Rapid Homogenization of the U.S. Financial Services Industry

Elbert V. Bowden
Judith L. Holbert

Reston Publishing Company
A Prentice-Hall Company
Reston, Virginia

Library of Congress Cataloging in Publication Data

Bowden, Elbert V.
Revolution in banking.

Includes bibliographies and index.
1. Banks and banking—United States. 2. Banking law—United States. I. Holbert, Judith L. II. Title.
HG2491.B59 1984 332.1'0973 84-3363
ISBN 0-8359-6682-8

A Prentice-Hall Company
Reston, Virginia 22090

10 9 8 7 6 5 4 3 2 1

Printed in the United States of America.

Preface

Profound changes are occurring in the nation's financial services industry. These changes are more basic and far-reaching than anything that has happened in banking since the near-collapse of the banking system during the depression years of the 1930s. A revolution in banking in the 1980s? Yes.

Dramatic Change Since the First Edition of this Book (1980)

The first edition of this book was written in 1980 just after the March 1980 banking act was passed. That act was a truly revolutionary package of legislation. But it was clear even at that time that the 1980 act didn't come close to resolving all of the serious problems of the American financial system. Many unrealistic and no longer tenable anti-competitive distortions remained.

What has happened since then? So much and so fast that it's difficult to comprehend.

During the first few years of the 1980s the financial services industry has broken loose from the past. Truly, it's a "new world" in the nation's financial markets and in the industry. How did it happen? And what does it mean for all of us (individuals, businesses) as users of financial services? And what does it mean for the economy? And for the Fed's monetary policy? And for the individual depository institutions (commercial banks, savings and loan associations, savings banks, credit unions)? And what's the outlook from here on? Those are the things you'll be reading about in this book.

Market Forces, New Technology, and New Legislation Are Breaking Down the Barriers

What's happening? In a word, you might say that the basic laws of economics—the competitive forces of the marketplace—are deregulating our banking and financial services system. And the computer-telecommunications-technology revolution is tripling or quadrupling the speed of change. Also, some of the recent Congressional and state legislative actions are having a lot to do with it.

Anyone—any member of the general public—who wants to understand what's happening around them *must* somehow obtain an understanding of what's happening in the financial services industry during the 1980s. That's the exciting story that is told in this book.

No Specialized Knowledge Required

This book does not presuppose that you have any specialized knowledge either of banking and finance or of economics. When the sophisticated concepts and terminology of banking, finance, and economics are discussed, they are always explained in easily understandable terms. So to the student or to the "non-economist" this book can serve well as an exercise in applied economics.

We have tried to design this book to be interesting and informative reading, not only for bankers and other members of the financial community, but also for students and for those members of the general public who like to keep informed on vital current issues.

This book is not written in "traditional textbook style." Because of the excitement going on in banking and finance it hardly seems appropriate to "deaden" these exciting issues by using traditional textbook format and exposition. So we have tried to make this book *interesting,* as well as clear, accurate, and informative.

As you read this book you will gain a factual awareness and understanding of the vitally important changes that are occurring in the nation's financial institutions and markets. And you also will gain an "intuitive feel" about what is going on and why, and about the attitudes of the members of the financial community regarding these revolutionary changes that are having such profound impact on all of them.

Sources of Information

The book begins with an introductory part highlighting the current issues and placing all this in historical perspective. Then each of the subsequent parts contains explanations and discussion on one of these issues. The final part focuses on the future outlook and offers success strategies for the banks and thrifts in this "new world" of the 1980s.

Throughout the book the discussions are enriched by statements of senior bank officers. They are the ones who are dealing with these issues on a daily basis, and they recognize the significance of correctly assessing this rapidly changing environment as the key to the future success of their own financial institutions.

Information in this book also has been drawn from recent testimony before the Banking Committees of the United States House and Senate, data compiled by the American Bankers Association in Washington, various issues of the *Federal Reserve Bulletin,* research findings and articles published in the reports and papers of the various Federal Reserve banks, various issues of professional journals in economics, business, and finance, and from recent issues of *The Wall Street Journal, Business Week, The American Banker,* and other business news sources.

Acknowledgments

Most of the statements by various bank officers reported in this book have been condensed, edited, and sometimes paraphrased by the authors. Any errors that may appear are the responsibility of the authors, not of the bank officer quoted.

The authors hereby express their appreciation to the many members of the banking and financial community whose willingness to share their ideas has contributed greatly to this book, and to Betty Webb, whose cheerful willingness to put it all together and meet an impossible time schedule certainly has been performance far above and beyond the call of duty. Thank you, Betty.

Elbert V. Bowden
Judith L. Holbert

Contents

Foreword

The Banking Act of March 1980 (Depository Institutions Deregulation and Monetary Control Act—DIDMCA) was described as "revolutionary"—as "the most important banking legislation in the past half-century." Then two and one-half years later, the Banking Act of 1982 (the Garn–St. Germain Act) was again termed "revolutionary"—and as "the most important banking legislation in the past half-century."

Then in November of 1983, Senator Garn, Chairman of the Senate Banking Committee, introduced another major banking bill (not expected to pass before late 1984—or perhaps sometime in 1985—or 1986?). The new Garn bill was referred to in the same "revolutionary" terms as the banking laws of 1980 and 1982.

At the same time that the Congress was passing new laws, new banking laws were being considered by state legislatures all over the country. Since 1980 more than 15 states have passed new legislation dealing with the structure and functions of banking. Several states passed laws to try to attract out-of-state banks.

Why are all of these legislative changes happening so fast? And what about the other, non-legislative (*de facto*) changes? By early 1984 the changes are having an impact so profound that it's difficult to conceptualize. Once you succeed in getting it conceptualized, it's difficult to believe.

Market Forces Are Causing the Revolution

The conditions leading up to this revolution in banking have been brewing for the past 10 to 15 years or more. Back in the early 1970s the Congress and the state legislatures had an opportunity to make legislative and regulatory changes. But they didn't. So the pressures for change built in the nation's financial markets.

By the fall of 1979 and continuing on into the early 1980s, the revolutionary forces had become irresistible. The revolution was sparked mostly by enterprising entrepreneurs in the financial services industry finding loopholes in the laws and responding to the powerful forces of the marketplace.

So the Congress and the state legislatures were forced to respond—to take some kind of action. As you read this book you'll find out that many of the recent legislative changes have amounted to the ratification of conditions already existing (or changes already underway) brought on by the powerful forces of the marketplace.

The Homogenization of the Financial Services Industry

What will be the end results of all of these revolutionary changes? Profound. Not one person will remain untouched and unaffected by what's going on in the nation's financial services industry.

Even now (in early 1984), the banking industry as a clear and distinct entity doesn't exist anymore. It's a part of the broader "financial services industry." The same is true of the other industries that in the past have made up segments of the financial services industry: brokerage firms, credit card companies, insurance companies, etc.

In the mid-1980s it's necessary to group all these "industries" into one and call it "the financial services industry." Now we can only distinguish among firms on the basis of the *functions performed,* not on the basis of their *names.* Would you believe, for example, that Sears Roebuck and Company is the name of one of the nation's largest financial services institutions?

As you read this book you'll find out that in the mid-1980s many nonbanking and nonfinancial businesses are involved in banking—and that many banks are crossing the lines going the other way. Nobody is quite sure about the rules of the game or where the lines are drawn. And *competition is fierce*. What an exciting time to be involved in (or learning about) banking and finance!

The Specific Objectives and Content of this Book

It isn't possible to do everything in one small book. But it is possible to put this banking revolution into perspective and to provide an overview conceptualization of what's going on and why—and to give some insight into the future outlook. When you finish your thoughtful reading of this book, you'll have all of that.

Specifically, what does this book explain? The major topics are:

- How the conventional regulatory framework surrounding the banking and financial services institutions developed, and the controversy leading to the recent legislative (and *de facto*) changes.
- The reasons for and content of the new banking laws of 1980 and 1982 and additional proposed legislation, and the revolutionary impact of these legislative changes.
- The elimination of the distinctions between banks and thrift institutions (S&Ls, savings banks, credit unions) so that by the mid-1980s the thrifts (the ones that want to be) are commercial banks—except in name.
- The importance of the Fed's monetary policies and of macroeconomic conditions on this industry, and, on the other hand, the important ways that the revolutionary changes in the industry are influencing the Fed's monetary policies and targets.
- The way in which interstate and intrastate geographic barriers to banking expansion and competition are being eroded, leading to "nationwide banking," and an evaluation of the effects of this new "spatial competition."
- The electronic funds transfer systems (EFTS) that are rapidly developing and spreading nationwide and having an increasing impact on the structure of the industry and on all of us as individual and/or business buyers of financial services.

- The way in which the "homogenization" of the financial services industry is bringing all of the financial services into competition with each other—turning the marketplace into a jungle where survival of the fittest is the name of the game —where everybody is trying to get into banking and banks (and thrifts) are trying to get into everything!
- The impact on the depository institutions of this new competitive environment where any institution that wishes to survive in the "no-holds-barred financial free-for-all" of the mid-1980s must direct its very best efforts toward:
  - timely *innovation* in products, markets, delivery systems.
  - *efficient management* of all of its resources including (especially) people.
  - careful and constant *asset/liability management.*
  - *strategic planning*—deciding where we're going and how we're going to get there.

What a list of topics! Truly, an *entire book* could be written about any one of them. Hopefully, you won't be disappointed when this book doesn't tell you everything there is to know about each of these topics. This book didn't set out to do that.

The purpose of this book is limited. It only tries to give you an overview of the revolutionary changes going on in our financial services industry. What's happening? Why? How? What's the outlook? And what's the impact of all this on all of us? And what can the individual financial institutions do to try to survive this tidal wave of change?

If from this book you can gain an "overview understanding"—a conceptualization of this revolution that's going on right now in our financial services industry—then that's probably enough for one little book to try to do. We hope the book succeeds in doing that for you. And we hope you might even find it interesting and enjoyable along the way.

Part I
Introduction to the Issues

An Overview of the Revolutionary Changes
and an Explanation of How the Banking
Crisis of the 1980s Developed

Chapter 1

The Dual Banking System and the Fed: Setting for Controversy

This is an exciting time for observers and students to study the financial services industry. But for the banks and savings institutions it's a time of considerable uncertainty and more than just a little frustration. Changes in legislation and regulations are having a significant effect on the entire financial community.

The issues discussed in this book are among the most critical of our time. Whatever happens in the banking and financial community exerts an impact on the national economy, and is felt by businesses and individuals in every community throughout the country.

One way to say it is this: *Money is the life-blood of the market-directed economic system, and it is the banking and financial system that functions as the heart*. It is the banking and financial system that pumps money to the vital functions and places throughout the economy.

The importance of the banking and financial system in the functioning of the economy has long been recognized. In the deep depression years of the early 1930s under the Roosevelt Administration, financial reform was one of the most important parts of the program to bring about economic recovery. Far-reaching changes in the legal environment in which financial institutions in the United States operate were instituted at that time. New laws were passed, new agencies set up, and deposit insurance started, all in recognition of the fact that the economy can't function unless its "life-blood" is circulated by a healthy, sound, and effectively functioning banking and financial system.

Much of the legislation that influences and controls the banking and financial system even today dates from the time of the 1930s. As you will soon see, that was one of the problems. Until new revolutionary legislation was passed in the early 1980s, our banks and financial institutions functioned almost entirely under this depression-spawned (and no longer tenable) system of regulations and controls. You'll be reading a lot more about all this very soon.

If you can appreciate the central role that the banking system plays in the economy, then you can understand the vital importance of the changing circumstances and conditions that are having a serious impact on the financial institutions and markets right now. All these changes promise to significantly influence not only the banking (financial services) industry, but ultimately, the functioning of the entire economy and the lives of all of us.

The purpose of this introduction is to provide a brief description of the structure and functions of the American banking system and then to highlight the current issues that will be discussed in this book.

The Dual Banking System: State Banks and National Banks

The American banking system is often referred to as a "dual" banking system, meaning that some of the banks are chartered by the Federal government and others are chartered by the individual states. In the U. S. Department of the Treasury, the Office of the "Comptroller of the Currency" has been chartering banks for more than 100 years—since the time of the Civil War. And states have been chartering banks ever since the nation began.

So we have national banks and state banks. But, in fact, we have more than a "dual" banking system. We have nationally chartered banks, then we have fifty different banking systems of state-chartered banks, because each state passes its own laws regarding state-chartered banks.

One of the major differences among the states has to do with the question of whether or not banks can establish branches, and under which circumstances. In some states, absolutely no branching is permitted. A banking corporation can have one office and that's it. In other states, banks can establish branches within the city (or sometimes within the county) in which it is located but nowhere else. In several states, state-wide branching is permitted. But interstate branching now is prohibited, nationwide—except for the "exceptions," of which, as you'll soon find out, there are many.

Small Banks, Regional Banks, and Large Banks

One important cause of controversy among bankers is that the banking industry is not homogeneous—in fact, nowhere near it! The state bank–national bank distinction is significant. Often, even more significant is the small bank–large bank distinction.

Suppose you define a small bank as one with less than $100 million in assets. Then there are several thousand small banks. Compare that with BankAmerica and Citicorp, each with assets exceeding $100,000 million (over $100 *billion*). It would take more than two thousand small banks to equal the assets of these two largest banks. The assets of the five or six largest banks add up to more than the assets of all of the small banks put together! When you consider the tremendous size difference, you can understand why government policies favored by the giant banks might be opposed by the small ones, and vice versa.

In between the giant money-center banks and the small community banks there are several so-called "regional" banks whose positions on regulatory issues and government policies are often different from either the small banks or the giant banks.

Can you see how difficult it must be for "the banking industry as a whole" to get together and agree on anything? You'll be seeing evidences of this controversy at various places throughout this book.

Fed Member Banks and Non-member Banks

Another aspect of "duality" in the American banking system is the fact that some banks are members of the Federal Reserve System, while others are not. When the Federal Reserve System (the Fed) was established in 1913, all nationally chartered banks were required to join, to hold reserves in the Fed, and to meet the other requirements of Fed membership. In return, these banks were offered access to the services of the Fed.

State-chartered banks were not required to join the Fed, but they were offered the opportunity to do so if they wished to do so and if they were prepared to meet the Fed's requirements. Most of the state-chartered banks chose not to join the Fed. But many of the *larger* state-chartered banks have become Fed members.

Today there are, in total, about 14,600 commercial banking institutions in the United States. About 4,600 of those are national banks and are (by requirement) Fed members. Of the remaining banks (all state-chartered) about 1,000 are Fed members by choice. The others (approximately 9,000) are state-chartered non-member banks.

In the late 1970s the number of Fed member banks declined as banks exercised their option to withdraw from Fed membership. State banks are free to withdraw their membership, and national banks can apply for and obtain state charters, drop their national charters, and then withdraw from Fed membership.

During the late 1970s and the first quarter of 1980, the trend of withdrawing from Fed membership accelerated significantly. There was increasing concern about the effect of declining Fed membership on the ability of the Fed to exercise proper control over the money supply of the nation. So the "declining Fed membership" issue became very important. In this book you will find out why banks were withdrawing from the Fed, about various proposed solutions to the problem, and about the new legislation that was passed in March 1980—legislation that significantly altered the structure and functioning of our financial services industry.

The Fed's "New" (October 1979) Monetary Policy

During 1978 and 1979 the inflation problem became progressively worse. Public sentiment and government policy statements were showing increasing concern about inflation, and increasing determination to try to slow it down. Throughout 1978 and 1979, strict money-tightening measures were taken by the Fed. One effect of all this was to push interest rates to levels far higher than ever before experienced in this country.

On Saturday, October 6, 1979, the Fed announced strong money-tightening measures—actions that came to be known to some as the Fed's "Saturday Night Special" and to others as the Fed's "Saturday Night Massacre." On that Saturday the Fed announced an increase of its discount rate (the interest it charges when it lends reserves to banks) to a record 12%. It also imposed an additional 8% reserve requirement on bank holdings of certain types of "purchased money" (money borrowed by banks to permit them to meet their reserve requirements and to continue making loans).

In addition (and most important) the Fed announced that from then on they would stop being very concerned with how high the short-term (money market) interest rates might go—that from then on they were going to concentrate on regulating the availability of *total reserves* in the banking system (and therefore the total amount of money in the economy) no matter how high the money market interest rate might go. Following the October 6 announcements, interest rates soared and the stock and bond markets tumbled.

Impact of the Fed's "Tight Money" Policies

In the weeks following the announced new Fed policy, interest rates continued to rise. The rapidly increasing rates were having increasing impact on banks and financial institutions. The Fed member banks (which are required to hold millions of dollars in non-interest-bearing reserve deposits at the Fed) were well aware of the increasing "opportunity cost" they were paying for their membership. As money market interest rates soared, the cost of being a Fed member (and holding millions of dollars in non-interest-earning reserves at the Fed) increased dramatically.

Businesses began selling more of their own notes (commercial paper) in the money markets instead of borrowing from banks at the high interest rates. Commercial paper rates went up too, of course, but often were not as high as bank rates.

Another effect of the high and rising interest rates was felt by banks and by all other deposit-holding institutions. The depositors were withdrawing their savings and placing them in money market funds, bonds, and elsewhere to try to get higher interest. This is called *disintermediation*.

Since the 1930s, financial institutions have been limited by law (by Regulation Q) as to the amount of interest they could pay on deposits. In 1979, savings accounts became progressively less attractive as interest rates on other investments increased. Funds were pouring out of financial intermediaries and into money market funds.

The savings and loan institutions (S&Ls) were particularly hard-hit by all this. Much of their loan portfolios consisted of long-term home mortgages issued at significantly lower rates. If an S&L has to pay 10% or more to obtain funds and its loans only bring in 8 or 9%, then it can't stay in business for very long! Some of the S&Ls (and some banks, too) were caught in this condition.

What to do? Many people argued: "Kill Reg Q!" But many S&Ls and small banks were surviving only because they had some money in Reg Q-controlled, low-interest deposits. To them, "kill Reg Q!" meant "kill me!" So they fought to keep Reg Q. But it was a losing battle.

Two revolutionary banking acts (March 1980 and October 1982) called for the eventual phaseout of the Reg Q interest rate ceilings that had been in existence since the early 1930s. Soon you'll be reading about how this happened, and why.

Increasing Competition among Banks and Other Financial Institutions

The effects of increasingly tight money brought increased competition among the banks and other financial institutions. Each was trying to pull in depositors and maintain deposits and to find sound borrowers who could afford to pay the high interest rates.

Over the past several years the banks have constantly sought improved techniques to compete against each other, and against the "thrifts"—the "savings" institutions such as the S&Ls, credit unions, and mutual savings banks. Simultaneously, the thrifts have been competing against each other, and against the commercial banks. The banks and thrift institutions have used various means—"give-away" programs and such—to try to attract depositors.

Checks on Savings Accounts? Interest on Checking Accounts?

Historically, banks have had a monopoly on checking accounts. But then, during the 1970s some S&Ls were permitted to offer savings accounts that could be used as checking accounts. The depositors can write "negotiable orders of withdrawal," which work exactly like checks. One person can transfer funds to another simply by writing a "negotiable order of withdrawal." Such accounts are called "NOW accounts." Also, credit unions in some instances permitted depositors to write "share drafts," which, again, amount to checks written on savings deposits.

People were gaining these increasing opportunities to deposit their money in savings accounts, earn interest on the money, and also write checks against the account. So why would anyone want to put their money in a checking account that pays no interest? However, the banks fought back.

The banks (under a new regulation permitting them to do so) began to offer "automatic transfers" between a depositor's savings account and checking account. All of the person's deposit can be kept in the savings account. Then when a check is written against the (zero-balance) checking account, the funds to cover the check flow automatically from the savings account into the checking account, and the check is paid.

These "preauthorized transfer accounts" or "automatic transfer accounts" were first authorized in November 1978. But this arrangement soon was held by the courts to be illegal—at least until Congress specifically permitted these preauthorized transfers. The court allowed Congress until January 1, 1980, to make it legal. If the Congress had not acted by that time, all such accounts would have become illegal. But the Congress passed the necessary legislation and preauthorized transfer accounts became legal.

Dissolving Distinctions between Banks and Thrifts

This is an age of increased competition between banks, S&Ls, credit unions, and other financial institutions. The major distinctions between these institutions historically have been that banks for the most part hold checking accounts and make short-term commercial and consumer loans, while the thrifts hold savings accounts and make long-term mortgage loans. But now the clear distinctions between the banks and the thrifts are being rapidly eroded.

Both of the revolutionary banking acts of the early 1980s (March 1980 and October 1982) made significant reductions in the distinctions between banks and thrifts. And these revolutionary changes have been occurring in an atmosphere of great controversy. Why? How is it happening? What has been the effect of all this? And where does it seem to be leading? These are some of the issues you'll be reading about in this book.

Suggested Readings

Asay, Michael, R., and Kilcollin, Thomas E. "The Competitive Effects of N.O.W. Accounts on Financial Institutions in New England," Board of Governors of the Federal Reserve System (April 1980).

Benston, George J. "The Optimal Structure of Banking: Theory and Evidence," *Journal of Banking Research, 4* (Winter 1973), 220–38.

Berkman, Neil G. "Bank Reserves, Money, and Some Problems for the New Monetary Policy," *New England Economic Review*, Federal Reserve Bank of Boston (July–August 1980), 52–64.

Brown, William J. *The Dual Banking System in the United States*. New York: Department of Economics and Research, American Bankers Association, 1960.

"New Competition for Financial Services," *Economic Review*, Federal Reserve Bank of Atlanta, Special Issue (August 1981).

Paulus, John, and Hoffman, Stuart G. "The Burden of Fed Membership Revisited," *Economic Review*, Federal Reserve Bank of Atlanta (March-April 1979), 23.

Vrabac, Daniel J. "Recent Developments at Banks and Nonbank Depository Institutions," *Economic Review*, Federal Reserve Bank of Kansas City (July–August 1983), 33–45.

Chapter 2

Federal Reserve Policy: New Competition, New Challenges

Everything the Fed does influences the financial markets. Everything that influences the financial markets has an impact on the banks and other financial services institutions. Much of the turmoil and controversy during the 1979–82 period was born of inflation and of financial market conditions—tight money and high and volatile interest rates.

High Interest Rates and Controversial Fed Policy

The Fed maintained tight restrictions on money growth from October 1979 through mid-year 1982. The resulting money market conditions made Fed membership an infeasible alternative for many banks and made Reg Q interest rate ceilings intolerable. And that's what led to the near-crisis conditions that forced the passage of the two revolutionary banking acts: the first in March 1980, the second in October 1982.

During the last half of 1982 and on into mid-1983, the Fed took an easier stance and permitted the money supply to grow rapidly. But interest rates remained high by historical standards. This time it wasn't tight money but the fear of renewed inflation that got the blame.

Tight money brings high interest rates because the supply of loanable funds is restricted. Sure. But does easy money bring high interest rates too? Because of fear of renewed inflation?

These were (and are) some of the controversial issues of monetary policy in the 1980s. When you finish reading this book, you'll know a good bit more about what happened—and at least some of the reasons why.

Changing Geographic Structures and "Spatial Competition" in Banking

As competition in banking has increased in recent years, there is one kind of competition—spatial competition—which has been strictly limited by governmental regulations, both state and national. Within each state, regulations determine the geographic, or "spatial" areas in which the banks can compete. In the statewide branching states, one bank can compete with others throughout the entire state. In states that do not permit statewide banking, banks can only compete with each other in the geographic "space" specified by state law—perhaps the city or county in which the bank is located. Nationwide, banks are restricted by federal law so that they cannot openly compete across state lines. But all these restrictions are undergoing significant changes.

In recent years there has been increasing competition from foreign banks. Several hundred foreign banks have established offices in the United States. In some ways these foreign banks have had a competitive advantage over the American banks. For example, foreign banks have been permitted to establish banking offices in different states, whereas banks chartered in this country have not been permitted to do so.

Partly because of foreign competition and partly because of the (sometimes) clear economic advantages which could be gained by permitting interstate bank mergers, there is now growing interest in reducing restrictions on interstate banking. There are some small banks which probably should, for economic reasons, be merged into larger banks. And there are some circumstances in which the appropriate merger partner may be located in a different state. Until recently, all such interstate mergers had been prohibited.

Sometimes problems arise when a large bank is in danger of failing and therefore needs a "merger partner." Another bank in the same state which is large and strong enough to be an appropriate merger partner probably would not be permitted to enter into the merger because of antimonopoly laws. Until recently, a large bank from a different state would have been prohibited from merging with the troubled bank by the McFadden Act, the Federal law prohibiting interstate branches and mergers. So the only way a large "problem bank" could be merged was to be merged with one or a group of foreign banks. That's what happened in the failure of the Franklin National Bank in New York in 1974.

Sometimes interstate banking may be economically desirable from the point of view of the banks involved, the economies of the areas involved, and the increased efficiency of the American financial system. So the stringent restrictions have been somewhat eased in special circumstances. But in 1984 the basic prohibitions of the McFadden Act were still standing. And the question of whether or not to legalize interstate banking—and under what circumstances, and how—continued to be a topic of heated controversy. You'll be reading more about this issue later.

Banker-Brokers and Broker-Bankers

Are bankers prohibited by the Glass-Steagall Act (1933) from engaging in the stockbrokerage business? They thought so—that is, until recently. Then they found out the truth of the old song title: "It ain't what you do, it's the way that you do it!"

In January 1982 no major bank in the country was offering its customers brokerage services. By January 1983 some 600 banks and thrifts were offering (or had announced plans to offer) brokerage services. The securities industry complained and sued. But the regulatory authorities approved. You'll be reading about that soon.

The ties between bankers and brokers actually began from the brokerage side. Merrill Lynch started the trend in the late 1970s when it set up its Cash Management Account—clearly a banking service offered by a brokerage firm. Then American Express bought Shearson Loeb Rhoades, a major brokerage house, Sears bought the securities firm of Dean Witter, and there were several other instances of nonbanks moving into the financial services industry.

Soon the banks sought the freedom to undertake a counter-offensive. It is clear that during 1982 and 1983 the counteroffensive was effectively launched, bringing another major breakthrough in the "financial services revolution of the 1980s."

Explosive Growth of Nonbank Banks

While all these banker-broker things were happening, someone discovered the "nonbank bank." A nonbank bank is a bank structured so as to fall outside the narrow legal definition of "bank" as defined in the Bank Holding Company Act. To wit: a bank must (1) take deposits, and (2) make commerical loans. So if you eliminate either one or the other of these functions, you have a bank that falls outside the laws and restrictions that control the functions and activities of other banks.

In 1983 the number of nonbank banks was growing rapidly. Fed Chairman Volcker called for a moratorium on establishing new nonbank banks. He also called for a new legal definition of "bank" that would bring the nonbank banks under the banking laws. In 1983, while dozens of companies rushed to set up nonbank banks, bills were introduced into Congress to try to "close the nonbank loophole."

Who owns nonbanks? Several brokerage firms, insurance companies, finance companies, bank holding companies, and nonfinancial businesses—would you believe Control Data? J.C. Penney? Chrysler Corporation? Parker Pen Company? Yes, and many others.

What's the effect of all this? And the outlook on this issue? You'll be reading about that in the coming chapters.

New Technology and EFTS

An important influence underlying much of the dramatic change in the banking and financial services industry is that of new electronic technology. With the development of computer and communications technology, banks and financial institutions can now process great amounts of data and can make funds transfers more rapidly and efficiently than would have been possible only a few years ago. Much of the new equipment is expensive to install and bring "on line." The small banks are not able to set up the systems themselves, but need to depend on larger banks to help them in providing these electronic services.

The increased use of electronic funds transfer systems (EFTS) is sure to have an impact on the relationships among banks, large and small, on the relationships between banks and other financial institutions, on the relationships between the commercial banks and the Fed, on competition among the banks and other financial services institutions, on the issue of intrastate bank structure as well as interstate banking relationships, and on so many other aspects of the financial services industry. In short, the introduction of "electronic banking" is an important influence underlying many of the revolutionary changes that are occurring in the banking and financial services institutions during the 1980s.

The banking system in the United States is now clearing and processing more than 30 billion (that's 30,000 million!) checks per year, and the number is constantly increasing. The cost of handling this mountain of paper is the number one force that will speed the expanded use of EFTS in the coming years.

As individual bank customers find the cost of their banking services increasing in the next few years (as it is certain that most customers will) it is a safe bet that a large number of those customers will opt for the reduced costs of EFTS. Simultaneously, automated clearing house (ACH) services will be expanded, as will the use of automated teller machines (ATMs) and other applications of the new and rapidly developing computer and communications technology.

In this book you will be reading about the ways in which these new technological innovations will play an increasingly significant role in shaping the future of the banking and financial services industry during the 1980s.

Other Important Issues: Organizational Structure and "Consumer Protection" Laws

In addition to the several important issues already highlighted, there were other vitally important events and trends influencing the directions of change in the banking and financial institutions for the decade of the 1980s.

Two important kinds of changes shaping the future of all depository and lending institutions in the country—changes that already were having a very significant impact during the 1970s—are: (1) the rapidly changing organizational structure of America's financial institutions, including the holding company movement in the banking industry, the shift toward stock ownership by the "mutual" savings institutions, and the "merger movement" among financial institutions, and (2) the changing business procedures and practices resulting from the "consumer protection" laws (the equality in lending and truth in lending laws) and to some extent also the equal employment practices laws.

The Erosion of "Segmentation Barriers"

Much of what is happening in the financial services environment is resulting from "the changing rules of the competitive game." The various barriers that have been built to segment the overall financial services market are being rapidly eroded. Much of the erosion is resulting from the initiative of banks and other financial institutions seeking and finding legal ways to penetrate these barriers; some is resulting from reinterpretations by the regulatory bodies.

Far-reaching changes have come from new legislation: the two "deregulation" acts of March 1980 and October 1982. Major barriers now being eroded or eliminated include:

1. barriers preventing the thrift institutions from engaging in activities defined to be the "sole domain" of commercial banks.

2. barriers limiting mergers between financial institutions—between banks, between banks and thrifts, and between banks and brokerage firms and other businesses.
3. barriers between the banking business and the brokerage business.
4. barriers preventing interstate banking and (in several states) preventing statewide banking.
5. barriers preventing nonbank firms from entering the banking business.

In addition to the barriers separating and segmenting the various parts of the financial services industry, there are many *regulatory restrictions* circumscribing the activities of the banks and thrifts. There have been restrictions on the kinds of assets the depository institutions can hold, on the rates they can pay to depositors, and on the rates they can charge borrowers, and other restrictions.

All of these barriers and restrictions have served to limit the amounts and kinds of competition in the financial services markets. As the barriers are being eroded and the regulations and restrictions are being modified and/or removed, the competitive environment is changing rapidly. During the early 1980s, with the additional push from new technology and EFTS, the speed of change has been almost breathtaking.

The Impact on Banks and Bank Management

The events of 1979–83 had a profound impact on the industry. Several banks and hundreds of thrift institutions failed. All this has had an indelible impact on the psychology, philosophy, and techniques of bank and thrift management. The depository institutions were jerked out of their relatively easy existence in a secure, regulated world. They were faced with deregulated liabilities (which permit their cost of funds to go up) while the return on many of their assets was fixed. When an institution's cost of funds exceeds its return on assets by very much and/or for very long, it fails. Many did.

Asset-Liability Management

Now financial managements have new watchwords: "Careful asset-liability management." "Matched maturities between assets and liabilities." "Balanced interest rate sensitivity between assets and liabilities." All of these watchwords mean basically the same thing: "Don't get locked into a long-term, fixed-rate asset unless you have a long-term, fixed-rate liability to match it! That way, you're covered."

But there's more. The new competition is forcing up cost of funds and simultaneously holding down return on assets. So profit spreads are under pressure. How to make up the difference? Better management of resources. Cut costs. Raise service fees. And one more thing: Do some careful *strategic planning*.

Strategic Planning

Management must decide: Which banking functions will we offer? In which markets? In which directions do we want to grow? Which less-profitable activities should we curtail, or abandon? And even: Do we want to survive as an independent institution? And if so, how do we plan to go about doing that?

Yes, the impact of the recent revolutionary changes on bank management has been profound. In the final parts of this book you'll be reading statements by the officers of several banks and thrifts, small and large, from all over the country responding to the question, "How do you plan to cope with this new environment?" As you read these comments, you'll get an inside view of what these firms are up against as their secure, protected environment has turned into a jungle. Survival of the fittest (and sometimes the strongest) is the name of the game.

A Summary Comment

It is clear that we are experiencing a revolution in the commercial banking and financial services industry. Both the basic legal environment in which the banks and financial services operate and the *basic technology* supporting these institutions and activities are undergoing dramatic change. The conditions, issues, and developments that are mostly responsible for these changes have been highlighted in this introduction and will be discussed in much more detail throughout this book. Then the final chapters will describe the outlook and offer "prescriptions for success" for the banks and thrifts during this turbulent decade of the 1980s.

Suggested Readings

Albert, Andrew. "Rules for Bank Brokerages," *American Banker* (Friday, October 28, 1983), 1.

Carter, Michael G. "An Integrated Approach to EFT and Retail Service Delivery," *Journal of Retail Banking* (June 1982), 1–13.

Minsky, Hyman P. "The Federal Reserve: Between a Rock and a Hard Place," *Challenge* (May–June 1980), 30–36.

"Monetary Policy and Open Market Operations in 1982," *Quarterly Review*, Federal Reserve Bank of New York (Spring 1983).

Rosenblum, Harvey, Siegel, Diane, and Pavel, Christine. "Banks and Nonbanks: A Run for the Money," *Economic Perspectives*, Federal Reserve Bank of Chicago (May–June 1983), 3–12.

"S&L Interstate Expansion Inexorably Continues," *Banking Expansion Reporter* (September 19, 1983), 9.

"Statements to Congress" by Federal Reserve Chairman Paul Volcker on appropriate guides for the conduct of monetary policy, *Federal Reserve Bulletin* (August 1983), 617–622.

Watro, Paul R. "Geographic Banking Markets," *Economic Commentary*, Federal Reserve Bank of Cleveland (September 12, 1983).

Chapter 3

Flashback: The 1930s Legislation and Developments Through the 1970s

In the two previous chapters you read about the revolutionary changes going on in our banking and financial services industry. How did all these problems arise? How did such a crisis develop?

The U.S. financial system functioned largely under a depression-born system of regulations and controls until 1980. Many of the crisis issues of the 1970s and 1980s stemmed from this 1930s legal and regulatory environment.

This chapter takes a look back at what was happening between the early 1930s and the late 1970s. When you finish this chapter you'll have a better understanding of what happened and why.

In 1933 the Banking System Nearly Collapsed

The depression years were tough times for bankers, for individuals—for the entire nation. Between 1930 and 1933 more than 8,000 banks failed. Thousands of people saw their money evaporate as one bank after another collapsed. Everyone was running to the bank and demanding cash. But there wasn't enough cash.

In March of 1933 President Roosevelt declared a "bank holiday" and closed all the banks. There was no more running to the banks and demanding cash, because the banks were closed. The banks stayed closed until things calmed down a bit. So the 1933 "bank holiday" succeeded in preventing an entire collapse of the banking system.

Aims of the 1930s Legislation

Out of this traumatic experience arose financial reform legislation—new laws designed (1) to alleviate the crisis and (2) to create a sound financial system. How? By restoring confidence in the banking system and by insuring its stability. And how did they propose to do that? They used three approaches: (1) limiting competition among banks, (2) increasing federal regulations and supervision, and (3) establishing deposit insurance to make sure that depositors don't lose their money when a bank fails.

Most of the financial legislation of the 1930s dealt with commercial banks, because they were by far the most prominent form of depository institution at that time. Then later (after World War II), as the thrifts became more important, most of the 1930s regulations were extended to those depository institutions as well.

What were the *specific provisions* of the 1930s legislation—of these new laws that had such profound effects on our banking and financial system right up to the 1980s? That's what you'll be reading about in the following sections.

The Banking Act of 1933

The Banking Act of 1933 was really a "bundle" of acts. What did it do? It revolutionized the business of banking, as you'll see as you read the following provisions of the Act:

1. It established the Federal Deposit Insurance Corporation (FDIC) to insure demand, savings, and time deposits at commercial banks and at mutual savings banks. It was hoped that the FDIC would restore confidence in the banking system. As is turned out, it really did. The FDIC legislation has been referred to as one of the most successful, most effective pieces of legislation ever passed.

2. It supported the provisions of the McFadden Act (1927) that (a) prohibit banks from branching across state lines, and (b) require all national banks to observe the branching laws of the states in which they are located.
3. It separated the banking business from the brokerage business. Banks were prohibited from acquiring or underwriting corporate stock. This was to eliminate these "risky assets" from bank portfolios. This provision of the 1933 Act requiring the banker-broker separation is popularly referred to as the Glass-Steagall Act.
4. It authorized the Federal Reserve Board to set interest rate ceilings on savings and time deposits at all member banks and prohibited member banks from paying any interest at all on demand deposits. When the Fed issued regulations implementing this authorization—setting interest rate ceilings—it decided to call this "Regulation Q." You'll be reading a lot more about Reg Q later on.

The Banking Act of 1935

The Banking Act of 1935 wasn't "revolutionary" as was the 1933 Act. Mostly what it did was to extend the provisions of the 1933 Act to non-member banks. Specifically, the 1935 Act did the following:

1. It extended Reg Q to non-member banks and authorized the FDIC to set interest rate ceilings. It also prohibited non-member banks from paying interest on demand deposits.
2. It extended the powers of the Fed by giving the Board of Governors powers to set reserve requirements. And it cre-

ated the Federal Open Market Committee (FOMC) which, as you know, has become the nation's most powerful deliberative body on matters of monetary policy.

1930s Legislation for the Thrifts

Although commerical banks were by far the predominant form of depository institution at the time, the thrifts were important enough to attract some legislative attention.

1. Legislation in 1932 established the Federal Home Loan Bank System, headed by the Federal Home Loan Bank Board (FHLBB). This agency was created to perform for the S&Ls more or less the same kinds of functions (and exercise more or less the same kinds of supervision and controls) as the Fed does for the commercial banks.
2. Legislation in 1934 created the Federal Savings and Loan Insurance Corporation (FSLIC). This agency was created to provide deposit insurance for the S&Ls, much as the FDIC provides deposit insurance for the commercial banks.

Effects of the 1930s Legislation: The 1940s–Mid 1960s

During the 1940s, 1950s, and early 1960s, the financial system functioned well enough within its depression-born regulatory framework. One obviously positive effect was that the FDIC did restore confidence in the system—no more "runs on the banks." Also the FSLIC helped to create confidence in the S&L industry.

In the years following World War II, bank failures were averaging only about six a year—much lower than in pre-FDIC years. And on the rare occasion when a bank did fail, depositors didn't lose their money.

Throughout this period, Reg Q had little effect on the industry—except perhaps to create some complacency among bankers. Market interest rates remained approximately equal to or below Reg Q ceilings. There was a "comfortable spread" between the interest rate paid for the *cost* of funds—zero for demand deposits and about 3% or less for savings deposits—and the interest rate earned on the *uses* of funds—about 6% for loans. This comfortable spread, plus the lack of substitutes for demand-deposit accounts, truly let the bankers relax. These comfortable years for bankers led to the term "3-6-3 bankers"—bankers who "pay 3% on deposits, charge 6% on loans, and are on the golf course by 3."

Distinctions between Banks and Thrifts

Under the 1930s legislation the banking industry was completely separate from the thrift industry. The banks had always had a monopoly over demand deposits. Then the 1930s legislation allowed banks significantly greater freedom than the thrifts in their uses for funds. The S&Ls were generally required to put most of their loans into home mortgages. They were prevented from making significant amounts of consumer loans and from holding commercial paper.

This artificial heterogeneity resulted partly from the fact that the thrifts and the banks operated under completely different regulatory and supervisory agencies. The banks were under the Fed and the FDIC; the S&Ls were under the FHLBB and FSLIC.

It was not until 1966 that Reg Q interest rate ceilings were extended to cover the thrifts. In that year the FDIC was authorized to set interest rate ceilings on rates paid by the mutual savings banks and the FHLBB was authorized to do the same for the S&Ls. These agencies were supposed to get together with the Fed and coordinate their Reg Q ceilings.

The Reg Q ceilings for the thrifts were set slightly higher than for commercial banks. This was to give the thrifts a little more power to attract deposits and thereby channel more money into home mortgage loans. The idea was also that the thrifts "deserved" this competitive edge, since the banks could offer checking accounts (and get *interest-free* money!) while the thrifts were prohibited by law from doing this.

It was not until 1970 that the National Credit Union Administration (NCUA) was authorized to impose interest rate ceilings on credit union deposits. The NCUA ceilings were not tied to Reg Q and usually have been set slightly higher than the S&L ceilings.

Problems with Reg Q in the 1960s and 1970s

Reg Q was originally imposed to prevent the banks from competing with each other by offering higher interest rates to attract deposits. What's supposed to be bad about that? It's just that as banks pay more for their deposits, they have to earn more on their loans (or go broke!).

Which loans can generate the highest interest income for the bank? Risky loans! But risky loans can lead to defaults—and sometimes to bank failures. So the Reg Q ceilings are supposed to give the banks a low-cost source of funds, and thereby keep the banks out of the risky loan business—let those borrowers go to the consumer finance companies and the pawn shops.

How well did it work? As long as market rates were low, the Reg Q ceilings really didn't have any effect. But what happened when market rates went up? Disintermediation. Lots of depositors pulled their money out of the financial intermediaries (banks and thrifts) and put their money where it would earn the market rate (not the Reg Q rate). So what actually happened? Nothing much until the mid 1960s.

The Disintermediation Problem Gets Worse

In 1965 the inflation rate accelerated. Interest rates rose rapidly. Market rates of interest in 1966 reached a 100-year high—significantly above the Reg Q ceiling rates. Did disintermediation occur? Of course.

As interest rates on unregulated financial instruments (T-bills, commercial paper, etc.) increased rapidly, funds flowed out of time-, savings-, and demand-deposit accounts and into these higher paying alternatives. So what happened to the "guaranteed low-cost source of funds" for the banks and thrifts? It disappeared.

Disintermediation occurred every time market rates of interest significantly exceeded Reg Q ceilings. The problem was repeated in 1969, 1974–75, and 1979–80. Problems with Reg Q seemed to multiply as time went on.

New Financial Institutions and Instruments

As disintermediation occurred because of Reg Q restrictions, many more nonregulated intermediaries and nonregulated financial instruments began to appear. The power of the "free marketplace" at work? Right!

The explosive growth of money market mutual funds (MMMFs) provides the best example of this financial innovation. The MMMFs pool the smaller deposits of many shareholders and invest this money directly in short-term money market instruments. The MMMF shareholders have complete liquidity and earn market rates of interest. The best of all possible worlds!

The first MMMF was established in 1972. In 1978 the MMMFs held less than $4 billion. But by 1980 MMMF "deposits" had surged to over $60 billion. And in 1982? Would you believe more than $230 billion? That's right: about half the size of the total U.S. M1 money supply!* Where did all of that money come from? Most of it was "disintermediated" from the banks and thrifts. So how did the intermediaries survive? Several hundred didn't. You'll be reading about that throughout this book.

*The M1 money supply includes currency, travelers checks, and most checkable accounts at banks and thrifts. A complete explanation of the various "monetary aggregates" (the different definitions of the money supply) is presented in Chapter 21.

Basic Problem of the Thrifts: Unbalanced Portfolios

Beginning in the mid-1960s, the banks sometimes had a tough time during periods of financial disintermediation. But the thrifts suffered even more. Their limited kinds of deposits (no-demand deposits) and the structure of their loan portfolios (mostly home mortgages) made them more vulnerable to the credit crunches of the 1960s and 1970s.

By design, the S&Ls and mutual savings banks have always allocated most of their funds to long-term mortgage loans. So their asset portfolios have always been dominated by long-term, fixed-interest loans.

While their *uses* of funds (mostly mortgage loans) are long term, their *sources* of funds (mostly savings deposits) are short term. Such an unbalanced portfolio would be no problem during normal, stable, low-interest-rate times. But during the credit crunch, high-interest periods of the 1960s and 1970s? A serious problem! During these times the thrifts lost deposits. So they had to go to the money markets (and pay high market rates) for funds. The rates they were paying were sometimes much higher than the rates they were earning on their home mortgage portfolios. What happens when you pay out more than you bring in? You don't last very long. Many didn't.

The Rising Cost of Funds

The thrifts saw their cost of funds rising during the 1970s for several reasons:

1. Reg Q ceilings were raised at various intervals. So the thrift either paid the higher rate or experienced a large run-off of deposits to other thrifts and to the new, nonregulated accounts and financial instruments.
2. The new unregulated deposit accounts—for example, time certificates and large CDs—carried higher interest cost than passbook savings and other time deposits.

3. Even though institutions were prohibited from explicitly paying more to their depositors to compete for funds, they did compete by paying "implicit interest." They offered free services to attract and hold customers. And their increased operating costs (the costs of providing the services) became a part of their cost of funds.

Proposed Solutions: The Hunt Report and the FINE Study*

In the late 1960s it was becoming obvious that some changes were going to have to be made. So several studies were conducted and reports prepared offering specific recommendations. The most important of these studies are the Hunt Report (1971) and the FINE Study (Discussion Principles, 1975; *Compendium of Papers,* 1976). Both are very thorough studies. Both identified major structural problems of the financial industry and suggested sweeping—you might say *revolutionary*—changes in the American banking and financial services industry.

It's interesting to note that the major recommendations of both of these studies are the same: *Deregulate the industry*! Specifically, both of the studies recommended:

1. Abolish Reg Q ceilings on savings and time deposits and remove the zero ceiling on demand deposits.
2. Remove distinctions between banks and S&Ls. All depository institutions should be allowed to offer demand deposits, and all should have the same range of uses for funds.

*The official title of the Hunt report is: *Report of the President's Commission on Financial Structure and Regulation* (U.S. Government Printing Office, Washington, D.C., 1971). For an overview of the Hunt Report, see "Policies for a More Competitive Financial System" (Federal Reserve Bank of Boston, Conference Series No. 8, 1972).

The full title of the FINE Study is: *Financial Institutions and the Nation's Economy, Discussion Principles* (U.S. Congress, House, Committee on Banking, Currency, and Housing, 94th Congress, 1st Session, 1975) and *Compendium of Papers* (2nd Session, 1976). For more information on the FINE Study, see William G. Dewald, "FINE Principles and Prospects for Financial Institutions Reform," Carnegie-Rochester Conference Series on Public Policy, Vol. 7, Amsterdam (North-Holland Publishing Co., 1977), pp. 131–52.

That is, all should be permitted to make the same kinds of investments and to hold the same kinds of assets in their portfolios of loans and securities.

3. Remove the restrictions on intrastate and interstate branching.
4. Combine the regulatory and supervisory functions of the federal banking and thrift agencies to eliminate overlapping authority.

As you can see, these studies recommended removing the anticompetitive restraints enacted in the 1930s. The recommendations of the Hunt Report led to the proposed Financial Institutions Act of 1973, but the Act never passed. The FINE Study proposals were incorporated into a similar attempt at legislative reform in 1975, but this one didn't pass, either. Both proposals were defeated largely as a result of intensive lobbying by S&Ls and small banks. They didn't want to lose their umbrella of anticompetitive protection, to which they had become accustomed and under which they had grown and prospered.

So financial reform was not accomplished in the 1970s despite increasing recognition of the problems and of the need for reform. But the events of the mid- to late-1970s further exposed structural problems that could be ignored no longer. It was not until near-crisis conditions developed in the early 1980s that the political obstacles were overcome and some of the much-needed reform legislation was passed.

The 1970s: The Revolution Begins

The lack of financial reform legislation in the 1970s did not prevent financial innovation from occurring in the industry. The inflation rate was high and rising. So were interest rates. The banks and thrifts, in order to survive, had to somehow slow or stop the disintermediation process. But the problem wasn't just disintermediation. The years of complacency in a protected environment of regulation were slipping away. Suddenly banks were competing against each other and against the thrifts for funds. And the thrifts were fighting back. The competitive game got tougher.

Some bank and thrift managers forgot that they were supposed to be genteel "3–6–3 bankers."

The banks faced the problems of the growth of nonbank intermediaries and the growth of demand deposit substitutes. The thrifts suffered from their restrictions on sources and uses of funds—especially their lack of demand deposit accounts.

At the same time, all of the financial institutions were being hit by the computer-telecommunications revolution, by high and rising interest rates, and by serious inflation.

A few banks and thrifts failed. And many of these institutions that survived began to look quite different from the depository institutions of the 1960s. Thrifts were beginning to look more and more like banks. The barriers creating artificial differences between the thrifts and the banks were eroding—with or without Congressional approval. Another example of the power of the marketplace? Right!

New Interest-Bearing Checking Accounts

In 1972 the first Negotiable Order of Withdrawal (NOW) account was offered by a savings bank in Massachusetts. A thrift institution was offering a checking account—and one that bears interest!

By 1978 the thrifts in six New England states and in New York were offering NOW accounts. In 1978 some credit unions began offering share draft accounts, which are also interest-bearing checking accounts. The thrifts were fighting for survival against the banks and against all of the new nonregulated financial instruments and institutions.

But the banks fought back. In 1978 automatic transfer service (ATS) accounts were first authorized for commercial banks. With the ATS account, the depositor's money is held in an interest-bearing savings account, and when the depositor writes a check the funds to cover the check automatically flow from the savings account to the checking account. So, from the point of view of the depositor, is the ATS account an interest-bearing checking account? Yes.

Not only the thrifts and the banks were competing against each other. In the 1970s Merrill Lynch made headlines with its CMA (cash management account). In cooperation with a bank, Merrill Lynch had introduced an account offering money market interest rates and check-writing privileges. And it was available nationwide!

What Merrill Lynch started soon spread. Big cracks in the walls between bankers and brokers? Yes. What about the Glass-Steagall Act. Also big cracks in the walls preventing interstate banking? Yes. And what about the McFadden Act? Are the brokers and banks and thrifts and others all ignoring the laws and doing illegal things? Maybe so. Sometimes it's hard to know what's legal and what isn't. That's the way it is when a major revolution is going on. And that's what you'll be reading about in the chapters coming up.

A Summary Comment

It was in the late 1970s that the situation for the banks and thrifts became intolerable. They were entangled in an antiquated, depression-induced legal and regulatory framework that didn't allow them to meet the demands of a rapidly changing marketplace.

The high and increasing U.S. inflation rate and the seriously low international value of the dollar exacerbated the problem. As you might guess, OPEC's thousand-percent increase in the price of oil since the early 1970s had something to do with it. Oil in the international marketplace is priced in U.S. dollars. When the oil price goes up 1,000 percent, that means the value of the oil-purchasing dollar drops to ten cents! Serious inflation? Yes. No wonder the dollar was weak.

The Fed's "shift to monetarism" and tight money policy instituted in October 1979 was designed to overcome (1) domestic inflation, and (2) the international weakness of the dollar. Viewed from the perspective of 1984, it was easy to conclude that the Fed's policy worked. Domestic inflation rates in 1983 were the lowest in more than a decade. And the international value of the dollar had soared to such heights that foreign central banks and heads of state were calling on the U.S. government and the Fed to "ease off a bit!"

But the interesting part from our present point of view is not the question of the ultimate success or failure of the Fed's policy. It's what happened in the meantime. What happened to the depository institutions when they were hit with very high and very volatile interest rates? while strapped with (or supported by, depending on your point of view) antiquated Reg Q interest rate ceilings? and with each Fed member bank required to forego millions of dollars of interest income because of required non-interest-bearing reserves?

How did the depository institutions cope? And survive? Hundreds didn't. So what happened? The rules were changed. And the institutions changed. The introduction of new computer-telecommunications technology was greatly accelerated. A revolution was triggered in the financial services industry—a revolution that was destined to continue throughout the 1980s.

What will be the ultimate result? We can't describe it for you, but we can tell you this: The United States will have a banking and financial system that barely resembles the one with which we entered the 1980s. By the time you finish this book, you'll know what's been happening. And you'll have a pretty good idea what's going to happen from here on as this *Revolution in Banking* continues.

Suggested Readings

Colton, Kent W. "Financial Reform: A Review of the Past and Prospects for the Future," *American Real Estate and Urban Economics Association Journal* (Spring 1980), 91–117.

Fisher, Gerald C. "The Commercial Banking Environment: The 1960s Through the 1980s, Part IV-A, The Structure of the Commercial Banking System, 1960–1985," *Journal of Commercial Bank Lending* (September 1979), 44–61.

Friedman, Milton, and Schwartz, Anna J. *A Monetary History of the United States,* Princeton: Princeton University Press, 1963.

Klebamer, Benjamen J. *Commercial Banking in the United States: A History,* Hinsdale, Illinois: The Dryden Press, 1974.

Weil, Leonard. "Banking in the 1980s and How We Got There," *Journal of Commercial Bank Lending,* 63 (May 1981), 2–9.

Part II
What To Do About Fed Membership and Reg Q?

In 1979 Soaring Interest Rates Brought Falling Fed Membership and Rapid Disintermediation

Chapter 4

The Fed Membership Issue

The Federal Reserve is the central banking system in the United States. It consists of a Board of Governors in Washington and committees which assist the Board in making overall policy for the system. There are twelve Federal Reserve banks located in different geographical regions throughout the United States. But Fed policy is determined by the Board of Governors and the Federal Open Market Committee. Fed policy, once established, is carried out nationwide.

Functions of the Fed

The Federal Reserve provides many services to the banks and to the Federal government in its financing activities. But the primary and most important function of the Fed is in controlling the money supply of the nation—influencing expansions and contractions of the money supply, and influencing interest rates. The overriding purpose of Fed policy and actions is to stabilize prices, while at the same time providing sufficient money and low enough interest rates to permit the economy to operate at a high level of production and employment.

When the Fed was established by Congess in 1913, it was created as an independent organization, not under the direct political control of either branch of government. The purpose of this "independence" was to reduce political influence over the nation's money managers.

The Membership Problem

At the time the Fed was established, all the "National Banks"—that is, commercial banks which had been chartered by the Federal government—were required to join and follow the directives of the Federal Reserve system. Other banks (those chartered by the individual states) were given the option of joining the Fed if they met the requirements. Some of the state-chartered banks joined the Fed (mostly large ones) but most of them did not.

One reason for the reluctance of state banks to join the Fed is that Fed membership carries certain requirements. The most important requirement—at least it's most important during times when interest rates are high—is that member banks must hold non-interest-bearing reserves on deposit in the Federal Reserve Bank in their district.

State banks are also required by state law to hold reserves. But state banking laws allow the banks greater freedom in choosing how to hold their reserves. State banks can sometimes obtain interest on a part of their reserves, and they can obtain "free" banking services from correspondent banks in which they place their reserve deposits.

As interest rates increased rapidly in the late 1970s it became increasingly costly for member banks to hold their reserves in non-interest-bearing deposits in the Fed. A number of banks withdrew from the System. Some officials expressed concern that this trend might interfere with the effectiveness of the Fed's ability to control the nation's money supply.

This issue was discussed by the Fed, by banker's organizations, by representatives of other financial institutions, by politicians, by congressional committees, and by others. Various kinds of legislation were proposed.

The proposals ranged all the way from leaving the existing system "as is," to requiring that all banks and other financial institutions either be required to join the Fed, or be required to hold reserves at the Fed and follow the Fed's regulations. By the end of 1979—just three months before the Depository Institutions Deregulation and Monetary Control Act (DIDMCA) was passed in March 1980—the Fed membership problem was becoming critical. It was becoming more clear every day that the "as is" alternative wasn't viable.

Why not? And what were the major issues? And the arguments? The statements of senior bank officers presented in the following sections will answer these questions. These statements were made at a conference on current banking issues at Appalachian State University in December 1979. As you read them, you'll gain an understanding of the bankers' thinking on this issue some five years ago, just prior to the passage of the DIDMCA.

Rideout's Comments on the Fed Membership Issue*

The Fed membership issue depends on your perspective. For instance, what is the Fed membership issue from the point of view of the Federal Reserve?

A survey that Chairman Paul Volcker of the Fed has conducted indicates that up to a total of 575 banks are currently considering dropping their membership in the Federal Reserve system. Those banks represent a total of about *$70 billion* in deposits.

Currently there are approximately 5,480 banks that are members of the Federal Reserve system with total deposits that run on the order of *$720 billion.* If all of those 575 banks were to drop from the Fed, approximately *10 percent* of the deposits now under Fed control would no longer be under Fed control.

Ten years ago, 84 percent of all bank deposits in the country were represented by member banks. Currently that figure is 70 or 71 percent. Should all of these 575 banks drop out, that figure would drop to about 62 percent. The Federal Reserve's fear, then, is whether their ability to effectively implement monetary policies will be impaired.

*Statements in December 1979 by Thomas P. Rideout, formerly Senior Vice President, Wachovia Bank & Trust Co., Winston-Salem, North Carolina; more recently Chairman and CEO of Savannah Bank and Trust Co., Savannah, Georgia.

A second point of view is that of the Fed member banks. They look at the issue somewhat differently. One feeling is that the opportunity cost of holding non-interest-bearing reserves in the Federal Reserve system is higher than the values received from being a member of the Federal Reserve. The values received are such things as access to the discount window, various types of operating services, and payment services which the Federal Reserve provides.

A third perspective on this issue is that of the non-member bank. There are two major points here:

1. One is the concern about the bank's loss of choice about where, and in what form, reserves are to be held. Legislation could mandate that reserves be held at the Fed by all banks—and perhaps by all depository institutions. Such legislation could effectively mandate membership in the Federal Reserve while not legally requiring it.
2. The other concern that non-member banks have (and member banks have as well) is that our dual banking system—a system that provides some checks and balances—might be threatened by a mandatory reserve maintenance bill. Such a move could, in time, lead to a single regulator with a consequent lack of regulatory sensitivity to the needs of the financial marketplace.

Fourth, there's a congressional perspective which focuses on the need to make sure that the Federal Reserve can carry out monetary policy. The congressional perspective is concerned also with the issue of competitive equity.

Another important focus of the Congress is this: It would be possible to make Fed membership more attractive—to lower required reserves (and/or to pay interest on required Fed reserves)—but what impact would this have on Treasury revenue? Currently, the Federal Reserve turns over approximately 6 to 7 billion dollars a year in earnings to the U.S. Treasury. About one and one-half billion dollars of this comes from the non-interest-bearing, required reserves of member banks. So you can see that if reserve requirements were lowered, and/or if interest were to be paid on these reserves, the Treasury could lose some 300 to 500 million dollars per year. This is a matter of deep concern to the Congress.

I would like to say that if we are really going to achieve "competitive equity" among the financial institutions, then *all* depository financial institutions—such as the Merrill Lynch money market funds—should carry universal and uniform reserves on transaction accounts. With equal requirements, everybody would be carrying precisely the same burden. If we're going to have a "level playing field," that means we should have reserves on the same categories and at the same rates for everybody.

As you can see, the Fed membership issue is very complex. There are conflicting points of view. At this point, the ultimate solution to the problem is impossible to predict.

Buchanan's Comments on the Costs and Benefits of Fed Membership*

The Federal Reserve has petitioned Congress for several years to change the law with regard to the membership in the Federal Reserve. The Fed has been concerned about the loss of members. But this problem really hasn't created much interest other than among bankers.

Every time we find the issue of Fed membership being discussed, it's tied to something else with a little more appeal. It's tied to NOW account legislation, which certainly has consumeristic overtones, or to the change in Regulation Q or to some other issue that is more interesting, more appealing to the public and the Congress.

So this issue has not received a great deal of *press* exposure. But from the standpoint of the Fed and the bankers, it obviously has received a great deal of discussion.

The question of the "Fed Membership Problem" has been debated by bankers and Congress for some time. There has been

*Statements by Donald D. Buchanan, Executive Vice-President, North Carolina National Bank, Charlotte, North Carolina, December 1979. NCNB is a Fed member bank. NCNB Corp. has assets of about $13.5 billion.

considerable debate as to whether the basic premise that the Fed sets forth is valid, that is, that they need the member bank reserve base to enable them to effectively carry out monetary policy. There are those who believe that this basic premise is not valid—that the Fed has not fulfilled its obligation of supporting that position.

Here is another aspect of change—the question of "the pricing of Federal Reserve services." The Federal Reserve today provides services in the settlement of transactions between banks. When you give a check to a local merchant, that merchant may bank with another bank. So it's necessary to "settle the accounts" between these institutions. The Fed plays a key role in this area of check settlement and in the movement of funds from one bank to another throughout the country. Ever since the inception of the Fed, these services have been priced at "zero charge" to banks. I didn't say that they were at zero *cost* to banks. I'm saying that they have not been *priced* to the member banks.

A few years ago the Fed began to allow *non-member* banks access to certain Fed check-collection services. What did the member banks think about that? Picture yourself as a member of an expensive tennis club where you pay your initiation fee and monthly dues and then suddenly you find there are a lot of non-members (non-dues-payers) playing on your courts. That's what happened when the Fed started making some of its services available to nonmember banks.

Another significant event that allowed access to Fed services by non-member banks was the development of the *Automated Clearing House* (ACH). The ACH allows for direct deposit (without writing checks) of such items as payroll, social security payments, and an increasing number of private sector transactions, such as payments of insurance premiums.

The Automated Clearing House is a program that the commercial banks, in cooperation with the Federal Reserve, developed to stem the flow of paper in the banking system. Initially this service was offered only to member banks. But later it was made available to non-member banks and, more recently, to non-bank financial institutions.

These events certainly have had an influence on the "Fed Issue." Services that were provided by the Fed only to member banks, have become available to non-member institutions. It's impossible to tell how much that had to do with the current problem.

There are some complex questions posed with regard to the pricing of Fed services. We find in Congress a perception on the part of many that the banks have been getting something for nothing from the Fed. The Federal Reserve has been providing services "free" because there was no direct charge. But the member banks have reserves with the Fed. These reserves represent a portion of bank assets on which the member banks receive no earnings. These are "sterile" reserves that amount to a significant loss of potential interest income.

There are many bankers who now believe that the Federal Reserve should price and make direct charges for its services, provided that it also will reduce the cost of membership—that is, the cost of lost interest income that results from maintaining high levels of sterile, non-interest-bearing reserves.

When new legislation comes, it's likely that a lot of banks will be excluded. There will be an "exemption level" that says that if you're less than six feet tall, you can get free services. If you're *over* six feet tall, you pay for them. So if you happen to be one of the smaller banks, less than six feet tall, you're likely to be very interested in that kind of a solution.

The fact is that about 14,000 of the banks affected are "smaller banks"—under six feet tall. That only leaves about five hundred banks which are big enough to be required to abide by the new rules. So you say, "Well, let's let those five hundred big banks go around with long faces—because we've got 14,000 banks that are happy!" That's what you can call a political solution.

Today, the Federal Reserve is providing services that are similar to the services provided by some commercial banks. Many banks offer check-clearing services to other banks. We clear checks for them and handle settlement transactions from one bank to another. So in this area the Fed is clearly in competition with some of the larger commercial banks. The equitable pricing of Federal Reserve services would, in fact, allow commercial banks to more effectively compete with the Fed. And it's likely that many of these services could be provided at lower cost.

We're going to see a number of changes in all this. There are legislative proposals that will bring about pricing of services by the Fed. When the Fed provides services without charges, the development of private sector alternatives is discouraged. Obviously, when there is a service available for which no direct charge is made, it's very difficult for the private sector to compete.

It costs too much to be a member of the Fed. That's why the Fed has a declining membership—the *cost* exceeds the *benefits.* So the Fed has a problem. In order to make membership attractive, it must lower the cost of membership. The Fed, however, is being held hostage by the Treasury due to the substantial revenues that the Fed generates for the Treasury. A significant part of those revenues are derived from earnings generated on reserve deposits of member banks—reserves on which the Fed pays no interest to the member banks.

The high cost of membership is, in effect, an additional tax on banking—and the money goes to the Treasury. The resolution of this complex problem will not come quickly. When it comes it will be the result of considerable compromise. The final outcome cannot now be foreseen.

Adams' Comments on Fed Membership and Competitive Equity*

Northwestern Bank is one of the largest non-member banks in the country. But although we aren't a member of the Federal Reserve System, the Fed is a regulator of ours just the same. Northwestern Financial Corporation is a one-bank holding company and our holding company's activities come under the purview of the Fed. We find the Fed to be a fair, competent regulator—one with which we have frequent contact.

I want to deal primarily with one aspect of the Fed membership issue—the inequity issue. One of the most frequent charges leveled at the present system of Fed membership is that it is inequitable because member banks have to meet Federal Reserve requirements while non-member banks do not. However, an in-depth analysis of the earnings performance of non-member banks casts serious doubts on the accuracy of this inequity allegation.

*Statements by Austin A. Adams, Group Executive Vice-President, Northwestern Bank, North Wilkesboro, North Carolina, December 1979. Northwestern is a non-member bank with assets of about $2.33 billion.

A recent study was conducted of member and non-member banks in the asset category of one to two billion dollars in size. This study indicated that an earnings comparison (based on the frequent criterion of return on average assets) showed almost identical levels of earnings performance for member and non-member banks. The reason for such similar earnings performance seems to be that non-member banks above a certain size *consciously* structure their business in quite different ways than do Fed member banks. Recent balance sheet data indicate that non-members tend to concentrate in areas where membership in the Federal Reserve is not particularly helpful, while members tend to concentrate in areas of business where membership is helpful and sometimes necessary.

One measure of the degree of consumer orientation of a bank is its ratio of mortgages on one- to four-family residences plus consumer loans, to total assets. The recent study indicates that member banks in the one to two billion dollar size have 18 percent of their assets in consumer oriented loans, while non-members have 24 percent of their assets in such loans.

It seems clear that the large non-member bank is more consumer-oriented.

My point by this analysis is that any solution to the Fed membership issue that would increase dramatically the amount of sterile reserves that a present non-member bank would be required to hold would test the financial strength of some of these institutions. But more importantly, it would diminish the pool of funds available for consumer loans. It would be likely to result in a restructuring of many of our loan portfolios so as to include less consumer lending. The key point is this: any solution that would dramatically, in the short term, increase the amount of sterile reserves that we would be required to hold would likely reduce our consumer lending.

As an individual and as a banker I agree that effective monetary policy is critical to a sound economy. If the Congress deems that mandatory Fed membership is essential to having an effective central bank, then Northwestern's position is that two key points should be a part of that legislation.

The first point is that the phase-in period for bringing non-Fed members into the system should be ten years. If Fed membership must become mandatory, we can live with the ten-year phase-in and I think that's reasonable.

The second key point is that *all* financial intermediaries (not just banks) should be required to hold reserves at the Fed. We think this is an issue that is *absolutely critical* to an equitable resolution of the problem.

Suggested Readings

(See list of suggested readings at the end of Chapter 5.)

Chapter 5

McTeer's Comments on the Falling Fed Membership Issue*

When the Fed was set up by the Federal Reserve Act which was passed in 1913, Congress provided that all National Banks be members of the Federal Reserve system. Membership was left voluntary for state banks; they could either join or not. As a practical matter, though, it's voluntary for everybody, because if a national bank wants to drop Fed membership, it can exchange its federal charter for a state charter and then withdraw from the Fed System. So all banks do have a means of dropping out.

The Costs and Benefits of Fed Membership

Over the years, until recently, there's been a sort of balance between the cost of membership and the benefits of membership. The cost of membership primarily is that member banks, by law, are required to hold reserves in forms that *do not earn any interest.* The two legal ways they can hold reserves are: (1) cash (currency and coin) in their vaults, and (2) deposits at their Federal Reserve Bank. None of these reserves earns any interest. That's

*Statements by Robert D. McTeer, Jr., Vice President, Federal Reserve Bank of Richmond, Virginia, December 1979.

the primary cost of Fed membership—forfeiting the interest which could have been earned on that money.

On the other hand, there are several benefits that Fed members get. One of the benefits is access to the discount window. Member banks are able to borrow temporarily, in time of need, reserves from the Fed. Most of the time, that's not such a big deal. But now and then the economy and the banking system go through periods of stresses and strains, and access to the Fed's discount window is a tremendous asset. It's an asset to the banking system as a whole because it gives needed flexibility to the reserve base. But it's also an asset from the viewpoint of those individual banks that might be in trouble.

Other benefits of Fed membership include such things as free coin and currency services, free safekeeping services for securities, check collection, etc. But, as you already know, the exclusive value of some of these benefits has eroded over recent years because the Fed has made some of these services available to non-member banks. That's one of the current problems.

As Interest Rates Rise, Membership Cost Increases

The most fundamental factor that has led to the membership problem has been *the effect of the recent inflation on interest rates.* Back when interest rates were around three or four percent, the income lost by holding non-earning assets (as reserves required by the Fed) was not all that significant. But now the inflation rate has built up to 13 percent, so you have interest rates that are going above 13 percent and becoming real (i.e., higher than the inflation rate). So the burden of this cost has increased significantly.

So we now have a reassessment by many bankers of the relative cost of membership and the relative benefits. This is causing a lot of banks to drop out, wisely or not.

Traditionally, the banks that have dropped out have been the smaller ones. This is partly because the benefits of membership seemed to be greater for the larger banks. Large banks can resell a lot of Fed services to smaller (correspondent) banks. They have access to the Fed's check collection services and they can, through that access, provide similar services to smaller banks. But recently, one of the most disturbing aspects of the membership problem has been that a lot of the larger banks are beginning to consider dropping out.

Fed Membership and Monetary Control

Is the declining Fed membership problem really a problem? Actually there are two problems that the Fed emphasizes. One is that at some point (a point not clearly defined, even within the Fed) eroding membership (meaning an eroding base of reserves, that the Fed has control over) will reduce the Fed's effectiveness in conducting monetary policy. Nobody knows just at what point this problem becomes serious. I don't think there is a serious problem in that regard yet. I don't even think it would be too serious if we lost a few more and the Fed's deposit base shrank somewhat more. But I do think that at some undefined point, the ability of the Federal Reserve to conduct monetary policy will be hampered—perhaps not destroyed, but at least seriously eroded—because of the declining reserve base under the Fed's jurisdiction.

As you know, when banks make loans, new money is created. If the Fed is going to conduct monetary policy, it must do so through the banking system. Even so, we have this unique situation in this country—a relationship with the central bank is not mandatory for all banks. The banks in this country have a choice. They can pick and choose among the various bank regulators. (Which is fine. I have no problem with that.) But at the same time, they can choose whether or not they're going to have a relationship with the central monetary authority (the Fed). We think that's going to cause some problems with respect to monetary control. But in addition to control problems, we think there is a basic unfairness here.

Reducing the Costs of Membership

You have a lot of organizations creating money in the process of their operations. Some of those are being penalized because they're members of the Central Banking System and must hold reserves in non-earning form while others that are competing with those banks are not having to bear that burden. There are two ways to deal with that kind of problem. One would be to reduce the burden for the member banks to the point where the benefits and the cost pretty well balance out again. That way you provide a financial incentive for them to keep their Fed membership.

Over the years the Fed generally has favored this voluntary approach. We don't like the idea of dragging banks into the Fed System against their will. We like the idea of their wanting to have an association with the Fed. So traditionally, we have favored a voluntary approach to the solution, which primarily would involve paying interest on member bank reserves. In the past, the Fed has proposed to Congress that we be allowed to pay interest on reserves, but it now appears that this approach is just not politically feasible.

Some would say that if the Fed pays the banks interest on their reserves, that is in effect taking money out of the taxpayer's hands and giving it to the nasty bankers. During the past year or so the Fed has switched to another approach: that is, *mandatory reserve requirements for all money-creating institutions*. The required reserves would be set at a fairly low level so as not to be terribly burdensome, and they would apply equally to all financial institutions that are (in effect) creating money.

The approach in the Proxmire bill is primarily one of requiring reserves of all financial institutions that have transactions deposits—that is, deposits that can be transferred from one person to another without any cash being involved, such as checking accounts, NOW (negotiable order of withdrawal) accounts, ATS (automatic transfer from savings to checking) accounts, and share drafts. I believe the Fed now prefers this approach primarily because it deals more directly with the question of *competitive equity* among the various financial institutions in the nation.

Charging Prices for Fed Services

Another approach to this problem would be to begin pricing Fed Services. Just about all the major bills that are before Congress include some provisions for the Fed to charge prices for the services it performs for commercial banks. The idea is that there will be a lot more efficiency in the marketplace if the Fed puts prices on its services. If the Fed offered to perform services at higher cost than a commercial bank could do them, the Fed wouldn't be able to compete. The commercial bank would take over the service. The bank would benefit because it would get the business; society would benefit because resources would be allocated more efficiently. The business would go to the most efficient, lowest-cost producer of the service.

I have no basic problem with that approach. There might be some transitional problem within the Fed if we lose a great deal of our business. There are also different kinds of services, and they raise different potential problems. It seems to me that it makes more sense to price things like check collection, for example, than the distribution of coin and currency. One might argue that providing the public with coin and currency, which is a purely governmental operation, should be performed by the government rather than by private enterprises.

We at the Richmond Federal Reserve Bank have no fundamental problem with the concept of the pricing of Fed services. Most of the emphasis and push for that comes from the larger banks who see themselves as major competitors of ours. If the smaller banks studied the issue carefully, I'm not so sure they would be in favor of it. It seems to me that they might worry just a little about the implications of all this, for themselves—but we don't hear much about the pricing idea from the smaller banks.

What About Charging for Float?

A new issue that's come up recently is the question of Federal Reserve float and whether that ought to be treated as one of our charged-for services. Essentially, Federal Reserve float is created when some banks are credited for the proceeds of checks deposited before that amount has been subtracted from the reserve accounts of other banks. So, in effect, there's a temporary loan of reserves to the banking system by the Fed. I would think that the banking system as a whole wouldn't object too strenuously if we did not charge for this temporary loan by the Fed. But the banks—mainly with large banks as spokesmen—are objecting to the idea of the Fed not charging for float. Many of the large banks seem to feel that if we charge for float, it will raise our prices and make us a less effective competitor in providing services. So there's disagreement on this issue too.

The Allocation of the Burden

It should be remembered that the whole question here is one of the allocation of cost within the banking system. There's really no such a thing as an *absolute* burden of Fed membership. If all banks were treated equally, then whatever the burden might be, the Fed would have to take the appropriate action to make the whole system work.

If we had higher reserve requirements, for example, the Fed would simply have to pump more reserves into the banking system to meet the needs for more reserves. If we had lower reserve requirements, we'd have to take the necessary actions to pull reserves out of the banking system. So the whole question is how to divide up and allocate the burden. It isn't a question of whether there is going to be a burden.

If we have a legislative solution that involves a substantial reduction of bank reserve requirements (in the aggregate), the Fed is going to have to go into the market and mop up those reserves by selling government securities. Banks in the aggregate aren't going to be all that much better off. It's just a question of the allocation of the burden.

The Loss of Treasury Revenues

The key to understanding one source of opposition to reducing the aggregate amount of required reserves is that it's going to be a *cost* to the U.S. Treasury. Suppose we reduce reserve requirements to the banking system. To keep that from being inflationary, we have to go into the market and sell off government securities from our own portfolio to mop up the excess reserves. Then the Fed will own a smaller portfolio of government securities. Since most of our earnings come from our interest income on government securities, as we sell off those securities our earnings are going to be reduced. And since almost all of our earnings are turned over to the Treasury at the end of the year, the Treasury will get less money from us. Some people would oppose this proposed solution for that reason. Senator Proxmire has expressed a great deal of concern about this potential loss of Treasury revenues.

As you can see, the "falling Fed membership" issue is really many different issues. And it's clear that it will involve many difficult and controversial decisions before satisfactory long-term arrangements are worked out for the future.

Suggested Readings

Benston, George J. "Federal Reserve Membership: Consequences, Costs, Benefits and Alternatives," Study prepared for the Association of Reserve City Bankers (September 1978).

Board of Governors of the Federal Reserve System. *The Federal Reserve System: Purposes and Functions* (Washington, D.C.: FRS, September, 1974).

Cacy, J. A., and Winningham, Scott. "Reserve Requirements Under the Depository Institutions Deregulation and Monetary Control Act of 1980," *Economic Review,* Federal Reserve Bank of Kansas City (Sept.–Oct. 1980), 3–16.

Goodfriend, Marvin. "Discount Window Borrowing, Monetary Control, and the Post-October 6, 1979, Federal Reserve Operating Procedure," Federal Reserve Bank of Richmond Working Paper 81–1, January 1981.

Goodfriend, Marvin, and Hargraves, Monica. "A Historical Assessment of the Rationales and Functions of Reserve Requirements," *Economic Review,* Federal Reserve Bank of Richmond (March–April 1983), 3–20.

Paulus, John. "The Burden of Federal Reserve Membership, NOW Accounts and the Payment of Interest on Reserves," Federal Reserve Board of Governors, Staff Economic Study (June 1977).

Rose, Peter. "Banker Attitudes Toward the Federal Reserve System: Survey Results," *Journal of Bank Research* (Summer 1977), 77–84.

Chapter 6

Reg Q Deregulation and New Powers for the Thrifts

If one bank (or other financial institution) can provide a better or more desirable service than another, then that bank can win customers. That's competition through improved products or services. Whenever banks or other financial institutions can attract customers in this way, that usually is good business. But sometimes it's impossible to convince people that your products or services are better than those of your competitors. Then if you want to attract customers you may need to use "price" competition.

Price competition in banking and in other financial institutions consists of offering your customers more money if they will bring their deposits to you. And it also means offering to lend money to your customers and charge a lower interest "price" than charged by your competitors. It also means pricing the other services you offer at lower rates than your competitors.

In the American "free enterprise" economy, almost all businesses are free to introduce any kind of product or service they wish, to pay as much as they wish for the "input" goods and services they require, and to charge whatever prices they wish for the goods and services they sell. The force of competition induces them to produce high-quality goods and services, to pay approximately the "going rates" for their inputs, and to charge approximately the "going rates" for their outputs. The point is, it is *competition, not government,* which regulates most businesses in the American economy. But that is not the way it works in the banking and financial services market.

Government Regulation of Financial Institutions

In the banking and finance markets, both services and prices have been regulated by government. The kinds of services that could be offered, the prices (interest) that could be paid to depositors for their funds, and the prices (interest) that could be charged to borrowers—all of these aspects of competition have been limited and controlled by government regulations. So in the banking and financial markets, the kinds of competition that banks and other financial institutions engage in have been strictly limited.

Why has there been so much regulation limiting the kinds of competitive services that can be offered by the financial institutions? And the prices that can be set by these institutions? One of the concerns has been that we can't have a healthy, stable, growing economy unless we have healthy, stable, growing financial institutions and markets. And there are short-run periods during which unrestricted competition can have very disruptive influences on an industry.

There have been many "financial panics" in the history of the American financial markets—about one every ten years from the end of the Civil War until the time the Federal Reserve System was set up in 1913. When you look at that historical experience and at the experience of the depression of the 1930s, it is easy to see why so much of the legislation relating to the banks and other financial institutions has been aimed toward achieving safety and stability.

In recent years many aspects of the old restrictions became more detrimental than beneficial. By late 1979 it was clear that changes were absolutely necessary—changes in the direction of *deregulation*.

Tight Money and High Interest Rates

In October 1979 the Federal Reserve Board announced a new decision about how it was going to control the money supply. Until that time, the Fed had looked more at *interest rates* as an indicator of "the tightness of money." But in October 1979 the Fed's target became the "monetary base"—that is, the reserves available to banks. If the monetary base is not permitted to expand, then the ability of the banking system to make new loans is cut off.

The significance of this shift in Fed policy is this: By controlling the monetary base, the Fed can *absolutely prevent* the money supply from expanding. When it does this, if the demand for money goes very high, then interest rates are pushed up very high—and not only do they go high, they also become very volatile. Since the supply of money becomes more or less fixed (unresponsive), demand changes cause interest rates to fluctuate widely. And that's what happened.

How do the financial intermediaries, bound by Reg Q, function in an environment of high and widely fluctuating interest rates? Not very well. They suffer disintermediation. They see their cost of funds go up—often to more than their return on assets. This is exactly what was happening in the late 1970s. By the end of 1979 the issue was becoming critical. What were the banks and thrifts doing? And what did their managers think should be done to relieve the crisis conditions? That's what you'll find out as you read the following statements made at the Appalachian State University Banking Conference in December 1979.

Brewer's Comments on Reg Q and the S&Ls*

We should recognize that these deregulation issues have been going on for some time now. All this talk about financial reform didn't just begin in the last year or so. Over the past ten to fifteen

*Statements by James T. Brewer, Senior Vice President, Wachovia Bank & Trust Co., Winston-Salem, North Carolina, December 1979. Wachovia is a Fed member bank with assets of about $7.2 billion.

years the S&Ls—at least some of the institutions in that industry—have been pushing very hard for expanded powers. They want to offer different kinds of deposit services, such as checking accounts.

There are reasons—very sound economic reasons—why the S&L industry has sought broader powers. One reason is that they would like to become more "full-service" institutions. When they acquire a customer they would like to get the customer's home-mortgage loan, savings account, and also provide the customer with a checking account. Also many S&Ls would like to balance their loan portfolios—now predominantly in long-term mortgages—with a mix of consumer loans. Perhaps that would make for better asset-liability management.

Let's look at all this from the side of the commercial banks. The commercial banks are saying: "That's O.K. with us. You can have all the powers of commercial banks if you want. But if you do, then you are going to have to give up the special advantages you have."

There have been debates on this within the banking industry. There's the small bank position and the large bank position, the midwest position and the southern position, and on and on. I think that if commercial banks could get together on this issue it would be much easier for Congress to act. Right now there's no unanimity, either within the commercial banking business or within the S&L business, as to what should be done.

There are three issues here. One is the issue of extending the powers of the S&Ls. Another is the equalization of differentials between commercial banks and S&Ls. Then there's the third issue, also closely related: Should we do away with Regulation Q altogether? Should we just let interest rates on deposits be determined by the market?

The law setting up Reg Q was passed in 1933. The original limit was three percent. That was the maximum rate of interest that could be paid on time deposits at banks. During the early years, Reg Q had no effect anyway, because the money market rate was much lower than the Reg Q ceiling rate.

There were a few changes in Reg Q in the 1950s and several changes in the 1960s. In 1966 the S&L industry was brought under Reg Q for the first time. The 1966 law required that the Federal Home Loan Bank Board and the Federal Reserve Board agree mutually on new regulations regarding interest ceilings for the S&L industry.

The S&Ls were permitted to pay more than the banks. In 1966 the differential between the ceiling interest which banks could pay and that which the S&Ls could pay was set at $\frac{3}{4}$ of a percent for most categories of deposits. Then in the years following 1966 there were several changes. The trend was toward reducing the Reg Q interest rate differential between the banks and the S&Ls.

In 1975 there was a law passed that said no more changes in the differential could be made without Congressional approval. Right now the Congress is trying to resolve this regulatory issue—the question as to what powers should be given the S&Ls and what should be done about the interest rate differential—or should we perhaps get away from interest rate regulations altogether?

I think Congressional action is going to *formalize* or *ratify* what has already happened.

Some of the larger, more aggressive S&Ls are involved in many things other than home mortgages, and several kinds of new deposits are being offered. In my opinion, it is just a matter of time before all of this is ratified by Congress.

Anyone who recognizes the complexity of these current banking and financial issues can see already the kinds and the significance of the changes that are sure to come. But as to exactly what changes will occur, and in what time frame, we must wait and see.

Marsh's Comments on the Impact of Deregulation on the Savings and Loan Industry*

For years, many S&L managing officers sat and watched the simple process of their operations sustain profits and build reserves. Loan forms were a simple matter—usually one page. Many people in the industry simply took deposits and made loans. Today, it's a new ball game. No longer can the S&L industry exist as an independent entity unless it gets out and competes.

*Statements by James P. Marsh, President, Watauga Savings and Loan, Boone, North Carolina, December 1979.

How are our savings institutions coping? Nearly all are experiencing heavy outflows of deposits—that is, disintermediation. Some outflow is going into bonds and government securities. Heavy outflows are pouring into money market funds offered by brokerage firms. This savings decline is eroding profits, straining reserve positions, and testing old and new management techniques.

The phenomenal growth of money market funds has paralleled the slowdown in housing and mortgage financing nationally. Anticipated government regulation may soon change this.

But government regulation can't provide a blanket of protection to the thrift industry. We don't expect that or want that. That's why the majority of savings and loans are watching so closely the process of certain Congressional legislation: HR4986—*The Financial Institutions Deregulation Act*. Passage of this act could change the entire complexion of our industry overnight. Bogged down in conference committee currently, time is running out on this particular legislation for this session of the Congress. However, passage of a portion of this far-reaching bill will simply signal a beginning to the kind of change that is sure to come.

The seed has been planted and many of the aspects of this legislation will most assuredly come to pass. These changes will help to spur the move toward mergers in the S&L industry all across the country. The final result will be a stronger savings and loan industry. However, in the process, there will be some wailing and gnashing of teeth.

NOW accounts will be something that many savings and loan associations will be slow to offer—and even slower to adjust to. This is not only going to require a great *capital outlay* by the associations, but it is also going to add to *expenses*. A different type of personnel expense will surely be required of each association.

As a result of the NOW account innovation, some would say that we're all destined ultimately to develop into single "full-service" financial units. Certain economic seers even say that some day, not too far in the future, we'll have a completely Fed-controlled financial system, with singular insurance of accounts. Be that as it may, it must be recognized that these regulatory changes add to our cost of operation.

It's a simple fact of economic life that we are not in business to give away our services. We are, both mutual and stock associations, profit motivated. And as more of us become stock-owned associations and deal with the innovations brought about by new legislation, our profit motivation will be more "up front" in all of our decisions and procedures. So NOW accounts will bring us a pricing problem. The customer is going to gain a new service, but you can be sure that the customer is going to have to pay for it.

The cost of money to us—and to the consumer, in turn—is going to continue to hold high as a freer marketplace develops. In the 1980s this is certain to happen. And as a result, mortgage rates are going to stay up, too.

Regulation, deregulation, governmental interpretations of statutes, legal opinions, etc.—all of these affect us daily. Our once simple business has become complex. But this is part of the growing process. Just as in the basic law of nature, those who can adjust will survive and become stronger and more viable participants in the economic community.

Farthing's Comments on Reg Q Deregulation*

One thing Reg Q limits have done in the American economy is provide cheap capital. If a bank can pay a depositor two or three percent and then lend that money to a business at seven or eight percent, and the business can invest the money and earn 20 percent, the whole economy will grow rapidly. But the depositors are indirectly subsidizing the borrowers by receiving less than the market rate of interest on their savings. So the underpaid depositors allow the bank to charge its borrowers relatively low rates for loans.

In the short run, eliminating interest rate ceilings and allowing banks to begin paying interest on checking accounts is likely to have a serious effect on the banking industry's ability to generate stable, consistently increasing profits. Why? Because the old spread between what banks pay their depositors and what banks charge when they make loans has been pretty well established over time as a fixed percentage, and taken for granted. Generally

*Statements by Larry Farthing, Vice President, Northwestern Bank, North Wilkesboro, North Carolina, December 1979. Northwestern is a non-member bank with assets of about $2.33 billion.

it has been sufficient to cover all operating expenses. That just isn't going to be true anymore.

The banking industry never has had to deal very much with pricing. The profitability question has always been covered by the spread that we've been able to get because of the regulations we've been living with. So when this regulatory situation changes, initially some banks may have a lot of trouble.

Banks are going to have to start realistically pricing all of the services that they provide. And I mean not just loans, but all of the other services that banks have been giving away over the years. These realistic prices are going to have to be much higher than in the past.

What I am saying is that you can probably expect deregulation to bring, in the short run, higher expenses for you, the customer, whether you're a borrower or whether you're using some of the other services of a bank. I think in the longer run the banks will price loans at a high enough rate of interest to again offset much of the cost of doing business. However, I also think that in the long run the less efficient banks and other financial institutions—the ones which react slowly to the new market conditions—will be eliminated.

Poole's Comments on Reg Q Deregulation*

For many years, banks could generate all of the funds they needed to lend, just from the checking accounts of their customers—primarily commercial checking accounts. The value of funds generally was so low that it didn't provide much incentive for the treasurer of a corporation to look for alternative places to put their funds in order to earn interest. So they left a lot of money lying idle in their checking accounts. Consumers did the same thing.

During this period an interesting thing happened. We developed a pricing system in the banking business that would defy all logic from the point of view of the ordinary businessman. Most

*Statements by Winton R. Poole, Senior Vice President, North Carolina National Bank, Charlotte, North Carolina, December 1979. NCNB is a Fed member bank. NCNB Corp. has assets of about $13.5 billion.

businesses must look at their *cost of producing* products or services and compare that with what they get—*revenues received* when they sell those products or services in the marketplace. That's how a business figures its profit. But it was different with banks.

Since banks were receiving all of these funds free of charge from the demand deposits of their customers, they could afford to give away all kinds of services to those customers—and to the rest of their customers, too. As a result of all of this, the old "80-20 Rule" came into effect. The idea is that only 20 percent of our customers carry 80 percent of the deposit balances in our banks, and the other 80 percent of the customers carry only 20 percent of the deposit balances. So the free funds provided to the banks by the top 20 percent of the customers make it possible for the bank to provide free services to the other 80 percent who, in fact, are not paying their own way.

About 80 percent of the checking accounts in banks these days are not profitable to the banks. If you take an average checking account of the lower 80 percent of our customers (which costs about $70 a year to service) and look at the income generated by the balance on that account, you'll see that it just doesn't generate $70 a year in interest to pay that cost. Once we start paying the interest we should be paying to the people who have money on deposit with us, we will have to turn around and charge people for all of the services we are providing to them.

Everybody seems to agree that we're going to have to start paying interest on checking accounts. Many people believe that this will happen in 1980. Also the differentials between the rates that banks can pay and the rates that savings and loan institutions can pay probably will be eliminated. Other limitations such as limitations on the kinds of services which savings and loans can offer (checking accounts and consumer loans, for example) will probably be eliminated also.

Over the next three to five years it's going to become increasingly difficult to see any difference between various types of financial institutions. Commercial banks, savings and loan associations, credit unions, and others—all of which in the past have performed specialized financial services—soon will begin to look more and more alike. All probably will be permitted to offer all of the services that anyone else can offer.

Bank personnel are going to have to become more skilled at

marketing. The strange kind of pricing system we have had in the banking business in the past has caused a generation of bankers to grow up as "order takers"—not as salespeople. That has already been changing for several years, but the change so far has been gradual. It is going to accelerate.

Banks are going to have to do a lot better job of selling and competing in the future. It will be absolutely essential for banks to understand their costs and to use these costs as the basis for pricing their services. No longer is it going to be possible for banks to continue to offer their customers all kinds of free services, or services at costs which bear no relationship to the actual costs of providing those services.

In some ways it's going to be a lot tougher to be in the banking business. But for the long term, I think our industry and our customers are going to profit from the increased efficiencies that will result from deregulation and the resulting competition.

A Summary Comment

This chapter and the two previous ones have given you a "flashback" to December of 1979. That was two months after the Fed's new money-tightening initiative of October 1979. And it was three months before the March 1980 Banking Act (DIDMCA) was passed.

The issues discussed by the bankers in these three chapters were the issues that ultimately pushed aside political differences and forced the passage of the 1980 Act. By the end of 1979 the Fed membership issue was becoming critical. And disintermediation (because of Reg Q interest rate ceilings on deposits) was bleeding the depository institutions to death. The chapters coming up in Part III explain what happened after that—and why and how.

Suggested Readings

Benston, George. "Interest Rate Payments on Demand Deposits and Bank Investment Behavior," *Journal of Political Economy*, Vol. LXXII, No. 5 (October 1964), 431–449.

Chase, Kristine L. "Interest Rate Deregulation, Branching, and Competition in the Savings and Loan Industry," Federal Home Loan Bank Board *Journal* (November 1981), 2–6.

Flannery, Mark J. "Removing Deposit Rate Ceilings," *Business Review*, Federal Reserve Bank of Philadelphia (March–April 1983), 13–20.

Gilbert, R. Alton. "Will the Removal of Regulation Q Raise Mortgage Interest Rates?," *Review*, Federal Reserve Bank of St. Louis (December 1981), 3–12.

Marcis, Richard G. "Implications of Financial Innovation and Reform for the Savings and Loan Industry," *American Real Estate and Urban Economics Association Journal*, 8 (Spring 1980), 148–155.

Morris, Frank E. "The Cost of Price Control in Banking," *New England Economic Review*, Federal Reserve Bank of Boston (May–June 1979), 49–54.

"Trouble Anew at the Thrifts," *Business Week* (September 15, 1980), 119–20.

Part III
The Banking Act of 1980 (DIDMCA) and the Regulatory and Financial Environment

The 1980 Act Addressed Several of the Problems and Solved Some, But It Didn't Stop or Even Slow the Disintermediation Process

Chapter 7

Events Leading to the Passage of the 1980 Banking Act (DIDMCA)

The new banking Act was passed in late March 1980. This chapter describes and explains the conditions and events preceding the passage of this Act. The following chapter explains and discusses the provisions of the Act itself. Then the final two chapters in this Part describe and evaluate immediate reactions to the new Act and the changing conditions and events in the bond and money markets and in the financial services industry following its passage.

Trouble at the Thrifts

During 1979—especially after the Fed's drastic money-tightening moves of October 6—serious financial problems were faced by some of the nation's financial institutions. Seriously unstable conditions existed in the nation's money and capital markets. The November 19 issue of *Business Week* carried an article entitled "Trouble at the Thrifts: The Pain of High Interest Rates." This article began:*

**Business Week*, November 19, 1979, page 120.

> After a decade of dazzling growth, the nation's $700 billion thrift industry is suddenly on the verge of a massive shakeout. The Federal Reserve Board's credit-tightening program on Oct. 6 threw all the nation's financial markets into a tailspin, but no sector has been harder hit than the thrifts. Indeed, the industry—composed of 4,500 savings and loan associations across the nation and 500 mutual savings banks, primarily in the Northeast—is now in nothing less than a race for its economic life, a race that many small and unsophisticated institutions seem certain to lose.

The article went on to explain how the thrifts were being forced to pay more for the funds they were acquiring in the money markets than they were earning on their investments—mostly home mortgages. Then the article explained various ways that some of the thrifts were trying to cope with this new environment, and discussed the impact of some of the proposed regulatory changes—such as expanded services for the thrifts, NOW accounts, and the impact on the thrifts if Regulation Q were abolished. The article ended with the conclusion that a shake-out is definitely coming in the thrift industry, and that it's going to be both long-lasting and severe. That was the view in November of 1979.

The Worsening Problems of Early 1980

During the first several weeks of 1980 the situation worsened. The inflation rate increased and interest rates continued to move up to record levels. Many of the thrifts and an increasing number of banks were facing financial difficulty. And many more Fed member banks were threatening to withdraw from the Federal Reserve System. There was increasing concern about the financial safety of some of the smaller banks, and some large ones too.

On Tuesday, February 26, 1980, *The Wall Street Journal* carried a feature article emphasizing the problems that some banks were facing. The title of the article was: "Many Small Banks are Short of Money, Long on Worried Customers." The article gave several cases in which the tight money policies of October 1979 had caught small-town banks in a profit squeeze, making it almost impossible for them to provide the credit needed by their local communities.

The Fed's money tightening moves had pushed up interest rates in the urban areas, and also in the rural areas. Most of the urban banks in early 1980 still had plenty of money to lend. But money at many of the smaller "country banks" was in short supply, and appeared likely to remain that way for some time.

Problems of the Small Country Banks

The small country banks generally had been in the practice of making loans at fixed rates of interest. It had been possible for them to do this because of their own relatively stable cost of money. So in early 1980, many of the country banks were faced with a situation similar to that which had trapped the S&Ls and other thrifts. They were "locked in" with fixed-interest income on their loans, while facing variable (constantly increasing) interest costs on the funds they were acquiring. Under these circumstances, businesses in the local rural areas—including farmers, small manufacturers, distributors, retailers—were finding it very difficult to borrow the funds needed to carry on their operations.

The Havoc of High Interest Rates

The very high and rising interest rates were having their impact throughout the money and capital markets. The construction industry, particularly residential home-building, was moving into a seriously depressed condition. Farmers were having difficulty obtaining the funds needed to support agricultural and livestock production. Businesses of all kinds were feeling the pinch of tight money and the increasing cost of the very high interest rates.

The value of bonds in the nation's bond markets plummeted. Individuals, banks, insurance companies, trust funds—everyone who held long-term bonds that had been issued with interest rates as low as 4% or 5% or even 9% or 10%—saw the market values of their bonds going down. These low-interest bonds, when sold in the market, had to be sold for deep discounts. Who would buy these low-interest bonds at face value when interest rates in the short-term money markets were in the mid or upper teens, and interest rates on new long-term bonds being issued were also in the teens?

Some state and local governments and some large corporations, needing to obtain long-term funds for capital improvements and long-term investments, were finding the interest cost sometimes so high as to be prohibitive. Some cities and states decided to defer scheduled capital expenditure programs because of the high interest cost—to wait, and hope for a drop in interest rates.

The savings and loan associations and mutual savings banks and other thrifts were losing billions of dollars in deposits because of "disintermediation"—the withdrawal of savings by people who were dissatisfied with the low interest on their savings accounts. Savers were withdrawing their savings and investing them in money market certificates, money market mutual funds, and other short-term investments that paid much more interest. As the days and weeks went by, it became increasingly obvious that changes in the basic regulatory structure surrounding the banks and the thrifts—changes of a basic, fundamental nature—were needed, and quickly.

Wriston Calls for Decontrol of Prices on Money

It was in this near-crisis environment that Walter Wriston, Chairman and Chief Executive Officer (CEO) of Citibank in New York, appeared on the CBS program "Face the Nation" (March 23, 1980) and called for deregulation of interest rates on deposits and loans.

Mr. Wriston referred to the "price controls on money" that have existed in this country for many years, and said that a person who saves "has been ripped off by government regulations that prohibit banks from paying more than 5% or 5½% on your savings account. And state usury laws control the amount of interest that can be paid [by borrowers]." Wriston explained that the existing system is penalizing the saver and encouraging borrowing. He blamed many of the problems existing in the American economy on the price controls on interest, and on the tax laws that discourage saving and make it profitable to have large debts.

Mr. Wriston emphasized that *saving* is what is necessary for building capital in an economy, and that when laws are designed to penalize people who save, then investment will suffer and employment and productivity will suffer. Wriston said: "We have to reorient the laws of this country to make it not only fashionable but profitable to save money and to create capital—and to discourage borrowing."

Mr. Wriston was clearly in favor of phasing out Reg Q and eliminating the restrictions imposed by state usury laws. In the bills that were being argued in Congress at that time (March 1980) there were provisions designed to eliminate the former and reduce the impact of the latter.

Events Leading to the Passage of the New Bank Bill

During the first three months of 1980, both the House and the Senate Banking Committees continued to meet and talk with members of the banking and financial services industries, with members of the Fed, and with members of the Administration—and, in several joint sessions, with each other. There were many "hot issues" discussed, but the two most critical were these:

1. The question of what to do about the declining Fed membership problem (whether to pay interest on deposits, require all banks to hold reserve deposits at the Fed, or what), and
2. The "Reg Q" issue (whether or not to increase the interest rate ceilings that banks and S&Ls could pay on savings deposits, or whether to phase out these controls altogether—and if to phase out the controls, over what period of time).

The House had already passed a bill addressing the Fed membership issue, and the Senate had already passed a bill calling for the phase-out of interest ceilings on savings accounts (Reg Q) over a 10-year period. One of the big arguments during the early months of 1980 was this: The Senate was refusing to consider legislation on the Fed membership issue until after the House had considered the interest rate deregulation issue. But the House was refusing to consider interest rate deregulation until after the Senate had taken action on the Fed membership question. But fortunately, some representatives of the two banking committees (House and Senate) did get together and begin to talk about these issues, and try to work them out.

Volcker and Miller Urge Congress to Pass New Legislation

In early February of 1980 Fed Chairman Paul Volcker spoke to the Senate Banking Committee about the seriousness of the declining Fed membership problem.* He told them that during the fourth quarter of 1979 and the first few weeks of 1980, 69 banks, with aggregate deposits amounting to some $7 billion, had given notice of their plans to withdraw from Fed membership. He said that the loss of deposits during this short period of time was greater than in any full year in the past.

Volcker emphasized the seriousness of the problem, saying that such continuing erosion of membership would reduce the Fed's power to control the nation's money supply. He warned that unless remedial legislation could be passed quickly, the exodus from the Fed system would reach "flood proportions." He said that during the past three years (1977–79), Fed member bank deposits, as a proportion of overall deposits in the nation, declined from 73 percent to 70 percent.

Volcker said that some 670 banks were considering withdrawing from the system, and that Congress should produce a legislative solution quickly to avert the possibility of a serious disruption of the Fed's power of monetary management.

On the day following the appearance of Fed Chairman Volcker, Secretary of the Treasury G. William Miller met with the Senate Banking Committee to testify on the same issue. Miller urged Congress to consider extending reserve coverage to all financial institutions providing transaction accounts—including commercial banks, savings and loans, credit unions, and all others. Miller said that the administration supported this proposed extension of re-

*Volcker's various statements to Congress can be found in the *Federal Reserve Bulletin*, and in the *Congressional Hearings*.

serve requirements to non-member banks and to nonbank financial institutions, and the lowering of reserve requirements. Miller referred to the proposed universal reserve requirement as "the key to our solution to the problem of effective monetary control."

Miller explained that the lowering of reserve requirements was necessary to reduce the burden of non-interest-bearing reserves on the nation's financial institutions. He said this approach would cost the Treasury about $74 million annually in revenue losses, because the Fed would hold a smaller *total* amount of reserve deposits. So the Fed would have less "free funds" to invest in government interest-bearing securities. This would reduce the amount of interest income the Fed earns—which it turns back over to the Treasury.

The expected loss to the Treasury of $74 million annually would be considerably less than the loss that would result from some other approaches being considered. The House bill called for paying interest on reserves and would cost the Treasury about $357 million in lost revenues. The Senate version of a bill that would pay interest on reserves would cost the Treasury about $579 million. Miller told the Congressional Committee that the administration would like to hold down the loss in Treasury revenue to less than $200 million.

Heiman and Partee Testify About Reg Q

The House Banking Committee established a subcommittee to work on the interest ceiling deregulation issue. In February of 1980 this subcommittee heard testimony from John Heiman, Comptroller of the Currency, and from Charles Partee, a member of the Federal Reserve Board, both recommending that interest rate ceilings on savings accounts be phased out, and not over a 10-year period, but over a 5-year period. Both of these bank regulators noted the recent high inflation and interest rates and emphasized the fact that market developments were changing too quickly for a 10-year phase-out. Mr. Partee said that "a 5-year phase-out of deposit interest rate ceilings—beginning toward the end of this year (1980)—should provide the regulatory agencies sufficient flexibility in managing the transition."

Congress Passes the New Banking Act

The House Banking Subcommittee began holding meetings in March with members of the Senate Banking Committee, trying to resolve the differences on this issue and work out an agreement. Everyone concerned was aware of the urgency of passing some kind of legislation and doing it quickly. This awareness of the urgency was strong enough to overcome the disagreements.

Differences between the House bill (which had been passed in 1979) and the Senate bill (passed in early 1980) were worked out. Near the end of March, a compromise bill was introduced and quickly passed, first by the House and then by the Senate. On March 31, the *Depository Institutions Deregulation and Monetary Control Act of 1980* was signed into law by President Carter. The provisions of the Act and its implications will be explained in the following chapters.

Suggested Readings

"Are We on the Way to 19,000 Banks?," *American Bankers Association Journal* (May 1980), 99.

Dince, Robert R., and Verbrugge, James A. "The Right Way to Save the S&Ls," *Fortune* (Aug. 10, 1981), 134–144.

Federal Reserve Bank of Chicago. "The Depository Institutions Deregulation and Monetary Control Act of 1980," *Economic Perspectives* (Sept.-Oct. 1980), 3–23.

Hendershott, Patric, and Villani, Kevin. "The Likely Impact of Increase in Deposit Rate Ceilings on Thrift Earnings and Housing," Paper presented at the annual meeting of the American Real Estate and Urban Economics Association, New York (Dec. 30, 1977).

"Is Your Money Safe in a Savings and Loan?," *U.S. News & World Report* (Aug. 17, 1981), 72–73.

Chapter 8

The Depository Institutions Deregulation and Monetary Control Act of 1980 (DIDMCA)

It was in the near-crisis environment of the first three months of 1980 that the Senate and House Committees worked long and hard to settle their differences and agree on a compromise package of banking legislation. They tried to design a Bill that would not only meet the emergency needs of the crisis but also set the stage for the economic health and growth of the nation's financial services institutions during the decade of the 1980s and beyond.

In late March the final compromises were worked out. The Bill was passed by both Houses of Congress, and on March 31 the *Depository Institutions Deregulation and Monetary Control Act of 1980* (Public Law 92-221) was signed into law by President Carter. The following sections of this chapter explain and discuss the provisions of the Act.

The Act

The Act contained nine titles, each an act in itself. The nine titles, or "sub-acts," are:

Title I–Monetary Control Act
Title II–Depository Institutions Deregulation Act
Title III–Consumer Checking Account Equity Act

Title IV–Powers of Thrift Institutions
Title V–State Usury Laws
Title VI–Truth in Lending Simplification and Reform Act
Title VII–Amendments to the National Banking Laws
Title VIII–Financial Regulation Simplification Act
Title IX–Foreign Control of the United States Financial Institutions

Many of the provisions of the total Act are not directly relevant to this discussion and need no explanation here. But several provisions are extremely relevant, and these are explained, in easily understandable language, in the following section.

Important Specific Provisions of the Act

Reserve Requirements. Reserve requirements were set for *all depository institutions* at 3 percent of the first $25 million in transaction account deposits, and 12 percent for deposit balances in excess of $25 million. But the Fed was empowered to adjust the rates within a range of 8 percent to 14 percent on deposits above $25 million.

For non-personal time deposits, the reserve requirement was set at 3 percent. But the Fed was authorized to adjust that requirement down to zero or up to 9 percent. Also, the Fed could require *additional reserves* of as much as 4 percent of *total* transaction account deposits. But on these additional reserves the Fed must pay interest.

The new reserve requirements were to be phased in over a 4-year period for Fed member banks and over an 8-year period for all non-member depository institutions (banks and thrifts).

Interest Rate Ceilings. Interest rate ceilings on savings deposits were to be phased out over a six-year period. The adjustments to interest ceilings during this period were to be worked out by the Depository Institutions Deregulation Committee (DIDC).

The legislation specifically called for an increase in interest rate ceilings on savings accounts of 0.25 percent within the next 18 months, 0.5 percent during the following 18 months, and 0.5 percent each year after that during the three final years of the phase-out—at which time Reg Q was to be abolished.

The Depository Institutions Deregulation Committee. The Depository Institutions Deregulation Committee (DIDC) set up by the Act was charged with the responsibility of adjusting deposit interest rate ceilings (by majority vote) during the Reg Q phaseout period. The members of the committee are the Secretary of the Treasury, and the Chairman of each of the regulatory agencies that supervise and regulate the banks and thrift institutions—the Federal Reserve Board, the Federal Deposit Insurance Corporation (FDIC),the Federal Home Loan Bank Board (FHLBB), and the National Credit Union Administration. The Comptroller of the Currency serves as a non-voting member.

S&L Lending and Asset Powers. The S&Ls were authorized expanded lending powers and were allowed to invest up to 20 percent of their assets in consumer loans, commercial paper, and corporate debt securities.

NOW Accounts. The Act legalized NOW accounts, effective January 1, 1981, with a uniform interest rate ceiling on NOW accounts for *all depository institutions.* Also legalized were share drafts, automatic savings-to-checking transfers (ATS accounts), and remote service units.

Pricing for Fed Services. The Fed was authorized to establish prices for its services. Access to Fed services by non-member banks was to be delayed until the pricing system for Fed services had been established.

Non-member Banks. Non-member banks were not required to become Fed members and were permitted to pass their reserves through a member bank, or through a non-member and then a member bank, to the Fed.

NOW Account Reserves. The Fed's new reserve requirements for all NOW accounts were imposed immediately with no phase-in period, *except that* in those eight states where NOW accounts were already in existence, the reserve requirement on those accounts would be phased in gradually over an eight-year period.

State Usury Laws. State usury laws limiting the amount of interest that could be charged on various kinds of loans were overridden for all *Federally insured* lenders (which includes almost all banks and thrifts). But these usury provisions were temporary except for home mortgage and mobile home loans. However the individual state legislatures could act to override this Federal law. On business and agricultural loans, the Federal provisions overriding the state usury laws only extended for three years.

Federal Usury Laws. The new Federal Act established its own "usury limits" in terms of "percentage points" above the Fed's discount rate—as the discount rate goes up or down, the interest that can be charged on the various kinds of loans also goes up or down. The usury ceiling for Federal Credit Unions was raised from 12 percent to 15 percent, and the National Credit Union Administration was authorized to raise the ceiling even further.

Truth in Lending. Truth in Lending (TIL) requirements were simplified to reduce problems of administration. Agricultural loans received exemptions from TIL restrictions; the Fed was required to develop simple "model TIL disclosure forms" which, when used properly would exempt lenders from liability to civil suits. The period during which lenders can be held liable under the Act cannot extend back beyond January 1, 1977, and liability is limited to provable cases of systematic abuse (not just clerical errors).

Other Provisions.

- Federal Deposit Insurance was increased to $100,000.
- Rules for S&Ls stock conversions were liberalized.
- A moratorium was imposed until October 1, 1981, on formation of trust companies outside the home state by a bank or S&L.
- The Fed was signalled to be less restrictive in approving financing arrangements for establishing one-bank holding companies.

- Financial regulators were required to conduct a cost-benefit analysis of all new regulatory actions.

Brief Analysis of the Effects of the Act

Fed Chairman Paul Volcker expressed pleasure with the way in which the compromise Bill was worked out and finally passed. He said that this Act would strengthen the Fed's ability to conduct monetary policy by eliminating the incentive for member banks to withdraw, and by bringing non-member banks under the Fed's reserve requirements.

As the provisions of the Act are phased in, fundamental changes will be occurring among the financial institutions throughout the country. The S&Ls will lose the quarter-point interest rate advantage that they have been authorized to pay on savings deposits. But at the same time they receive authorization to offer a variety of new services—lending powers and other services that previously only commercial banks have been permitted to offer. The competitive impact of these changes among the nation's financial institutions, and the ways in which the various financial institutions will respond to this new competitive environment, will significantly change the nature of the financial services industry in this country.

It is clear that this piece of legislation was the most significant, far-reaching, and revolutionary change that had occurred in the banking and financial industries in this country since the depression of the 1930s. The new legislation signaled great change in the structure and operation of banking and other financial services institutions. As these changes are phased in, the impact will be felt throughout the economy.

It is clear that small savers will receive more return on their savings as the banks and S&Ls and other depository institutions compete for the small saver's deposits. And borrowers in all segments of the market are likely to find themselves paying interest rates that more accurately reflect the "time value" of the funds that they are borrowing. This change is likely to have some significant effects on the uses of borrowed funds and on the success and growth (or failures) of businesses, large and small.

A Summary Comment

The March 1980 DIDMCA was a revolutionary Act to be sure. But it left many questions unanswered. Soon it became obvious that additional reform legislation was needed. You'll be reading all about that later.

But first: What happened after the 1980 Act was passed? What problems did it solve? And which ones did it leave unsolved? That's what you'll be reading about in the chapters coming up.

Suggested Readings

"America's New Financial Structure," *Business Week* (Nov. 17, 1980), 138–144.

"Banking's New Competition: Myths and Realities," *Economic Review,* Federal Reserve Bank of Atlanta (January 1982), 4–11.

Board of Governors of the Federal Reserve System. "The Depository Institutions Deregulation and Monetary Control Act of 1980," *Federal Reserve Bulletin* (June 1980), 444–53.

"Reserve Requirements Undergoing Change," *DallasFed Roundup,* Federal Reserve Bank of Dallas (November 1982), 3.

Warner, Arthur E. "A Legislative Bombshell," *Business and Economic Review,* Division of Research, College of Business Administration, University of South Carolina, Columbia, SC (Dec-Jan 1981), 18–26.

West, Robert C. "The Depository Institutions Deregulation and Monetary Control Act of 1980: A Historical Perspective," *Economic Review,* Federal Reserve Bank of Kansas City (February 1982), 3–13.

Chapter 9

Conditions and Events Following the Passage of the DIDMCA in March 1980

Following the signing of the *Depository Institutions Deregulation and Monetary Control Act,* the Federal Reserve Board issued this statement:

> *The Depository Institutions Deregulation and Monetary Control Act* of 1980 initiates wide-ranging changes in the nation's monetary system that will enhance the efficiency of financial markets, promote competitive balance among depository institutions, and facilitate the implementation of monetary policy.

Perhaps the new Act did not contain precisely all of the provisions that the Fed might have wished. But it is clear that the Act satisfied the major objectives that the Fed was seeking through new legislation. Clearly, the single most important of these objectives was to reduce the high cost of Fed membership and to place member and non-member banks on a more equal basis. And the Act did that—at least well enough to succeed in stemming the exodus of Fed-member banks from the System.

The Effect on Fed-Member Banks

During the weeks following the passage of the Act, several banks decided to reconsider their prior decision to withdraw from the Fed. Before the Act was passed there were as many as 60 banks in the Philadelphia Federal Reserve Bank's area which were planning to withdraw from membership. But after the Act was passed, one banker commented: "There just isn't any incentive to withdraw from the System, now."

From the point of view of most of the Fed member banks, the new Act was clearly favorable. Not only did it reduce the amount of non-interest-bearing reserves that they are required to hold, it also required that the other depository institutions offering transaction accounts hold the same reserves. This created a "more level playing field," which many of the Fed member banks had been asking for.

The larger Fed member banks had long been saying that they did not object to having non-bank financial institutions enter the transaction account market or other lending markets in competition with banks if they were required to abide by the same rules that applied to the commercial banks. And that was approximately the situation established by the Act.

The Effect on the Thrifts

The larger and more aggressive S&Ls, savings banks, and other thrifts also welcomed the new Act because it unleashed them to compete more effectively. It gave them a much broader range of "competitive tools" with which to work. The smaller financial institutions also were given an advantage by the Act.

The reserve requirement on the first $25 million in transaction account balances was set at only 3 percent; for amounts above $25 million it jumps to 12 percent.* Therefore, small banks and thrifts with $25 million or less in transaction accounts had a very low reserve requirement. As the institution's transaction account balances increase above $25 million, the reserves that it must hold with the Fed become a constantly increasing percentage of that institution's total transaction account balances.

*The Act specified that this $25 million figure would be adjusted upward in future years to reflect 80% of the future increase in total checkable deposits in the country. For example, by the time total checkable deposits in the country increase by 20%, the $25 million figure will be increased by 80% of 20% (16%); 16% of $25 million is $4 million, so the base figure will become $29 million.

Here's an example. A bank with only $25 million in transaction account balances would be required to hold reserves of only 3 percent ($.75 million). A bank with $50 million in transaction accounts would be required to hold 3 percent ($.75 million) on the first $25 million and 12 percent ($2.0 million) on the second $25 million, for total reserves of $2.75 million—which is an average reserve requirement of about 9 percent of its total transaction account balances. A bank with $500 million in transaction account balances would be required to hold very nearly 12 percent of that amount in reserves. So in this way the small financial institutions are favored by the legislation. But this advantage is not sufficient to make all of the small financial institutions happy with the Act.

Some representatives of the thrifts were not pleased with the new "rules of the game." Some were saying that without the Reg Q differential, people are likely to be more inclined to keep their money in banks than in savings institutions, and that therefore as Reg Q is phased out, the thrifts will be at a competitive disadvantage.

Many of the smaller thrifts had been satisfied with their "niche" as it existed before, and had no desire to offer transaction accounts. Many were satisfied with the interest rate differential on their savings accounts as a sufficient attraction, and had no particular interest in competing aggressively for new kinds of business. But under the new rules of the game, all financial institutions were more or less forced into this new situation of more aggressive competition. Their survival depends on how effectively they can cope with this new environment.

The Effect on Non-Member Banks

It appears that, in general, the non-member banks—which were required by the Act to hold non-interest-bearing reserves with the Fed—are the most obvious losers. The Act doesn't specifically give them very much that's "new" to enable them to compete more effectively. Yet it places on them this new burden of required reserves.

It should be noted, however, that many non-member banks are small and will benefit from the fact that the reserve requirement is lower for banks with small transaction account balances. And now they can borrow from the Fed. Sometimes that may be important. Also, the fact that the reserve requirements were to be phased in over an 8-year period would provide them time to make some necessary adjustments.

What About the Effect on Monetary Policy?

Some monetary analysts were saying that the new Act, contrary to the position of the Federal Reserve Board, could *reduce* the Fed's ability to control the growth of bank reserves, and thereby limit inflationary expansions of the money supply. The argument is that the Act opens up the Fed's "discount window" to an additional 15,000 depository institutions. This provides the opportunity for these institutions to borrow more reserves and to permit the money supply to expand beyond the Fed's targeted rates of growth.

At this time, no one is sure just how much the newcomers will try to borrow from the Fed's "discount window," and no one knows what limits the Fed will place on this borrowing privilege. Judging from the Fed's past relationships with its member banks, it isn't likely that the Fed is going to offer the S&Ls and nonmember banks an "open window policy." But the fact that this issue has been raised points up the fact that the Fed will need to monitor (and perhaps place specific limits on) discount window borrowing by the new "members of the club."

What About the Federal Deposit Insurance Increase?

Another area of dissatisfaction with the Act concerns the increase in Federal deposit insurance from a maximum of $40,000 to a maximum of $100,000. The question comes up, "How could the government pay off all those depositors if widespread failures developed among the banks and other financial institutions in the economy?"

Considering the difficulties that many financial institutions (including some major banks) were facing in 1980, some financial analysts were not certain of the ability of the government to prevent (under all conceivable circumstances) a serious financial panic. And such a panic could result in the collapse of banks and financial institutions throughout the nation. What then?

The fact is that the Federal Deposit Insurance Corporation (FDIC) has a very small reserve, relative to the total size of deposits now covered. The ratio of FDIC reserves to insured deposits is only a little more than $1.00 of reserves for every $100 of insured deposits. Some observers are concerned that a few major bank failures would begin to use up the FDIC's reserve fund. People might become concerned about the ability of the FDIC to pay off, and begin running to their banks to demand their money. If this ever happened it would certainly destroy the banking and financial system.

This kind of scenario doesn't appear likely, of course. In the first place, the FDIC doesn't usually pay off the depositors of a failing bank. What it does is to find a "merger partner" for the troubled bank and the FDIC takes whatever loses are incurred by the merger.

One analyst, Professor Jack Guttentag, a senior banking professor at the University of Pennsylvania's Wharton School, suggests that it would be wise to eliminate the FDIC reserve fund altogether—to recognize that if necessary the FDIC must be supported by the full financial power of the federal government. In that way no one would have a reason to worry about what would happen in the unhappy event that the reserve fund was becoming depleted.

The Interstate Banking Question

Another kind of legislation that was not dealt with in the new Act was legislation dealing with interstate banking. One section of the Act imposed a moratorium (until October 1, 1981) on the formation of trust companies by a bank, bank-holding company, or savings and loan institution in any state outside the home state of the parent financial institution. But beyond this, the Act was silent on the issue of interstate banking.

Continuing Problems of the Thrifts

In the months immediately following the passage of the Depository Institutions Deregulation and Monetary Control Act, an increasing number of financial institutions found themselves in trouble. The thrifts—especially the ones that had been aggressively expanding their mortgage loans in the 1970s—found themselves in a very high-interest-rate environment, and with long-term loans bringing in less than 10%.

As the depositors "disintermediated" their savings to put their money into higher-yielding investments, the thrifts were in trouble. They had no choice but to go into the high-interest money markets to obtain funds.

In mid-May of 1980, it was estimated that some 40 percent of the nation's thrifts were losing money. The thrifts asked, "How can we make long-term, fixed-rate mortgage loans when we must pay fluctuating (and unpredictable) money market rates for our funds?"

The 1980 Bond Market Crash

In early 1980 the bond market lost some $300 billion in value—its biggest crash since the Depression of the 1930s. Why? Because of the rapidly increasing interest rates. In early 1980 many financial institutions were following a policy of not buying *any* long-term bonds or other long-term debt obligations. They just weren't ready to take the risk.

Many corporations were deferring bond financing and turning instead to the commercial paper market, and to borrowing from banks. This created an extraordinary demand for loans by corporations and caused Paul Volcker, Fed Chairman, to instruct banks to make no loans that would help corporations to avoid long-term financing in the bond market. But there is no question that corporations were using bank loans and other short-term borrowing to delay issuing new long-term bonds and having to pay such high interest rates.

The prime rate reached a peak of 20 percent in April of 1980. But then the drop began. The downward turn in interest rates had a dramatic impact on the seriously depressed bond markets. Some long-term treasury bonds increased as much as 5% in value in one day—the largest single-day rise for treasury bonds, on record. But at that time there were many economists who were skeptical about the continued decline in interest rates and the continued revival of the bond market. At that time there was no solid evidence to indicate that the inflation rate had slowed significantly. And it was generally recognized that as long as inflation rates stayed as high as they had been in the recent past, interest rates would stay high to reflect that.

Real Rates and Nominal Rates

Why were interest rates so high? The fact is that in *real* terms they weren't so high. In fact, in real terms they weren't high at all! Would you believe they were *negative*? Less than zero? That's right.

The *nominal rates*—the rates actually quoted, the rates you have to pay—had gone up very high. But the *real rates*—the nominal rates *adjusted for inflation*—were negative. Why adjust for inflation? Here's why.

The *nominal interest rate* you earn on your money is the nominal rate of *increase* in the value of your money assets over time. The inflation rate is the rate of *decrease* in the value of your money assets over time. If you're earning 10% nominal interest and the inflation rate turns out to be 15%, that's a *negative real rate* of 5%. You're losing money!

Negative Real Interest Rates 1972–81

People don't like to deposit their savings and earn negative real rates of interest. And financial institutions don't like to make loans at negative real rates, either. But both things were happening in this country (with a brief exception in 1975–76) all the time from mid-year 1972 until near the end of 1980.

Depositors were receiving negative interest. The value of their money assets was eroding all the time—sometimes quite rapidly.

And financial institutions were making negative-interest loans subsidized by the savers. Why would the savers (and the banks) accept negative interest? Mostly because they didn't know.

You Don't Know the Real Rate until Afterwards

You never know what the inflation rate is going to be during the next 90 days—or year, or two or three years. If the inflation rate keeps speeding up (faster than expected), then interest rates are likely to turn out to have been negative during that period.

Here's another reason why depositors would accept negative real interest rates on their savings: Many people felt that the only completely liquid and completely safe (insured) place for their savings was in savings accounts at the banks and S&Ls. And those accounts could only pay 5¼ or 5½ percent—take it or leave it! A lot of people took it, at least for awhile.

Many People Sought Higher Paying Deposits

As time went on, more and more people moved their money into money market mutual funds (MMMFs) and often doubled (sometimes tripled!) the nominal rates they had been earning from the banks and thrifts. So were they earning a *positive real interest return* on their savings? Usually, no. The inflation rate (until late in 1980) was higher than most of the money market rates. But you can be sure that those depositors who "disintermediated" their funds and shifted into the MMMFs came out better than those who didn't. The ones who shifted certainly reduced the size of the *negative real rates of return* on their money assets. As a result of this experience, many saver-depositors these days are being much more careful where they put their money. And they aren't ashamed to shop around for the best deal they can get!

The Bond Markets Rally

The turbulent events in the money and bond markets during early 1980 had a serious and no doubt lasting impact on the investment psychology of bond-buyers. The trend toward shorter-term maturities was clearly evident. In May and June of 1980, as the bond markets strengthened, corporations moved quickly to restructure their debt, selling long-term bonds and using the proceeds of their bond sales to pay off their high-cost, short-term liabilities (commercial paper, and money borrowed from banks).

But even in the more favorable bond markets of early June 1980, interest rates were still high by historical standards. Some municipal governments still were postponing their bond offerings in the hope of lower rates in the future. And corporations were issuing shorter-term bonds because these bonds could be sold at lower rates of interest.

The sharp rallies in the bond markets that occurred during April, May, and June of 1980 indicated that a great number of investors had not yet completely lost confidence in long-term bonds. But it is impossible to know what percentage of those investors were planning to buy, wait for a short-term reduction in interest rates to push bond values up, and then sell—rather than holding the bonds as a "dependable source of income and capital value" until maturity.

As a result of these experiences, we are likely to see some changes in the direction of short-term bonds and other debt instruments. And we're likely to see greatly increased use of variable interest loans and deposits—instruments that can adjust to reflect changing conditions in the bond and money markets.

Financial Market Conditions 1980–81

The unstable, widely fluctuating financial markets of early 1980 settled down some during the last half of the year. But not much. Nominal interest rates eased somewhat during the summer, but then climbed again and stayed high. By the end of 1980 the "prime rate"—the "quoted rate" that commercial banks charge their most creditworthy customers—stood at 21.5%. In early 1981 it eased some, but throughout the summer of 1981 the prime rate fluctuated between 20% and 21%.

It was during this period (beginning in the fall of 1980) that a positive real rate of interest reappeared in the U.S. economy. This initiated the first sustained period of positive real rates of interest in this country since 1972.

During 1981 some money market funds were paying rates of 15% or more. How could passbook savings paying 5¼% or 5½% hope to compete with that? They couldn't. The disintermediation problem worsened. Some banks and many of the thrifts were threatened by bankruptcy. How bad was it? And what could be done? That's the subject of the chapters coming up.

Suggested Readings

Buckley, John M. Jr. "The Savings and Loan Environment in the 1980s," *Federal Home Loan Bank Board Journal,* 14 (January 1981), 19–20.

Cacy, J. A. "Monetary Policy in 1980 and 1981," *Economic Review,* Federal Reserve Bank of Kansas City (December 1980), 18–25.

"Deposits Without Interest Rate Controls," *Wall Street Journal* (Sept. 22, 1981), 2.

"Interest Rates Show Unprecedented Swing," *Wall Street Journal* (Oct. 2, 1981), 56.

"It's A Horrible Environment," *Fortune* (June 29, 1981), 7.

"S&Ls Had Record $4.6 Billion Loss in '81," *Wall Street Journal* (April 6, 1982), 5.

"S&L Officials Attack Decision To Permit Higher Interest Rates on Passbook Savings," *Wall Street Journal* (Sept. 24, 1981), 3.

Part IV
Worsening Conditions in 1981–82 and the Garn–St. Germain Act

The DIDMCA Did Not Do the Whole Job,
So Additional Legislation Was Required

Chapter 10

The Situation in 1981: High Interest Rates and Disintermediation

Two of the most important objectives of the Depository Institutions Deregulation and Monetary Control Act of 1980 (DIDMCA) were:

1. Stop the Fed membership exodus!
2. Phase out Reg Q and stop all this disintermediation!

There's no question that on the first objective it succeeded. On the second, it failed.

Reg Q Deregulation by "New Deposit Instruments"

The DIDMCA authorized the DIDC to phase out Reg Q over a period of time. Initially the DIDC planned to achieve phaseout by raising the amount of interest the depository institutions could pay on their existing kinds of deposits. But it soon became clear that this approach was not at all feasible. Pressure from the thrift industry helped the DIDC to decide against this approach.

Consider this: Suppose a depository institution is paying 5½ percent on savings deposits while at the same time money market funds are paying 15 percent. How much more funds could the depository institution attract if it raised the rate on its savings accounts from 5½ percent to 6 percent? None!

So what would the increase of ½ percentage point (50 basis points) accomplish? It would simply increase the cost of funds to the depository institution and exacerbate the already serious problem of high-cost liabilities and low-return assets. So how could the DIDC proceed to deregulate? It could do exactly what it did.

The only feasible approach was to phase out Reg Q by introducing new kinds of "products"—permitting depository institutions to offer new kinds of deposit instruments, and permitting them to pay rates on those new deposit instruments that were competitive with money market funds and the other alternatives available to the depositor.

Cost of Funds Goes Up and Disintermediation Continues

The use of interest-bearing checking deposits as authorized by the DIDMCA spread rapidly. This increased the cost of funds to most depository institutions. The increasing cost of funds brought some banks and many thrifts under serious financial pressures. The cost of their liabilities kept going up but there was no corresponding increase in their return on assets. Several institutions failed. Many insolvent banks and thrifts had to be merged into other, stronger institutions.

Throughout the financial services industry there was increasing recognition of the need to increase return on assets and to increase revenues from other sources. Many of the free services that most bank customers had come to expect as "free" suddenly became "fee" services. And charges for existing fee services were increased.

During 1980 and 1981, interest rates remained high. Disintermediation continued. The drain of funds from the depository institutions to the money market mutual funds continued at the average rate of two to three billion dollars a week. This outflow of funds spelled disaster for one institution after another.

Finding Ways to Get Around Reg Q

Several banks were finding various ingenious ways to offer checking accounts tied to money market funds. For example, in the fall of 1981 the Bank of San Francisco began offering a checking account tied to money market rates. Some banks used repurchase agreements (RPs, explained later) tied to NOW Accounts to offer their depositors money market interest rates. The Bank of New York during the summer of 1981 offered checking accounts to small businesses in which the idle cash was invested in money funds. These examples are but a few of the many ways banks around the country were "avoiding Reg Q" and attracting and holding deposits in the face of high-interest competition from the money funds.

The Plea for a Money Market Deposit Account

During this period some members of the financial community were urging the Congress or the Depository Institutions Deregulation Committee (DIDC) to authorize some kind of money market deposit instrument. There were many kinds of new deposit instruments, but none that would permit the depository institutions to compete openly with the money funds. The depository institutions couldn't offer money market rates and complete liquidity to their depositors.

The DIDC did authorize additional depository instruments on which money market rates could be paid. But all of these instruments had sizable minimum deposit amounts. And all of them tied up the deposit for some time—until the maturity of the certificate.

The continuing drain of deposits from the depository institutions showed clearly that these new "time deposit instruments" weren't enough. Fixed-time CDs just were not effective competitors with the money funds. The money funds offered money market rates *with complete liquidity*—you could get your money out any time you wanted to. Rapid disintermediation continued.

By mid-year 1981, some 15 months after the DIDMCA was passed, what was the situation among the banks and thrifts? For many it was not so good.

FSLIC Capital Injections for Failing Thrifts

As cost of funds stayed high and disintermediation continued, many thrifts were facing the threat of bankruptcy. In September 1981 the FHLBB approved a plan to inject new capital into ailing thrifts. A troubled institution could get cash or notes from the FSLIC to add to its capital base and thereby avoid insolvency. In exchange, the thrift would issue "income capital certificates," which were sort of "conditional promissory notes"—the institution promised that, if and when it became profitable again, it would pay back the money, plus interest.

New Troubled-Thrift Merger Powers

But some thrifts were too far in the red to be bailed out by the income capital certificates. Several had to be merged into other, stronger institutions.

The Emergency Powers Act of 1981 (the so-called "Regulators Bill") was designed to permit the depository institutions regulatory authorities greater powers to work out these "failing thrift" mergers—for example, by approving interstate mergers and thrift-bank mergers.

How serious was the situation? In mid-1981 FHLBB Chairman Richard Pratt was calling for new legislation to give the thrifts new powers—including commercial lending powers—to let them diversify their asset portfolios. Pratt argued that to survive, the thrifts must have new sources of higher-interest-earning assets.

In July of 1981, the largest S&L in the state of New York, West Side Federal Savings and Loan Association, was facing bankruptcy or forced merger. Pratt urged Congress to act. He said: "If Congress does not act in the short run to address this matter, there will be no long run for a very substantial segment of the thrift industry."

Increased Numbers of Troubled S&Ls

In 1981 the FHLBB's list of "troubled" S&Ls jumped from 121 in January to 404 (about 10% of the industry) in July. Then, as the numbers continued to rise, the Board decided (with the agreement of the U.S. League of Savings Associations) to stop maintaining a "problem list." During 1981 the FSLIC provided almost $1 billion in aid to the ailing thrifts. And mergers involving total assets of $13.9 billion were arranged for 30 troubled S&Ls.

It was in these troubled times that the November 1981 banking conference was held at Appalachian State University. The officers of several banks and thrifts were invited to express their views on recent conditions and events in their industry and to offer suggestions as to what should be done. The remainder of this chapter presents some of the statements made at that conference.

Brewer's Comments on Reg Q Deregulation and Problems of the Thrifts*

Most of the thrift industry and many banks would like to delay or stop the deregulation of Reg Q called for in the 1980 Act (DIDMCA). This resistance to deregulation arises primarily from concern about the increasing cost of funds already on deposit.

In September of 1981 the Depository Institutions Deregulation Committee (DIDC) voted to increase the limit on savings accounts by ½% (effective on November 1) to 5¾% for banks and to 6% for federally insured savings and loans. Under pressure from the savings and loans and some banks, the DIDC at its October meeting deferred indefinitely its decision on this savings-ceiling adjustment. While the 1980 law requires the phaseout of Reg Q by 1986, lobbying pressure will almost certainly be used to try and delay the schedule—or to scuttle it entirely.

The grave situation facing the savings and loans today is most regrettable, especially since, to a great extent, it is not of their

*Statements by James T. Brewer, Senior Vice President, Wachovia Bank & Trust Co., Winston-Salem, NC, December 1979. Wachovia is a Fed member bank with assets of about $7.2 billion.

making. They simply have been the primary instruments of a government policy that encouraged home ownership, along with broader consumption, through usury ceilings on loan rates and tax deductibility of loan interest.

However, basic changes in consumer markets and in public policy are taking place. The high inflation rates in recent years have caused consumers to seek more return on their money, and the higher returns frequently have been found outside depository institutions. Government policy is beginning to shift to more encouragement of savings and investment and to somewhat less emphasis on consumption. These changes require fundamental adjustments on the part of financial institutions.

Survival is a compelling instinct in all of us, so it is not surprising that the thrift industry and some banks are trying to hang on to the Reg Q life-support system. But, while Reg Q provides oxygen to relieve the gasping for *short-term earnings*, the brokerage houses are *bleeding away our deposit base* through their money market mutual funds and cash management accounts. It does not make much difference whether you suffocate or bleed to death. Dead is dead.

While it is premature to predict the demise of the depository institution industry, there are, in fact, three health-threatening forces that both the thrifts and the banks are facing today:

- The loss of cheap deposits as deregulation unfolds.
- Rising operating expenses due to inflation and the people-intensity built into the banking system.
- Competition from nondepository firms.

These forces have converged on the savings and loans sooner than banks, largely because the S&Ls are caught with so many long-term, low-interest loans. But unless significant changes occur, banks will be under similar pressures in the not-too-distant future.

Depository institutions must find ways to cope with the loss of cheap deposits, rising operating expenses, and competition. Lower rates of inflation presumably would provide temporary earnings relief because of reduced pressure on cost of funds and operating expenses. However, reduced inflation will not solve all problems associated with funds costs and operating costs, nor will it eliminate the competition from nonbank entities. Nonbank competitors, having successfully invaded new financial territory, will not readily withdraw even though economic conditions change and depository institutions proceed toward deregulation. They will adjust their areas of emphasis and their product offerings, but they are here to stay.

The health of depository institutions is dependent upon having the latitude to serve the full range of consumer financial needs and expectations. Reg Q is no longer a tonic either for carrying out public policy or for preserving the economic viability of depository institutions. Instead, it has become a narcotic that temporarily relieves pain for the ailing or provides a temporary high for the healthy. But it also numbs the senses and prevents full function of all who take it. It is addictive and ultimately self-destructive.

The 1986 date for the complete phaseout of Reg Q strikes a reasonable balance between the resulting impact on current earnings and the continuing erosion of the base of business by non-bank competition. Hopefully, this aspect of deregulation will continue on schedule.

Marsh's Comments on Problems and Outlook for the Thrifts*

In the past the S&L industry did the only thing it could do under the laws of our state and our nation: We loaned money to people so they could buy or build a house, and we made those loans at the lowest interest rates possible. We got no argument at that point. We were housing America, and it was good. Then high interest rates came along, and other things started happening.

We have been put into a position in the S&L industry where it is extremely hard for us to move. We had nothing to do with that. We were serving the people well. But now we find ourselves in a position where it's almost impossible to do so with interest rates as they are. And we aren't happy with everything that is happening in the name of deregulation.

The S&L industry is having problems, true. But we did not create those problems. Don't make us out to be responsible for

*Comments by James P. Marsh, President and Treasurer, Watauga Savings & Loan Association, Boone, NC, at the Appalachian State University Banking Conference, November 1981.

something that we have not been responsible for. Give us a little credit for all those years that we have met the housing needs of the nation. I think we deserve that.

Also, we need some time. We need some time to be able to get out of low-yielding loans and to adjust our assets to rates we can afford. We did not get ourselves into this position. We were put into this position. Perhaps we could have stopped making loans, had we been permitted to do it. But under the law we were required to put "x number of dollars" into home mortgages. So our present problems are mostly not of our making.

What about the future? There are a number of things we will be doing. We are not going to be making a great number of mortgage loans in the near future. We've got the variable rate mortgage, but can you afford to loan to a young couple on a variable rate mortgage? Can you tie them into a rate that may look like 14 or 15 percent and then later adjust that rate to 20 percent or more? Right now we are putting our dollars into short-term government securities.

For the future, there are challenges out there, and we will be working to meet those challenges. There may be mergers. Perhaps you'll find many S&Ls coming together to create associations large enough to employ more expertise. We might decide to combine our resources to be in a better position to meet the challenges of the new environment.

We will meet those challenges. It's going to be hard, but we're going to continue to serve the average American person who needs and deserves to be served. Those are the people who make this nation great. We will serve them, and I'm proud to be a part of it.

Broadwell's Comments on Problems and Alternatives for the S&Ls*

It appears to us in the savings and loan industry that there's a good bit of difference between *banking deregulation* and *savings and loan deregulation*. We don't feel that there has been an im-

*Comments by F. Edward Broadwell, Jr., President, CEO and Director, Clyde Savings & Loan Association, Clyde, NC, at the Appalachian State University Banking Conference, November 1981.

pact on the banking industry anything like that which has happened to the S&L industry. The S&L industry would like to have the phaseout come more slowly than the commercial bankers want. The deregulation doesn't affect the rates we're earning on our loan portfolio. But it does affect the amount we have to pay to our depositors.

We in the S&L industry feel that we are in a straitjacket. In the past few years we have had our earnings locked in at low interest rates while the cost of our money has gone up dramatically. Finally, just recently, our industry is being permitted to offer a variable rate mortgage instrument. This will give us some relief, but it's about ten years late and $600 billion dollars short!

Deregulation has completely changed our business. We are now offering a whole range of new products—the all-savers certificate, Individual Retirement Accounts, and a wide range of other new alternatives. I believe we will continue to offer such new products, whether the deregulation phaseout schedule stays on track or not.

We are setting up these new kinds of "savings deposits" and trying to make them attractive. So it doesn't make so much difference what you do with interest-rate ceilings on the old kinds of "deposit instruments"—passbook savings, for example—because everyone is leaving those and going to the new, more attractive instruments.

As we offer these new and more attractive alternatives for our depositors, our cost of funds is going up. But we still can't pay interest that is competitive with the money market funds. If the funds were paying a small premium over what we are offering, that might be just fine. But when they're paying several percentage points more than we can pay, it's hard for us to compete.

Some people are complaining that they don't think it's right for consumers to have to pay home-mortgage interest rates that reflect market rates. But those same people would like for savers to get market rates on their deposits. How is it possible for the S&L industry to pay out market rates to its depositors unless it can earn market rates on its mortgages? There's just no way! With the availability of variable rate mortgage instruments I think the banks will see home mortgages as a more attractive investment for them. So I think we will see more commercial bank home mortgages in the future than in the past.

Another change I expect in our home mortgage industry is increasing use of the secondary market in the public sector, with the Federal National Mortgage Association and other agencies absorbing sizable parts of the mortgage supply. There will also be increasing use of private intermediaries including the pension funds, insurance companies, and others who have long-term, stable sources of funds.

I think that one of the ways that the S&L industry will respond to deregulation is that we will go very rapidly into the "mortgage banking business." We will use our expertise in mortgage lending and provide mortgages for the portfolios we will service for the insurance companies, pension funds, and for the public sector also. This will provide greater stability both in the flow of funds to the mortgage business and in providing a stable source of funds for the S&L industry.

We in our industry are confident about our ability to respond to the new environment. By taking advantage of the secondary market, we think we will be able to continue to use our expertise and to provide adequate financing for home ownership in the communities. Consumers will often find it harder to afford home ownership, but I think home ownership will continue to make sense. The S&L industry is about a $750 billion industry. It's going to go through a very fast metamorphosis. But it's not going to disappear. Right now I think we need some protection while we are undergoing this metamorphosis. We need a little bit more elbow room in the financial industry, and I believe we'll be able to hold our own.

Regarding the future of the S&L industry, I would like to paraphrase Mark Twain: Rumors of my death have been greatly exaggerated. It's not here yet. It's not going to occur!

Suggested Readings

"Bankers Getting Increasingly Upset About Unregulated Rivals," *Wall Street Journal* (October 5, 1981), 31.

Neikirk, Bill. "Interest Rates Defy 'Conventional Wisdom'," *The Charlotte Observer* (July 16, 1981) Section D, 1.

"No Early Let-Up in High Interest Rates," *U.S. News & World Report* (Aug. 24, 1981), 58–59.

"Panel To Decide Schedule for Lifting Controls on Rates Banks, S&Ls Pay," *Wall Street Journal* (June 25, 1981), 29.

Scharff, Edward J. "The Savings Revolution," *Time* (June 8, 1981), 58–69.

"The Cost of Saving Troubled Thrifts," *Business Week* (November 23, 1981), 44–45.

The Future of the Thrift Industry, Conference Series No. 24 (Boston MA: Federal Reserve Bank of Boston, 1981).

Chapter 11

Snellings' Overview of the Revolutionary Changes and the Need for More Deregulation*

It has become commonplace for people making speeches to banking groups to begin by saying that the banking industry is currently going through a period of revolutionary change. But like many commonplace expressions, it is nonetheless true. Banking today is very different from what it was two years ago. Before the end of this decade, it could be so startlingly different as to be almost unrecognizable.

Rapid Change in Banking

Things have been changing so rapidly that an old-timer is a fellow who continues to think of Merrill Lynch as an organization where he buys stocks and of Sears Roebuck as a place where he goes to buy a home appliance. We know, of course, that these businesses, along with other types of nondepository institutions, represent just the latest entrants into the ranks of competitors for the business that banks and thrifts used to call their own.

*This chapter is paraphrased from a presentation made by Aubrey N. Snellings, Vice President and Secretary, Federal Reserve Bank of Richmond, at the Appalachian State University Banking Conference, November 1981.

Another sign of the change that is taking place is that it is no longer fashionable to speak of the "banking industry." The preferred term these days is "financial services industry." This term is so broad that it can encompass brokerage firms, retailers, insurance companies, and presumably the local undertaker, all of whom may soon be involved in what used to be called banking.

Any period of rapid change is likely to create serious problems and major dislocations, simply because the institutions involved are unable to change as rapidly as the various forces impinging on those organizations change. In the case of financial institutions, changes in the legal and regulatory framework in which these institutions operate, their asset/liability mixes, and their organizational structures have all failed to change as rapidly as the competitive environment in which they operate. The result has been the emergence of a number of problems that will require the attention of the industry itself, the various regulatory agencies, and the Congress.

Over-regulation and Strict Segmentation

Most of the problems confronting the financial services industry today began to appear when our inflexible and over-regulated financial system entered an environment characterized by high inflation, escalating interest rates, and rapid technological change. Some of our financial institutions simply lacked the ability to make the changes called for by these new conditions. One reason was the *strict segmentation* that has characterized our system throughout its history. The financial needs of Americans traditionally have been met by a number of different kinds of institutions, each limited to a very narrow range of activities.

These highly specialized institutions came into being because existing institutions were not meeting a specific need of the public at a particular time, so a new institution had to be created. Mutual savings banks were created to meet the savings needs of industrial workers. The first S&L came into being because commercial and savings banks did not finance home purchases by industrial workers. The first credit union was formed in 1909 because working people had great difficulty in getting consumer credit.

Over the years, legislative bodies at the state and federal levels ensured the continued separation of functions by, in effect, *building legal walls* that kept the different types of institutions apart. Each specialized provider of financial services was given its own little piece of turf and was then protected from competition from other institutions.

The Regulatory Philosophy of the 1930s

The most important cause of the inflexibility that characterized our financial system for so long was the *regulatory philosophy* that developed in the 1930s and that shaped the financial system for the next forty years. Between 1920 and 1933 about half the banks in the United States, more than 15,000 banks, went out of business. The terrible conditions at that time brought about the most far-reaching changes in the body of laws regulating U.S. financial institutions that had ever occurred in a comparable period of time.

The overriding objective of the 1930s legislation was to protect the soundness of banks and other financial institutions. But in its efforts to protect the safety and soundness of the financial system, Congress made banking the most regulated industry in the U.S. economy.

The emphasis on "safety first" born in the depression of the 1930s became the guiding philosophy of the regulatory agencies. Few would disagree that these agencies have succeeded in maintaining the soundness of the system; over the past 40 years the number of failing institutions has been very small. But this low failure rate was achieved at the cost of a reduced level of competition in the industry and a significant reduction in the ability of the system to adapt to change.

The Forces of Change: A New Environment

In the last 15 years, several forces emerged that radically changed the environment in which financial institutions operate. Two of these forces, inflation and technological change, were especially important in bringing about dramatic changes in the financial system.

Inflation brought very high interest rates, perhaps the highest in our history. The higher market rates collided with the Reg Q ceiling rates on deposits and other regulatory restraints, and subjected depository institutions to periods of disintermediation and severe liquidity pressures. The high rates also provided the incentive for households and businesses to devote more time and attention to the management of their financial assets. They became much more sophisticated in seeking out the highest available return on those assets.

Increased Competition For and Cost of Funds

Depository institutions found they could no longer obtain funds by hanging out a sign saying, "we accept deposits." As a result, banks and thrifts developed imaginative new services, such as NOW and ATS accounts. And the regulatory authorities eased the restrictiveness of deposit-rate ceilings by authorizing new types of obligations, such as money market certificates of deposit (CDs). The higher interest rates also helped to bring about several new institutions, such as the money market mutual funds.

These developments resulted in a great expansion in the variety of financial assets available to savers, and they allowed small savers to obtain something like a market return on their funds. They also greatly raised the level of competition for deposit funds and caused a substantial increase in the cost of money to depository institutions. This has brought on some very serious problems for institutions holding a high percentage of their assets in the form of long-term, fixed-interest-rate loans. That's the major problem of the S&L's.

The New Monetary Policy of the Fed

The inflation also brought about a change in the way the Federal Reserve conducts monetary policy. For more than a decade the Fed has aimed at controlling the money supply in the conduct of policy. But prior to October 1979 it attempted to control the money supply by manipulating the federal funds rate. This was not very successful, so in October 1979 we changed the way we do things. We now try to control the monetary aggregates by controlling the growth in the reserve base.

I am not sure the new approach has been much more successful in achieving a slow steady growth in money. But it has had some important consequences for credit markets and financial institutions. Under the old approach, the federal funds rate fluctuated, but changes occurred gradually. The present approach is to control the reserve base and let rates go where they will, within a rather wide range. As a result, interest rates are a lot more volatile than they once were. That significantly increases the risk of doing business for many financial institutions.

The Technological Revolution

The development of computer and communications systems helped to make possible many of the new services we have seen in recent years, such as automatic-transfer services, pay-by-phone, point-of-sale terminals, automated teller machines, remote-service units, and the automated clearing house. But we are only beginning to see the first results of the technological revolution that is going on.

Once the proper economic incentives appear, these developments have the potential to transform the entire financial services industry as well as the nation's payments system. One of the most important aspects of all this in terms of its long-term implications is the fact that the new technology has had the effect of extending the geographic growth and reach of banking markets.

The Blurring of the Distinctions between Depository Institutions

The forces unleashed over the past couple of decades have blurred the distinctions between different types of depository institutions and have lead to the incursion of nonfinancial businesses into areas traditionally reserved to banks and thrifts. The easing of the barriers separating banks, S&L's, and credit unions, which had been in progress for some time, culminated in the Depository Institutions Deregulation and Monetary Control Act of 1980. This Act made significant changes in the competitive positions of the various depository institutions. These developments substantially raised the level of competition in the financial services industry.

The Aggressive Incursion of Nondepository Institutions

The thing that really stirred up the waters was the aggressive incursion of nondepository institutions, including nonfinancial institutions, into areas and activities previously reserved for banks and thrifts. We are all familiar with the phenomenal growth of money market mutual funds. But a number of other institutions are also getting into the act.

Merrill Lynch, with its nationwide network of offices, offers in connection with its cash management plan a package of consumer financial services that has many of the characteristics of an interest-bearing checking account. Brokerage houses and large conglomerates are acquiring banks that have divested themselves of their commercial loan portfolios and thus are technically no longer banks. Finally, we see the nation's largest retailer, Sears, threatening to become one of the largest financial services institutions. In announcing the inauguration of what is essentially a money market mutual fund, the Chairman of Sears said, "Our goal is to become the largest consumer-oriented financial service entity."

The Legal Barriers Are Crumbling

I think we can sum up what has been happening by saying that the nice, secure, tightly-regulated world that bankers knew a decade or so ago is nothing more than a fond memory. Financial institutions find that the legal barriers that were erected so painstakingly around them are crumbling, and they are living in a rapidly changing world. Many institutions have adapted fairly well to the changes that have occurred; others are experiencing extremely serious problems. The only thing we know for sure is that we cannot return to what used to be. We must adapt to the rapidly changing world.

The Need for a Level Playing Field

The above discussion brings me back to a point I made earlier. The ability of banks and other depository institutions to adapt to the recent changes in the industry is greatly hampered by the rules and regulations under which they must operate, while money market funds and other nondepository institutions that are competing in these areas are virtually free of such restraints.

It seems obvious that Congress must address the question of how to level off the playing field for all of the contestants. It could impose on the nondepository institutions the same restrictions that now apply to banks. Or it could deregulate the banks and thrifts so that they would operate under the same rules as the others.

The process of change will continue whether Congress acts or not. And, whatever course Congress elects, in the years ahead the world is likely to be a little less pleasant for the providers of financial services than it once was. Competition will be more intense. Risk and uncertainty will be higher. By the end of the decade there are likely to be a lot fewer institutions in the industry than there are now, and the different kinds of institutions will look much more alike than they do now.

Suggested Readings

"A Step Closer to Rescuing the Thrifts," *Business Week* (July 27, 1981), 72–73.

DeMott, John S. "Casualties of the Revolution," *Time* (January 11, 1982), 67.

"Financial Reform Does Not Stand Still," *Business Week* (February 16, 1981), 42–43.

Kane, Edward J. "Accelerating Inflation, Technological Innovation and the Decreasing Effectiveness of Banking Regulation," *Journal of Finance* (May 1981), 355–67.

"More S&Ls in Peril," *Newsweek* (April 5, 1982), 52–54.

"Now Bankers Turn to a Hard Sales Pitch," *Business Week* (Sept. 21, 1981), 62–68.

"S&Ls Need Broader Operating Authority, Not Bailout, Pratt Says," *Wall Street Journal* (June 12, 1981), 2.

Santoni, G. J., and Stone, Courtenay C. "The Fed and the Real Rate of Interest," *Review,* Federal Reserve Bank of St. Louis (December 1982), 8–18.

Chapter 12

The 1982 Crisis of the Thrifts

The year 1982 was a "turnaround" year in the U.S. money and financial markets. By mid-year 1982 we had the highest real rates of interest in the history of the country!

The Inflation Rate and Real Interest Rates

The prime rate remained between 15% and 17% throughout the first half of 1982. But the inflation rate kept coming down. So the real interest rate kept going up.

Back in 1979—the year the Fed clamped down on money supply growth—the average inflation rate for the year was 13.3%. In 1980 it was 12.4%. For 1981 the average for the year dropped to 8.9%, but it was considerably lower in the last part of the year. That's when the "real rate of interest" in this country turned positive for the first time in many years.

The real interest rate remained strongly positive from that time until this book went to press in early 1984. It appeared that positive real rates would continue for the foreseeable future—at least for the next year or two.

For the year 1982 the average inflation rate was down to an

unbelievable 3.9%—the lowest since the 3.4% rate one decade earlier in the (price-controlled) year of 1972.

Real Rates and Nominal Rates in 1982

As the inflation rate dropped, real interest rates climbed. Why? Because nominal rates stayed the same. Why didn't nominal rates drop? Because the money markets didn't believe the good news about inflation.

Who would be so naive as to think that inflation rates were going to remain in the 3% to 5% range? Anyone who thought that would be forgetting the experience of the 1970s and 1980–81. During those years almost all of the time the inflation rate was higher than expected, and the depositors and lenders wound up receiving negative real rates of interest on their money.

So in late 1981 and until mid-year 1982, real rates soared. (All of us should have put our money into non-callable 15% or 16% bonds at that time to "lock in" a real return in excess of 10%! Not many times in a lifetime does a person have a chance to do that!) But then, as the inflation rate stayed low, nominal rates began to fall. The following table tells the dramatic story.

THE BIG DROP IN NOMINAL INTEREST RATES
DURING THE LAST HALF OF 1982

	June 1982	Dec. 1982
Treasury Bills	13%	8%
The Fed's Discount Rate	12%	8.5%
Prime Rate at Major Banks	16.5%	11.5%
High-Grade Corporate Bonds	15%	11%
Home Mortgages	17%	13.5%

Why Did Nominal Rates Fall?

The table shows that nominal rates came down by about 30% during the last half of 1982. Why? There were several reasons, not the least of which was this: The financial markets began to believe that (1) the inflation rate really was down to stay, and (2) the Fed wasn't going to do anything drastic to shock the money markets and force nominal rates back up again. As it turned out, the financial markets were right.

During the last half of 1982 there was a continuing slowdown in inflation, slack business and consumer demand for borrowed money (the recession), and, last but not least, easier monetary policy announced by the Fed in October. All of these conditions helped to ease market interest rates downward. But even though nominal rates dropped precipitously, *real rates* remained at or near historic highs. You'll be reading more about the causes and effects of this later.

For the banks and thrifts—especially the thrifts—the drop in market interest rates was a most welcome development. The rates the money market mutual funds (MMMFs) could offer came down fast. And the cost of funds to the banks and thrifts came down, too. But for many institutions the help was too little and too late.

Worsening Problems of the Thrifts

You already know that 1981 was a bad year for many (almost all) of the thrifts. But 1982 was worse. It wasn't that something else "turned bad." It was just that there was a continuing loss of deposits because of disintermediation. And for many institutions the high cost of funds (compared with return on assets) was sucking out the capital base and pulling the institutions down ever closer to bankruptcy.

By the fall of 1982, failures of S&Ls were averaging about *three a week,* compared with an average of less than *three a year* prior to 1981. In September of 1982, H. Brent Beesley, Director of the FSLIC, said that although the majority of the S&Ls will survive, several are already so weak that there's no way they can survive.

The New Thrift Powers of 1980–81 Helped—But Not Enough

You probably remember that the 1980 Banking Act (the DIDMCA, March 1980) gave new powers to the thrifts. The Act allowed the thrifts to invest up to 20 percent of their assets in consumer loans.

Many of the thrifts began to take advantage of this opportunity to diversify their portfolios. But when some 60% of their assets were in long-term, fixed-interest home mortgage loans, how much diversity could they hope to achieve in the short run? Not much, right? Eventually, yes, but the problem of the thrifts was not "eventually." It was "now"!

The thrifts were authorized (beginning in January 1981) to offer interest-bearing checking accounts, called NOW accounts. Remember? These new "checkable savings accounts" helped the thrifts to hold customers, and sometimes to gain new ones.

Also in 1981 the ceiling-free Individual Retirement Accounts (IRAs) and tax-exempt All Savers Certificates provided welcome sources of funds for the thrifts. But not enough.

New Deposit Instruments of Early 1982

In the first several months of 1982 nothing happened to worsen the problem facing the thrifts. But the drain on capital caused by losses month after month (resulting from high cost of funds and low return on assets) continued. And disintermediation continued. To slow the disintermediation, the federal regulators introduced several new kinds of accounts that paid interest rates reflecting money market rates. These were: (1) the 91-day money market certificate, (2) the 3½-year (ceiling-free!) deposit certificate, and (3) the 7-to-31-day time deposit.

All of these new deposit instruments were quickly adopted by the depository institutions to compete with the money market funds. But the MMMFs continued to drain money from the depository institutions.

The Continuing Competitive Edge of the MMMFs

The MMMFs still had the competitive edge. They could pay money market rates and offer the depositor complete liquidity. There was no 30-day or 90-day (or whatever) waiting period.

The depository institutions had to remind their depositors of the "substantial interest penalty for early withdrawal." But when you put your money into MMMFs, you (1) got as much—maybe more—interest, and (2) could get your money when you wanted with no interest penalty. It's no wonder the depository institutions were losing billions of dollars to the MMMFs!

Thrift Problems Reached Crisis Proportions In Mid-1982

By mid-year 1982, before the dramatic drop in interest rates, the problems of the thrifts were reaching crisis proportions. During 1981, losses by S&Ls were a record $4.6 billion. But during the first half of 1982, S&L losses were running at the annual rate of more than $6 billion! In July of 1982 the net worth of the nation's S&Ls was down by 20% from the year earlier.

Now you can understand why S&L failures were running at the average of three per week. And you can understand why thrift industry representatives (and Richard Pratt, FHLBB Chairman) were urging Congress to pass new legislation to rescue the thrifts.

Legislative Proposals in 1982

Proposed legislation included (1) more *capital injections* into troubled thrifts through greatly expanded use of *net worth certificates* ("income capital certificates") financed by the U.S. Treasury, (2) expanded lending powers for the thrifts to include commercial loans and more consumer loans, and (3) expanded deposit powers to include holding business deposits.

The commercial banks were generally opposed to the idea of giving thrifts these additional banking powers. But there was one proposal on which many banks and thrifts agreed: "We need a deposit instrument that is completely competitive with the money market funds!"

Another legislative initiative during the summer of 1982 was a proposed bill to require the Fed to take some action to ease money—to bring down interest rates. It was generally recognized that the high market rates were the root cause of the disintermediation and high cost of funds—the two things that were killing the thrifts.

This "instruct the Fed" legislation proposal didn't get anywhere because, as it turned out, interest rates soon began to fall. By the end of September the downtrend in interest rates was clearly visible. But again, from the point of view of saving the ailing thrifts, the drop in interest rates was too little and too late for many of them.

Congress Tackles the Legislation

Even as far back as 1980 many members of the Congress had recognized the need to do something more to help the thrifts. So why was new legislation so slow in coming?

In 1981 and 1982 various bills were proposed. But there were seriously conflicting positions within the industry, within the Congress, and between the Senate and the House banking committees. So a lot of compromise was required. It wasn't until October 15, 1982, that the new legislative package was passed. That's what you'll be reading about in the next chapter.

Suggested Readings

"Ailing S&Ls See Early Return to Health," *Wall Street Journal* (November 19, 1982), 56.

"A Year of Financial Strains," *Sixty-Eighth Annual Report,* Federal Reserve Bank of New York, 5–24.

"Banks and Thrifts Urged To Compromise, Back Deregulation Bill," *Wall Street Journal* (January 11, 1982), 22.

Carron, Andrew S. *The Plight of the Thrift Institutions* (Washington, D.C.: The Brookings Institution, 1982).

Loeys, Jan G. "Deregulation: A New Future for Thrifts," *Business Review,* Federal Reserve Bank of Philadelphia (Jan.–Feb. 1983), 15–24.

"S&Ls Posted $3.3 Billion Loss in First Half," *Wall Street Journal* (October 12, 1982), 5.

"Will Interest Rates Come Down?," *U.S. News & World Report* (May 31, 1982), 26–27.

Chapter 13

The Garn–St. Germain Depository Institutions Act of 1982

The *Depository Institutions Act of 1982* (PL 97-320) is popularly known as the Garn–St. Germain Act after its sponsors, Senator Garn, Chairman of the Senate Banking Committee, and Representative St. Germain, Chairman of the House Banking Committee. This Act has been termed by some financial industry personnel "the most important financial institutional legislation in the last fifty years." William O'Connell, President of the U.S. League of Savings Associations, said of the Act: "We came out with 90% of what we wanted."

An Overview of the Act

The Garn–St. Germain Act authorized money market deposit accounts for banks and thrifts; it established "income capital certificates" to bolster the equity of ailing thrifts; and it significantly expanded the powers of the S&Ls to perform functions previously held by commercial banks.

Under the Act, the S&Ls are permitted to offer commercial loans in amounts up to 10% of their assets after 1983. They also can expand their non-residential real estate lending up to 40% of their assets, and make investments in consumer loans up to 30% of their assets. And they can hold the deposits of those businesses to which they have made loans.

The Act also says that interest rate differentials between banks and savings and loans must be eliminated by January 1, 1984.

A major section of the Act deals with emergency acquisitions to aid financial institutions in trouble. Provisions regarding mergers of troubled financial institutions across state lines are also outlined.

The "net worth certificates" authorized by the Act are backed by either the FDIC or FSLIC and can be used if the net worth of the institution falls below 3% of assets. But to qualify for this aid the institution must have 20% of its loan portfolio in residential mortgages.

The Act also provides greater powers for the regulatory authorities to authorize interstate mergers between thrifts, between banks, and between banks and thrifts. But on this merger issue, the Act only confirmed practices that the regulators had already been following in cases of troubled institutions in need of merger partners.

New FHLBB Chairman Gray Supports the Act

In May 1983, newly appointed FHLBB Chairman Edwin J. Gray expressed his approval of the Garn–St. Germain Act, and announced his intention to help the thrifts take advantage of their new powers provided by the Act. In a speech to the National Association of Mutual Savings Banks in Boston (May 17, 1983) he said: "A top priority of this Bank Board will be to seek to find appropriate ways to encourage the industry to make effective use of the Garn–St. Germain powers. . . . The success of the industry could ultimately turn on the wise and effective use of the new authority."

The Specific Titles of the Act

You probably remember that the 1980 Banking Act (DIDMCA) was an "omnibus act" consisting of nine titles, each a separate act in itself. So you won't be surprised to find that the Garn–St. Germain Act was like that too. It contained eight "titles," as follows:

Title I: The Deposit Insurance Flexibility Act—expands and defines functions and procedures of the FDIC, FSLIC, and National Credit Union Administration (NCUA) in aiding troubled institutions.

Title II: The Net Worth Certificate Act—provides capital assistance to ailing thrifts.

Title III: The Thrift Institution Restructuring Act—expands the powers of the thrifts, calls for the DIDC to establish new deposit accounts that pay money market rates to be offered by banks and thrifts, and shortens the time period for Reg Q phaseout.

Title IV: Provisions Relating to National and Member Banks—makes various amendments to prior laws regarding lending limits, insider loans, dealings with affiliates, etc., and exempts from reserve requirements all depository institutions with reservable liabilities (transactions accounts) that do not exceed $2 million.

Title V: Amendments to the Federal Credit Union Act—removes some restrictions and provides more flexibility and broader authority to local credit union directors.

Title VI: Property, Casualty, Life Insurance Activities of Bank Holding Companies—reduces the ability of bank holding companies to engage in the insurance business.

Title VII: Miscellaneous—makes several minor changes in previous laws and calls for a study by the FDIC, FSLIC, and NCUA to determine the desirability of future changes in the U.S. deposit insurance system.

Title VIII: Alternative Mortgage Transaction Parity Act—provides for non-federally chartered lenders to offer the same kinds of alternative mortgage instruments as authorized for federally chartered institutions.

Who Was Helped Most by the Act?

Most of the thrift industry (and the FHLBB and FSLIC) enthusiastically supported the Garn–St. Germain Act. The banking industry was less enthusiastic. In fact, the bankers were quite opposed to some of the provisions—especially the new commercial lending and deposit powers of the thrifts and the restrictions on insurance activities of bank holding companies.

The "thrift bailout" provisions were designed to inject new equity capital into troubled thrifts. This was hailed as a major victory for the thrifts. But was it? Consider this:

1. About 100 of the nation's thrifts were already in such bad financial condition that they weren't considered viable "turn around" candidates and therefore were not eligible for the "net worth injection" program.
2. Of the total of some 4,000 thrifts, only between 250 and 300 were considered eligible for the aid. With the drop in interest rates, many of these probably could have returned to profitability on their own. During 1983 the average net worth of the thrifts—which had declined sharply in the previous two years—turned around and began to rise.
3. For a number of institutions the bailout program spelled the difference between solvency and insolvency. True. But for the industry as a whole, the lower interest rates and the improved economic climate were much more beneficial than the emergency bailout provisions of the Act.

The new lending and deposit powers were also hailed as a major victory by the thrifts. Certainly these provisions freed up the larger, more aggressive institutions to compete in a broader market. But it was recognized that most of the S&Ls were not yet "tooled up" to take advantage of these new powers. Throughout 1983 most of the thrifts kept on doing what they had been doing in the past. But a few were moving rapidly to take advantage of their new powers.

Both the thrifts and the banks were helped by—and moved rapidly to take advantage of—the new money market deposit accounts (MMDAs). There's a special section coming up that tells what happened on that.

Who Were the Losers?

Who was hurt by the Act? The money market mutual funds (MMMFs), to be sure. Their funds dropped sharply during the weeks and months following the introduction of the MMDAs by the banks and thrifts. And the small commercial banks? Losers too? Probably.

The small banks will face increasing competition from the thrifts as more thrifts learn to exercise their new powers. And competition from the big banks in attracting deposits into the MMDAs will be intense. So the small banks will face continuing pressure on their cost of funds.

One ultimate result of the Garn–St. Germain Act may be to speed the consolidation of small banks (and thrifts) into larger financial services units. And ultimately bring an end to the distinctions between banks and thrifts? Maybe. But as of early 1984 that hadn't happened yet.

The New "Money Market Deposit Account" with No Reg Q Ceiling

By far the biggest step toward the elimination of Reg Q was called for in the Garn–St. Germain Act and was carried out by the regulations of the DIDC. After the Act was passed in mid-October, the detailed regulations were worked out by the Committee during November. Effective December 14, 1982, depository institutions became authorized to offer a *money market deposit account* with a minimum balance of $2500, immediately accessible without any waiting period and with limited check-writing privileges.

The committee also created a "Super NOW" account, effective in January 1983, requiring a minimum deposit and average balance of $2500, with no restrictions on the number of checks written and no interest rate ceiling on the account.

In early December 1982, as the authorization date (December 14) for the new money market deposit accounts approached, banks and thrifts advertised heavily to attract deposits into these new accounts. The depository institutions moved quickly to offer interest premiums to try to attract deposits from the money market funds. The money market fund industry, through its Investment Company Institute, sued the DIDC to try to prevent the authorization of this new money market deposit account. The Institute charged that it was unfair to permit the depository institutions to offer a money market account with a minimum balance as low as $2500 and on which federal depository insurance would apply. But the attempt of the Investment Company Institute to block the introduction of this new account was not successful.

Money Market Deposit Accounts Grew Rapidly

By late December it was clear that the depository institutions were pulling a lot of money into their new money market deposit accounts. And as the depository institutions pulled a flood of dollars into their money market deposit accounts, the money remaining with the money market funds declined significantly.

The money market funds had grown from very small (less than $4 billion on January 1, 1978) to more than $230 billion in the fall of 1982. But following the introduction of the new money market deposit accounts in mid-December, the money market funds saw a continual outflow. By early February 1983, the money market funds had lost more than $30 billion. The total amount of money in the money market funds in mid-February was less than $200 billion. The following quote from *The Economist,* February 12, 1983, p. 77, highlights the situation:

> After an intense two-month promotional campaign, America's banks have pulled into their money-market deposit accounts . . . almost as much money as the money-market mutual funds attracted in the previous ten years. The bank accounts now hold $213 billion, compared with the peak of $230 billion controlled by the money-market funds late last year.

An article in *Business Week* (January 31, 1983, p. 85) entitled "Billions of Dollars with No Place To Go" said that the banks have been "stunned by their own success" in attracting money into the new money market deposit accounts. The article explains that with all of this new, high-cost money, it's difficult for the banks to know where to invest to gain a profitable spread between their cost of funds and their earnings on their investments.

Not all of the great increase in the banks' and thrifts' money market deposit accounts (MMDAs) came from money market funds. Many billions of dollars were merely shifted from low-paying deposits to the new, high-paying deposits. Between mid-December 1982 and January 5, 1983, MMDAs at commercial banks increased by some $70 billion, while passbook savings plus time deposits decreased by some $40 billion.

The depository institutions, no longer limited as to the interest they could pay to attract funds to these new accounts, were competing vigorously and very successfully. The new challenge had become: "Where do we invest this money so that we can generate enough interest earnings to pay the high cost of our newly acquired deposits?"

The S&Ls Expand Their Lending

As the months of 1983 passed, funds continued to flow into the money market accounts at the banks and thrifts. By the end of June, more than $367 billion was accumulated in these accounts. About $100 billion of that amount was in the S&Ls. No other deposit account ever before had experienced such rapid growth! In addition, the Super NOW accounts that were introduced in January 1983 had accumulated more than $31 billion by the end of June.

What to do with all that money? Lend it! Mortgage lending by the S&Ls during the summer of 1983 was averaging between $13 and $15 billion a month—up from about $4 billion in 1981 and about $5 billion in 1982. Also, several of the thrifts were exploring and moving cautiously into commercial lending.

Reg Q: The Beginning of the End—Finally!

From one point of view, by early 1983, "Reg Q deregulation" was virtually complete. Small depositors with passbook savings accounts, regular NOW accounts, etc., still received "Reg Q" interest rates on their deposits. But with the MMDAs and Super NOWs, the depository institutions were free to pay market rates to attract funds. And they did so very successfully.

In December, when the DIDC announced the guidelines for the MMDAs and Super NOWs, it also reduced the size of the minimum deposit required on several other kinds of previously authorized time deposit accounts. The minimum denominations of (1) the $20,000 time deposit, (2) the $7500 time deposit, and (3) the $10,000, six-month money market certificates, all were reduced to $2500 (the same as for the MMDAs), effective January 1983.

So by January of 1983, deregulation of Reg Q had come a long way. But passbook savings were still under Reg Q. The banks were paying 5¼%, and the thrifts were paying 5½%. So who cared? The thrifts cared, for sure! They were still holding almost $100 billion in passbook savings accounts—despite the higher yields available elsewhere. But total deregulation of Reg Q was coming.

At its June 30, 1983 meeting, the DIDC *eliminated all interest rate ceilings* on all time deposits of more than 31 days, effective October 1, 1983. Why? Because with the MMDAs and the Super NOWs paying market rates, ceilings on the other time deposits didn't make much sense anymore. Then, at its October 1983 meeting, the Committee adopted a schedule for the completion of the phaseout of Reg Q.

The Deregulation Schedule of October 1983

The "handwriting on the wall" was finally put on paper by the DIDC at its October 1983 meeting. Here is the schedule (subject to political pressures and changes, of course!) that was adopted at that time:

1. January 1, 1984. Interest rate differential between banks and thrifts on savings accounts and on 7–31 day time deposits is eliminated.
2. January 1, 1985. The $2500 minimum on MMDAs, 7–31 day time deposits, and on Super NOWs is reduced to $1000.
3. January 1, 1986. The $1000 minimum on the above accounts is eliminated.

4. March 31, 1986. Reg Q ceilings on passbook savings deposits at all depository institutions are eliminated.

Will Reg Q deregulation proceed as scheduled? Maybe so. But maybe not. A lot depends on what happens to money market conditions and interest rates—and on macroeconomic conditions. You'll be reading about these issues in one of the chapters coming up.

The Relative Importance of the DIDMCA and Garn–St. Germain Acts

The DIDMCA was passed in March 1980. Following its passage it was hailed as the "most far-reaching" and "most important" financial legislation in this country in almost 50 years—since the depression years of the 1930s.

Some observers termed the 1980 Act "revolutionary" and called it the most important financial legislation in the history of the country. But soon after the Act was passed, it became clear that something more needed to be done.

Finally, 2½ years (and several hundred failed thrifts) later, in October 1982, the Garn–St. Germain Act was passed. This Act was also hailed as "far-reaching" and "revolutionary," and as the "most important financial legislation in 50 years"—maybe the most important ever. But again, a few months later, new legislation was being called for.

Throughout 1983, the banking committees of the House and Senate were working on new legislation to try to deal with the (mostly unlegislated) revolutionary changes going on in the nation's financial services industry. In November of 1983 Senator Garn introduced a comprehensive banking deregulation bill. Hearings were scheduled to begin in early 1984. But unless some crisis develops, it isn't likely that the bill will be passed before 1985 (or 1986?).

The bill deals with:

- securities activities by banks
- insurance activities by banks
- real estate activities by banks

- Fed payment of interest on required reserves
- bank dealings in rentals and leasing
- check-holding policies by depository institutions
- state usury ceilings on interest rates
- payment of interest on checking accounts
- credit card regulations and disclosure
- interstate banking arrangements
- nonbank banks, and the definition: what is a bank?

Banking Deregulation—A Continuing Process

You can see that it doesn't make much sense to argue about which banking act was most important. Both the 1980 Act and the 1982 Act were part of a continuing process—a process which by 1984 was nowhere near finished.

The 1980 Act probably was the most important of the two because it broke the ground. It signaled the ultimate end of Reg Q, it broke the banks' monopoly on checking accounts, and it let the thrifts begin to diversify out of home mortgage loans. The 1982 Act carried deregulation further in the same direction, and it freed the depository institutions to compete with the money market mutual funds.

We can be pretty sure that the 1984 (or 1985? or 1986?) banking act will be another step in more or less the same direction. How can we know that? Because of this: Much of this deregulation process has been initiated by aggressive firms in the industry—bankers, brokers, others—finding loopholes in the law, then stretching these loopholes until legislative action has become imperative. Also, new technology has played an important role.

All these market forces for change will continue. If the Congress can't reach agreement and *act,* then sooner or later near-crisis conditions will develop and Congress will be forced to *react.* That's how it has happened so far. Don't be too surprised if that's the way it happens from now on.

Much of the remainder of this book will be talking about the important areas where the market is forging ahead and on which the Congress hasn't yet acted. One such issue is interstate banking. That's what you'll be reading about in the chapters coming up.

Suggested Readings

"A Big Brawl in Banking," *Time* (January 17, 1983), 34–35.

"Conference Report on HR6267," *Washington Financial Reports* (Washington, D.C.: The Bureau of National Affairs, Inc. 1982).

Fischer, L. Richard, Gentry, Elizabeth G. and Verderamo, Petrina M. E. *The Garn–St. Germain Depository Institutions Act of 1982: What's in It for You?* (The Consumer Bankers Assoc., Arlington VA, 1982).

"Garn–St. Germain Act Summarized," *Banking Expansion Reporter,* Vol. 1, No. 19 (Oct. 18, 1982), 4–14.

Holland, David S. "Score: Insurance Industry 10, S&Ls 5, Banks 2½," *Banking Expansion Reporter,* Vol. 1, No. 19 (Oct 18, 1982), 1–2.

"Implementation of New Powers Awaits FHLBB, FDIC Rules: League Officials Laud Garn–St. Germain Act," *Savings and Loan News* (November 1982), 7–9.

McIntosh, Willard, Warner, Arthur E., and Gaines, James P. "The Garn–St. Germain Act and the Availability of Funds to the Real Estate Industry," *Federal Home Loan Bank Board Journal,* Vol. 16, No. 5 (May-June 1983), 16–25.

"Reagan Signs Landmark Banking Law," *DallasFed Roundup,* Federal Reserve Bank of Dallas (November 1982), 1.

Part V
Interstate Banking and Foreign Bank Entry

Rapidly Changing Geographic Structure and New Spatial Competition in the Financial Services Marketplace

Chapter 14

Do We Have Interstate Banking? Should We?

Do we have interstate banking? Federal law says: "No!" But do we? There's no question about the answer: "Definitely, yes!"

In a speech in October 1983 (as reported in *The American Banker*, 10/27/83, p. 1), Senator Garn, Chairman of the Senate Banking Committee, said that the chances of changes any time soon in the McFadden Act or the Douglas Amendment (both prohibiting interstate banking) were "zero to nil." But he went on to say that it didn't make too much difference because: "Interstate banking is already here."

One of the most significant developments in the revolutionary financial services scene of the 1980s has been the rapid development of new forms of interstate banking. It has been happening so fast it's almost impossible to keep up. Why? New Congressional authorization? No. Why, then? In the same way that most of the important developments have occurred in the American economy: by the responsiveness of profit-seeking, competitive private enterprises to the clearly expressed demands of the marketplace.

Interstate Competition Is Already Here

Interstate competition among the financial services institutions is very real and very important. The rapid changes that are occurring in this area would be difficult to overstate. The larger banks are offering almost all of their kinds of services on an interstate basis. About the only thing a bank can't do on an interstate basis is set up an office to take deposits. But some are finding ways to do that. Money market funds and brokers are taking deposits nationwide and are offering checkable privileges to depositors nationwide.

The states have the power to permit interstate banking between themselves if they wish to do so. An increasing number of states have taken advantage of this opportunity. Also, some states have "grandfathered" arrangements which permit out-of-state banks to operate full-service banks in their states. Several banks have moved aggressively to take advantage of these "grandfather" loopholes.

No important new national legislation regarding interstate banking has been passed. Nor is any expected. The opposition from small banks is too great. However, interstate activity by banks and other financial services institutions continues to increase.

There has been a large number of interstate mergers involving troubled savings and loan institutions. The most significant interstate merger in the early 1980s was approved during late 1982. It permitted Citicorp of New York (one of the nation's two largest banks) to acquire Fidelity Savings and Loan in California—over the strong protests of California bankers.

The bottom line on this issue is that there is, in fact, a great amount of interstate competition among the financial services institutions. New ways of entering this competitive arena are being discovered and exploited by various institutions almost daily. The demands of the marketplace for interstate financial services are being met, and without any change in the laws.

A Quote from *The Economist*

As far back as March 27, 1982, an article in *The Economist* said: "Nationwide banking has already arrived in America without any change in the law. The nation's bankers have found loopholes in the law." The article gives several examples of nationwide banking, including deposit-taking, nationwide automated teller machine (ATM) networks, and others. The article concludes that by the time the Congress gets around to changing the law, it won't make any difference anyway.

Is this *Economist* article on target? And if so, how and why has such a situation been permitted to develop? And what's the rationale on this issue? What are the pros and cons? That's what you'll be reading about in the sections coming up.

The Role of Competition in the Economy

Competition in its various forms plays a vital role in the American economic system. The antitrust laws and enforcement programs are designed to prevent the reduction of competition in American markets. Healthy competition ensures that the buyers of various products and services will always have a variety of choices.

With healthy competition, the producer-sellers of the most efficiently produced and highest quality products and services will attract customers, will make profits, and will expand. Those that are inefficient will lose their market shares and ultimately disappear from the marketplace. So healthy competition leads to the constantly increasing efficiency of the economic system, and to the improved quality and reduced cost of products and services to the final consumer. The better-quality and lower-priced products win out in the competitive race.

The importance of maintaining competition in an economy like that of the United States is clear. An economy like ours could not function without it. Nevertheless, there are many ways in which competition is restricted by governments—local, state, and national.

The Effects of Spatial Competition

One important kind of competition is "spatial competition." Spatial competition is concerned with the geographic area in which the competition occurs. For example, an important kind of spatial competition is seen in the international trade area, where foreign producers of automobiles are permitted to compete in American markets against American automobile producers. If the inflow of foreign automobiles were restricted by tariffs or quotas, this would amount to a restriction on "spatial competition." Any such restriction would remove some of the pressure on the American automobile producers to increase their efficiency and to produce the kinds of automobiles most wanted by the American public.

Any restriction on spatial competition has the effect of insulating the producer-sellers in the "protected geographic area" (whether it be a local city or county, a state, or the entire nation). Producer-sellers of goods or services who are protected from spatial competition are relieved of some of the pressure to provide the most desired kinds of goods and services to their customers, and to provide those goods and services at maximum efficiency and least cost.

Some producers would like to insulate themselves from spatial competition. Without so much competitive pressure they can be somewhat more relaxed—worry less about losing their customers and about keeping their costs and prices down. In general, any restriction on spatial competition tends to result in higher prices, a less desirable group of alternative products and services for the buyers, and more profits for the producers in the protected geographic area.

Spatial Competition in Banking is Restricted

It is clear that spatial competition is generally in the public interest. However, under certain circumstances unlimited spatial competition sometimes can result in an unacceptable degree of instability and disruption in certain industries and markets. When you look at the central role that the banking and financial services industry performs in the day-to-day functioning of the economy, it is obvious that not only the *efficiency* of this industry is important but that the *financial health* and *stability* of the industry is equally important—perhaps (at least in any short-run period) even more important.

The health and stability of the economy depends greatly on the health and stability of its financial institutions. And it is this consideration more than any other that has led to the high degree of governmental restriction on spatial competition in the banking and financial services markets.

Spatial competition in banking in this country is circumscribed by a maze of regulations. Within each state, bank location and branching is regulated by the state. Banks generally have been prohibited by Federal laws from branching into other states or acquiring banks located in other states. These restrictions apply to both state-chartered banks and to national banks. Banks can establish branches in foreign countries, and many of them have done so. But they aren't generally free to establish branches in other states in this country.

Although "interstate banking" is generally prohibited in this country, there are already several instances that actually amount to "interstate banking." And the number of instances is growing rapidly.

Also there are several financial service functions that bank holding companies are permitted to engage in, in states other than the state in which the holding company is established.

Foreign banks have been permitted to come into the United States and establish branches, sometimes not just in one state, but in two or more different states. With the increased entry of foreign banks in recent years, some bankers and other people are now suggesting that it would be desirable to permit our domestic banks to engage in interstate branching, either on a limited basis—regionally, or under special circumstances—or on an unlimited basis nationwide.

What Are the Issues?

Some banks in this country feel that they are being placed at a competitive disadvantage in dealing with foreign banks. It has sometimes been suggested that permitting either interstate branching or interstate bank acquisition is a necessary step toward equalizing the competition between foreign banks and domestic banks.

Also, problems sometimes arise when a large bank is in danger of failing and therefore needs a "merger partner." Another bank in the same state that is large and strong enough to be an appropriate merger partner probably would not be permitted to enter into the merger because of antimonopoly laws. A large bank from a different state would be prohibited from merging with the troubled bank by the McFadden Act, which is the federal law prohibiting interstate branches and mergers. So the only way a large "problem bank" can be merged is *with a foreign bank—or perhaps a group of foreign banks.*

You can see how the maze of state and Federal regulations concerning the geographic areas in which banks can operate—that is, restrictions on bank location—can have a considerable influence on the kind of competition that exists in the banking industry. And you can see how such regulations can have a significant influence on the kinds of banking services that will be available to people and businesses in all of the cities and communities throughout the country.

Some bankers, economists, and bank regulatory authorities are suggesting that in the turbulent days of rapid change in banking and finance in the next few years, sometimes interstate merging may become a desirable alternative. Sometimes, interstate banking may be economically desirable from the point of view of the banks involved, the economies of the areas involved, and the increased efficiency of the American financial system.

This is a very current and a very important issue—sometimes a very controversial one. This is the issue you will be reading about in the following chapters.

Suggested Readings

Breckonfeld, Gurney. "Little Delaware's Powerful Lure for Big Banks," *Fortune* (May 16, 1983), 147–48.

Gagnon, Joseph, and Yokas, Steve. "Recent Developments in Federal and New England Banking Laws," *New England Economic Review* (Jan.-Feb. 1983), 18–27.

"Hearing Set on Central Regional Zone: 11 States in Heartland Invited To Discuss Interstate Concept," *American Banker* (November 8, 1983), 1.

Hutnyan, Joseph D. "There's Life in Old McFadden Yet," *American Banker* (October 30, 1981), 4.

Kramer, Orin. "Winning Strategies for Interstate Banking," *Fortune* (September 19, 1983), 104–120.

Moulton, Janice M. "Delaware Moves Toward Interstate Banking: A Look at the FCDA," *Business Review,* Federal Reserve Bank of Philadelphia (July-August 1983), 17–25.

Pearl, Jayne A. "The Best Spots on the Beach," *Forbes* (February 15, 1982), 108.

Schellhardt, Timothy D. "U.S. Clears California Federal's Merger with 4 Ailing S&Ls in Georgia and Florida," *Wall Street Journal* (February 8, 1982), 16.

Chapter 15

Bank Officers Call for Changes in Interstate Banking Restrictions

The Chairman and President of Manufacturers Hanover, John F. McGillicuddy, addressed the School of Banking and Money Management of Adelphi University in November 1980 on the subject of "Bank Regulatory Reform." The interstate banking issue was one focus of his address. He called for ". . . the ability of banks to compete across state lines in the same way our nonbank competitors do."

The following section presents more of Mr. McGillicuddy's comments on this issue. Then subsequent sections of this chapter present comments made by North Carolina bankers at the 1979 and 1981 banking conferences at Appalachian State University.

McGillicuddy's Comments on Interstate Banking

I tend to approach the nationwide banking issue from four points of view.

- First, *who's involved.* The issue is defined frequently in terms of large banks against small banks, regionals against money centers, national against international. But we know that the arena is far greater. Our fiercest competitors today are more often than not the commercial paper market, foreign banks, insurance firms and brokerage houses. Money market funds advertise nationally and draw funds nationally. Merrill Lynch offers credit and checking account services from a national network. Sears stands poised to sell short-term retail notes to the public—again, nationally. In short, the issue challenges the very existence of banks.

- Second, *what's involved.* Customer demands for new, better, and cheaper services are growing, and we simply cannot fence out the future. We can step aside and let the times pass us by. But we cannot turn back the clock. Either the banking system will be permitted to evolve to meet new demands, or the demands will be satisfied outside the system by competitors not subject to the same rules as we are.
- Third, *what's already happened.* Much of the current debate tends to ignore the fact that we already have a national banking system, albeit without branches. Credit cards respect no borders. To the traveling bank officer, the suitcase has always been his branch and, in addition, Edge Acts and LPOs dot the national landscape. Moreover, the holding company legislation of 1971 has given a new impetus to nationwide banking. My own organization, for example, began the 1970s with 200 offices in a single state. We now have more than 700 offices in 28 states. Bank of America has more than 1,000 employees in New York.
- Fourth, *the political realities.* Despite the seeming urgency of the debate, those looking for any quick and sweeping dismantling of geographic barriers may be reading the wrong tea leaves, particularly where the matter of branching across state lines is involved. It is sobering to note, for example, that 30 of our 50 states do not even permit statewide branching. And 11 states are still on a unit banking system, the most notable being Illinois and Texas—fully industrialized states with massive credit requirements, but with banks restricted to single offices.

The issue is not going to evaporate. There are too many fundamental questions involved—questions that directly impinge on broader considerations. For example:

- Given the massive financing needs of our nation, does a system of 14,000 independent banks still suit the times?
- Given the existence of natural market areas made up, in some cases, of three and four states, is it logical to maintain 50 sets of banking laws, one for each state?
- Given the erosion of markets to foreign banks, does it make sense that when an American bank runs into trouble and is looking for a partner, only foreign banks need apply?
- Given the growing competitive importance of operations-based services and the large investments required to compete in that market, is there a viable future for as many independent small banks as we have today?
- Given shifting demographics along with a pressing need to gather and mobilize consumer savings, is it in the country's best interest to limit a bank's deposit-taking capabilities to a single state?

Clearly, there will always be room for a well-run community bank. But that is not an answer in and of itself. The questions I have raised are controversial. But they must be explored.

Carrier's Comments on Interstate Banking*

Once you set up regulations for an industry, what do the people in that industry immediately start doing? They start figuring some way legally, within the regulations, to engage in activities that are profitable. After all, in a profit-motivated economy, when you put restrictions on a company, that company is going to still try to make as much profit as possible within the restrictions.

Regulation tends to spawn the "loophole mentality." How can I find some way to stay within the law, but still bring in some more bucks? That's a real problem with regulation. This process is going on right now in the area of *geographic restrictions* on banks.

In 1927 the McFadden Act said that national banks cannot

*Statements by G. B. Carrier, Jr., Senior Vice President, First Union National Bank, Charlotte, North Carolina, December 1979. First Union is a Fed member bank with assets of about $6 billion.

branch across a state boundary. Within each individual state, the laws of that state determine whether or not banks in that state can branch.

In 1956 another act was passed, called the Douglas Amendment to the McFadden Act. It said that a bank in one state can't acquire banks in other states. Up until then, banks couldn't branch across state lines themselves. But they could acquire (particularly through a holding company structure) banks in other states.

There are still some corporations (holding companies) in some of the western states that own banks in more than one state. They're still allowed to do that because they were "grandfathered"—they were in existence before the Douglas Amendment was passed in 1956.

Banks are trying to find legal ways of establishing their presence in other states—partially to be ready for legalized interstate banking if and when it comes. It's legal now for banks to do anything they want to in another state, *except* take deposits. It's perfectly legal for us to make loans in other states. Until recently it was legal to open "loan production offices" in other states. You can't walk into a loan production office and make a deposit. But you can talk to a loan officer, and he can arrange to make you a loan.

Many banks or bank holding companies now have as subsidiaries separate finance companies that can establish branches in other states. Banks also have various types of finance companies, including operations that make loans on second mortgages, and operations that finance cars and make small loans. It's perfectly legal to have these kinds of offices in other states. There is an act called the Edge Act that permits banking operations for *international* purposes to be established in other states.

More and more, large banks are looking for sources of funds outside their local areas. Our bank, and certainly NCNB and Wachovia, is talking to corporate treasurers and other large depositors around the country on a daily basis. We're offering them certificates of deposit at whatever we think the proper rate of interest is on that day.

Through the Eurodollar market we can take deposits in a branch of our bank located in a foreign country. We can take deposits from all over the world in our foreign branches. Then we can use those deposits, either domestically or overseas, in accordance with our particular needs.

I don't want to leave you with the impression that this is a sleazy, under-the-table type of business for banks to be involved in—this business of trying to find ways of establishing a presence in other states. It's really a natural outgrowth of the growth of our economy, in many ways. As the economy gets larger, the amounts of credit required are growing.

Suppose a North Carolina company wants to build a new plant in the small town of Boone. Maybe twenty years ago the plant would have cost half a million dollars. Today it would cost several million dollars to build the same plant. If all we had was one small bank (or even three or four small banks) in Boone, that company would not be able to go to the local bank and find the means to finance the plant. The local banks wouldn't have enough money to make a loan of that size. So they would have to get the money from outside somehow.

In order for banks to get large enough to meet the needs, they've been branching intrastate (within the state), and now they also are looking for ways to bring in money from other parts of the country to be used in financing local activities in small towns and cities. And this sort of thing is going on in every state in the nation.

Interstate branching and statewide branching can offer greater public convenience and a greater availability of credit in the local areas. Also, interstate banking would allow greater competition and all that that implies. But there are some potential problems that could arise from interstate banking.

Interstate banking would tend to bring about larger and larger banks. Small banks might say: "If you let the big banks from all over the country come in and start trying to do business in this state, how can we survive? We're already having enough trouble, competing with the big banks and the little banks in our area as it is! Don't let those other sharks into our pool or they'll really gobble up us little fish!"

So the issue of interstate banking is an interesting issue. Like most other things, it doesn't fall neatly into a black or white category. There are some dangers that could come about because of it. But there certainly are some advantages that would be gained if more open interstate banking were allowed.

Kemp's Comments on Interstate Banking*

The McFadden Act is about 50 years old. The Douglas Amendment is almost 25 years old. In our opinion, neither one of them has improved with age. They were appropriate for the time in which they were passed, but a lot of things have happened in the financial world since that time.

Business activity is now much more national and international in scope. There have been changes in technology and communications—and attitudes, for that matter—that encourage all businesses (and the conduct of banking business in particular) to be broader in geographic reach than was once thought to be the case. And it's our view that the legislative restrictions in the banking structure need to accommodate themselves to these changes.

In the corporate banking business these restrictions have had no impact at all. Bankers travel throughout this country and throughout the world, doing business day to day. Foreign banks are now actively engaged in establishing a rather significant market share in our corporate banking business. So in corporate banking we already have interstate banking.

Banks have a lot of interstate "loan production offices" and "representative offices" in addition to traveling people. In the international area, changes are making it easier for banks to cross state lines, and easier for foreign banks to come into this country.

In retail banking, Citibank has gotten a lot of publicity from issuing credit cards on a nationwide basis. Merrill Lynch and other brokerage firms are doing what we consider to be almost banking business with their money market funds and things of that sort, all of which are available on a nationwide basis.

The point is, it's happening, even in spite of the regulations. Bank holding companies themselves are actively engaged in providing financial services in numerous states. At NCNB we have subsidiaries operating in virtually every state in the Southeast. They don't happen to be *banks,* at the moment. But they do, in fact, provide financial services—mortgage loans, consumer loans, some other services—to people throughout the Southeastern United States.

*Statements by Francis B. Kemp, Executive Vice President, North Carolina National Bank, Charlotte, North Carolina, December 1979. NCNB is a Fed member bank. NCNB Corp. has assets of about $13.5 billion.

There also are banks that operate in several states already. They are "grandfathered," or have some sort of special arrangement.

So the fact is, in our opinion it's not a question of whether or not you're going to have interstate banking. It's a question of what form that evolution is going to take. The position of NCNB's management is that the present statutory framework is anti-competitive, antiquated, and inefficient in an economic sense. In our judgment it is not in the public interest. We believe that some change in the statutory framework is essential, and we hope that some such change will take place in the not very distant future.

We would support legislation to modify the Douglas Amendment to allow bank holding companies in a particular region to begin merging with one another. We would propose that banks in the Southeastern United States be permitted to merge across state lines, and that banks in the Midwest, in the Northwest, on the West Coast, and in other regions be permitted to merge with other banks in their respective regions. This would be an initial step. We believe that this approach may be more palatable politically. And the impact on the marketplace may be a little less traumatic than to do away with the restrictions on interstate banking altogether. We think it would be somewhat more orderly to do it this way.

If the present interstate banking restrictions are not changed, we believe that these restrictions will lead to a massive concentration of banking resources in ten or twelve banks. They may be foreign banks, they may be New York banks, Chicago banks—I don't know. But our view in its simplest terms is this: If the banks outside the major money-market centers are restricted and required to sit and watch the world change around them, then they will miss a great opportunity. So there needs to be legislation that will allow major banks in each area to begin to merge with one another.

All of the traditional geographic boundaries are under pressure. It's only a question of how soon they will fall. We've had a very effective and progressive banking system in this state and could productively bring some of this management expertise to banking companies in other states. That's the strongest argument for *why* interstate banking makes sense for the country.

People who don't appreciate the importance that branch banking has had in the progress that's been made in North Carolina over the last several decades are really out of touch with reality.

We have a very strong network of independent banks. But it is unheard of to have five, *billion-dollar* banks—two, more than *five-billion dollar* banks—in a state like North Carolina. This state is hardly thought of as representing a major concentration of financial resources!

We've built large banks by combining resources throughout the state. That has had a very important impact on the ability of the state to make progress, and the ability of the banks in the state to finance that progress.

In our view, interstate banking on a regional basis is a concept whose time has come. Our primary concern is that North Carolina banks—which have done so well for themselves and for the state—not be left behind.

Gentry's Comments on Interstate Banking*

The new environment for banking is characterized by the dismantling of a regulatory structure that was put in place in the early 1930s and rested upon the premise that the most important aspect of banking was safety of deposit funds. Not only was this the most important function, it was viewed as the only significant public policy issue. To ensure that banks did not take too much risk, they were restricted in terms of price (interest rates), products (through such restriction as the Glass-Steagall Act), and place (banks cannot branch across state lines).

The regulatory structure set up in the 1930s did not impose serious costs on the economy so long as interest rates were low, financial products were relatively simple, and banking remained a local business limited by transportation and communication. These conditions, for which the regulatory structure was appropriate, began to disappear in the 1960s and have totally changed today. Because the regulatory structure did not change, we have seen an illustration of the truth that the marketplace gets what it wants. Money market funds were a response to the consumer's desire to preserve the purchasing power of his funds despite reg-

*Statements by Frank L. Gentry, Senior Vice President, North Carolina National Bank, Charlotte, N.C., November 1981. NCNB is a Fed member bank. NCNB Corp. has assets of about $13.5 billion.

ulations that prevented banks and savings and loans from being competitive on interest rates. Because those money market funds are offered by firms that are not banks, they are not subject to any geographic restrictions. They are a prime illustration of *interstate competition.*

Similarly, banks and bank holding companies themselves have been able to compete across state lines for most kinds of business other than deposit taking. NCNB, for example, owns a consumer finance company that makes consumer loans from offices in several states. Until recently, we owned a multi-state mortgage company. We still own a leasing company and commercial finance company that make asset-based loans. We, and other large North Carolina banks, have out-of-state loan production offices that seek corporate loans that are booked in the main office.

What we cannot do, and what, thus far, the money market funds seem to be able to do best, is to offer to individuals and small businesses deposit services that are accessible by check without regard to location. As a banker, these geographic limitations worry me, but as a consumer, they need not. It is now clear that deposit services will be provided efficiently whether or not they are provided by banks.

Savings and loans, in many ways, are banks. But they are not banks with respect to the restrictions that are placed on deposit taking across state lines. Recently a supervised merger of troubled institutions created a savings and loan headquartered in California with branches in New York and Florida. While this event was unusual, it was clearly permissible within the existing legal structure. By contrast, no banking agency could approve a similar merger of commercial banks.

Despite the obvious disadvantage placed on banks by these restrictions, the banking industry is by no means united in wishing to eliminate geographic restrictions on bank expansion. Many smaller banks seem to take the position that, since they are already having to compete with Gulf and Western, Sears, Merrill Lynch and American Express, the last thing they need is to have to compete with Citicorp and Bank of America. This view may be suicidal for the industry in the long run, but it is certainly understandable. I believe that this view will turn around if and when a significant number of banks become convinced that their best alternative is to be able to merge with other institutions. Under those circumstances, they would want to consider as many merger partners as possible, so they would no longer support geographic restrictions.

North Carolina has been considerably more progressive than the nation as a whole on the subject of interstate competition and geographic restrictions generally. We have and have had statewide branching in North Carolina for many years. And many bankers in this state have been willing to consider various types of reciprocal legislation that would allow banks to form holding companies across state lines within our region. An approach of this sort would allow the opportunity to create sizable bank holding companies headquartered in various parts of the country prior to any wide-open nationwide branching.

Action for interstate banking can come and is coming through the states. Clearly the Congress has the right to regulate interstate commerce. Yet only in the case of banking have they delegated that power to the states. So long as such power is delegated to the states, the states themselves have the option to take action.

North Dakota and Delaware have both invited out-of-state banks in, under limited circumstances, in order to attract jobs and capital. There are also statutes in Iowa and Florida that allow bank holding companies that have been operating in the state prior to a certain date to continue to operate there, and to expand their operations on equal footing with banks who operate entirely within those states.

While these developments are better than nothing, I believe the consumer will be served best by an environment that moves us quickly to elimination of restrictions on place as well as on price and product.

Suggested Readings

"A Yankee Test of Interstate Banking," *Business Week* (February 14, 1983), 39.

Calonius, Erik. "The Interstate Bank War Is More Than a Rumor," *Florida Trend* (October 1981), 97–102.

"Country Cousins: Small-Town Bankers Fight To Keep Curbs on Big Rivals' Growth," *Wall Street Journal* (June 3, 1983), 1.

Hill, G. Christian. "S&L Losses May Force Regulators To Ease Interstate Banking Rules," *Wall Street Journal* (January 12, 1982), 35.

"Interstate Banking Gets a Florida 'Yes'," *American Banker* (February 10, 1982), 1.
Salamon, Julie, and Conte, Christopher. "Firm with 31 Banks Over 25 States Is Proposed," *Wall Street Journal* (February 18, 1983), 10.
Sigale, Merwin. "Southeast Regional Banking Endorsed: 3 of Area's Big Banking Companies Approve Interstate Trend," *American Banker* (November 1, 1983), 1.
"Six S&L Mergers in Five States Cleared by U.S.," *Wall Street Journal* (August 3, 1982), 4.

Chapter 16

Rideout's Comments on Foreign Bank Entry*

Past history reflects the fact that in banking (as in other areas) nature does indeed abhor a vacuum. As long as there are ways for banks (or any other type of business) to do things that they perceive to be desirable, then those things somehow will be accomplished. With respect to the laws that have determined how foreign banks may operate in the United States (at least until July of 1978) this concept of "nature abhoring a vacuum" applies very well.

In July of 1978 a law was passed entitled *The International Banking Act of 1978.* Prior to its passage, foreign banks had the virtual ability to set up operations in the U.S. market on an interstate basis—and I'm talking about full-fledged operations—not only lending powers, but deposit-taking powers as well. Because of this flaw in the legislative-regulatory structure governing the banking system, there was a rather rapid rate of growth of foreign banks in this country. For instance, in 1972 there were 209 foreign bank entities operating in the U.S. domestic markets. By April of 1979, that number had increased by more than 50 percent—up to a total of 318 bank entities.

Estimates range widely on the market share of domestic com-

*Statements by Thomas P. Rideout, Formerly Senior Vice President, Wachovia Bank & Trust Co., more recently Chairman and CEO of Savannah Bank and Trust Co.

mercial loans that these banks hold. I've heard estimates ranging from 10 percent to 30 or 40 percent. Probably the number is somewhere in the range of 13 to 15 percent. I've heard estimates that these foreign bank entities in our markets have on the order of about $140 billion in total assets.

This incursion of foreign banks into our domestic markets created sufficient political pressure to result in the passage of the aforementioned *International Banking Act* in July of 1978. That Act did several things: First of all, it "grandfathered" all of the foreign banks who currently had interstate banking operations in the United States—that is, everybody who was already here was permitted to continue to operate as they had in the past. However, new foreign banks that seek to come to the United States will be required to, in effect, declare a "home office." They must say "my home office is in Houston" (or Atlanta, or Dallas, or New York City, or wherever). Then they will be subject to the same types of branching constraints as are the domestic banks in that state.

Edge Act Branches

The International Banking Act continued to permit the establishment of Edge Act branches. These are international-type facilities that U.S. banks (and foreign banks operating in the United States) have been empowered to establish for many decades. The Edge Act permits banks to establish these international banking facilities across state lines.

What the Federal Reserve proposed (under Regulation K—their regulation basically to implement the International Banking Act) was that Edge Act banks may now declare a "home office" and then, with the approval of the Fed, establish Edge Act branches on a nationwide basis. This is different from the old rule which required that each "Edge facility" be separately approved and separately capitalized with a minimum capital of $2 million. So now, under the new rules, we have a situation where Edge Act branching can take place.

More controversial than that, however, was a proposal under Regulation K that would allow Edge Act branches to perform a full-service domestic banking business with corporations in those marketplaces where they were established—but only with corporations that could meet a test called the "qualified business entity" test. In effect, the test is concerned with sales and other indications that prove that the customer is engaged predominately in international business. For those corporations that qualify, the Edge Act branches would be permitted to hold corporate deposits and to provide for those customers a full range of domestic and international banking services.

There has been a good deal of opposition from certain segments of the banking industry. But that's just another example of the way the interstate banking issue is beginning to evolve.

Acquisitions by Foreign Banks

Finally, there is another controversial aspect of this whole issue which has to do with the ability of foreign banks to acquire U.S. banks. Probably the key case now being considered in that regard is the attempt by the Hong Kong–Shanghai Bank to buy Marine Midland in New York State.

Why does this competitive pressure from the foreign banks exist? What is it that makes them want to expand into our market? There are a lot of reasons why a foreign bank might want to come in and merge with a domestic bank such as Marine Midland. By going the merger route, the foreign bank could establish an *immediate presence* in a marketplace. If they came in and established a *de novo* (entirely new) branch, they would have to start from scratch.

One reason why foreign banks want to come here now is the fact that there are a lot of what they perceive to be "cheap dollars" available to purchase banks. And there are some relatively attractive opportunities to buy, with market values well below book value. In addition, relatively stable sources of deposits are also available.

Foreign banks would cite the fact that they merely want to come to this market because their customers are moving here and they want to follow their customers on a global basis. And I think, finally, there is a perception (and I think it is valid) that the political and economic stability that is offered in this country makes the United States a very viable place for expansion.

How do the foreign banks differ from United States banks? They differ in a number of ways. First of all, many foreign banks really represent the banking arm of their governments. For instance, the Japanese banks, the British banks, and the French and German banks as well, are really the banking arms of their governments. There is a much closer relationship between the banks and the government of most western nations than is the case here in the United States.

Another lever, or advantage, that foreign banks have in terms of expanding in our market is what we call the "reciprocity threat." The fact of the matter is that United States banks expanded rather aggressively in the late 1950s and the 1960s into foreign banking markets. To the extent that we might try to restrict the expansion of foreign banks into the U.S. marketplace there is a threat that our banks operating abroad would feel some pressure from the regulatory authorities in those particular nations.

Another pressure affecting the marketplace is the fact that it is perceived here that the ability of foreign banks to lever themselves—in other words, the ability to leverage their capital in terms of loans—is much greater than is permitted here. Thus, they can afford to price their loans on a thinner margin basis, be more competitive, and thereby increase their share of the market.

Other Important Issues

There are some very important issues in all of this. One is the question that has been raised by Paul Volcker. He feels that any foreign bank that is to acquire a domestic United States bank should pass what he calls a "foreign bank takeover benefits test." In effect, he is saying that any merger that is proposed would have to meet the following tests:

- The merger would have to improve the capital of the bank being acquired.
- The merger would have to improve the management.
- There would have to be proof that the bank would be making a commitment to the local marketplace.
- There would have to be proof that the new ownership could stand on its own, *better than* the previous ownership.

- Finally, the nation represented by the bank merging with the United States bank would have to pass the "national reciprocity test"—that is, they would have to be as kindly toward the expansion of United States banks in their nation as we are to the expansion of their banks in our nation.

Another philosophical question concerns our regulators: Are our regulators being compromised to the extent that they are having to approve foreign bank expansions in this country because of the reciprocity threat? Are our regulators having to approve expansions of foreign banks which are going to hurt domestic competition? Are they allowing foreign banks to come in, and to leverage themselves in ways that our banks cannot? Does that somehow compromise the regulatory process in this country? I think that's a very important question.

You can see by the kinds of issues that are being raised here that there are some very difficult problems. One of the things that concerns domestic banks perhaps more than anything else is the fact that a foreign bank can buy a U.S. bank while a U.S. bank cannot buy that same bank. Suppose that a fairly large U.S. bank is about to fail. And suppose no bank within that state can merge with it because of antitrust regulations—restrictions designed to prevent the concentration of economic and financial power. Today, regulators have only one safety valve, and that is to bring in a foreign bank to merge with the failing bank. The McFadden Act, passed in 1927, prevents domestic banks from crossing state lines. So a bank in another state can't acquire the failing bank.

All this points to a basic unfairness here. Why, for instance, shouldn't it be possible for a bank like Texas Commerce of Houston to merge with Marine Midland instead of allowing only foreign banks the right to enter into that merger? That's a very real and very important policy-type question. It makes a strong argument for relaxing or removing some of the restrictions on interstate banking. It's a question which needs to be addressed by the Congress.

Suggested Readings

"American Pie," *The Economist* (October 8, 1983), 86.

Berkowitz, Peggy. "Big Canadian Banks Plan To Expand in U.S.," *Wall Street Journal* (October 15, 1983), 31.

"Breaking Wide in America (Fuji Bank)," *The Economist* (March 19, 1983), 100.

Dolan, Carrie. "BanCal Takeover Shakes U.S. Bankers Worried about Growing Foreign Interests," *Wall Street Journal* (August 25, 1983), 12.

"Here Come Foreign Banks Again," *Business Week* (June 26, 1978), 77–86.

"International Banking Facilities and the Eurodollar Market," (Summary of Federal Staff Study), *Federal Reserve Bulletin* (August 1983), 591.

Luse, Eric. "To Acquire a Big U.S. Bank, It Helps To Be a Foreign Buyer," *American Banker* (October 21, 1983), 4.

Chapter 17

America's Nationwide Financial Services Industry

You already know that many financial services institutions in the United States are offering their services on a nationwide basis. And you know that very few of the activities of the larger banks are confined to the banks' home states.

By 1984 the erosion of the barriers to interstate banking had come a long way—so far, in fact, that it would have been much easier to list the *exceptions to* rather than the *kinds and instances of* interstate banking. But you need to have an overview awareness of this maze of interstate banking activity—of the extent and kinds of things going on across state lines.

Interstate Bank Activities and Services

From the previous chapters you know that banks operate offices in other states. These offices arrange loans and are involved in consumer finance, mortgage finance, insurance activities, credit card services, financing international trade, providing trust services—in fact just about every banking service you can think of *except* accepting deposits.

So are banks limited to their home state for deposit-taking? Of course not. Many banks are out "beating the bushes" nationwide trying to generate new deposits. But the deposit must be sent by the depositor to the bank in its home state, so that the deposit is "received and recorded" by the bank in its home state. Interstate banking? Legally, no. In fact? I don't know. What does it look like to you?

But the point is this: The bank can't set up a full-service branch (or the bank holding company can't own and operate a full-service bank) in another state. It can't, that is, unless certain special circumstances are met, as discussed in the next sections.

Banks with "Grandfathered" Rights

Suppose a bank had branches in other states when the anti-branching law (McFadden Act, 1927) was passed. Then that bank can keep those branches, and (depending on state laws) perhaps expand its operations in the state or states in which it has this "grandfathered" position.

There are only two U.S. banks with grandfathered branches: Heritage Bank of New Jersey, which has a branch in Pennsylvania, and Bank of California, which has branches in Oregon and Washington. But there are at least 15 bank holding companies which owned banks in two or more states at the time the Douglas Amendment passed (1956). So these banks are grandfathered in their right to own banks in more than one state. Altogether there are more than 30 states interlinked through these "grandfathering" arrangements. And there are at least five foreign banks with grandfathered banks in at least two states—usually New York and California.

During the early 1980s several banks with grandfathered positions in other states were moving aggressively to expand their activities and gain large market shares in the other states.

Interstate Mergers Involving Troubled Thrifts

You already know about the problems of the thrifts in the early 1980s. In March 1981 the Federal Home Loan Bank Board (FHLBB) adopted a policy of allowing interstate thrift mergers when necessary to bail out an ailing institution. By January 1984 more than 30 such mergers had occurred.

Two of the troubled thrift mergers involved a bank acquiring a thrift. The first was in August 1982, when Citicorp of New York acquired Fidelity Federal S&L of San Francisco. The second was in September 1983, when Old Stone Corporation (bank holding company) of Providence, Rhode Island, acquired Perpetual S&L of High Point, North Carolina. These thrift–bank interstate mergers have been generally regarded as quite significant and precedent-setting. But their long-run effect on eroding interstate banking barriers remains to be seen.

By 1983 some banks and thrifts were talking about the possibility of applying for interstate mergers. We'll just have to wait and see how that turns out.

State Laws Permitting Out-of-State Banks to Enter

In 1982–84 one of the hottest issues on the revolutionary banking scene was state legislative action on establishing interstate banks. Both South Dakota and Delaware have invited outside banks to come in and set up limited-purpose banks and escape some of the restrictions imposed by their home states. Citicorp runs a nationwide credit card operation and offers insurance through its South Dakota subsidiaries. Delaware passed its law in February 1981. By December of 1983, 11 out-of-state banks had established offices there.

Before the end of 1983, 15 states had passed some form of law to permit out-of-state banks to come in. Some states required reciprocity—your banks can come into our state only if our banks are permitted to go into your state.

Several of the New England states passed laws requiring *regional reciprocity:* "only New England banks need apply!" In 1983 as the effects of this new legislation began to be felt, there was a flurry of interstate merger activity in New England, especially between Massachusetts and Connecticut.

By the end of 1983, "regional reciprocity" interstate banking legislation was being considered in many states. But there was some strong opposition from small banks, which feared the threat of out-of-state competition. And the political aspects of this issue are tough to deal with. Consider this: If the state legislature won't legalize state-wide branching (and almost 30 states haven't done that yet), how do you expect them to vote on the interstate issue?

But the more important point is this: Many states are passing enabling legislation to permit regional interstate networks to be established. If all goes well within these regional networks, the "good examples" may spread.

Interstate Banking-Type Services of Nondepository Institutions

In 1977 the Fed ruled that the Merrill Lynch Cash Management Account (CMA) did not violate banking laws. That was a door-opener. It opened the door to the "almost banking" business for brokerage (and other) firms. And it opened the door to nation-wide "special account banking." And the door has been pushed open wider ever since.

As a CMA account customer, you begin with a $20,000 minimum—in stocks, bonds, money market funds, cash, whatever. You can call your broker and buy and sell as you wish. Dividends and interest on your stocks and bonds are paid into the account and automatically put into money market funds. But that's not all. As a CMA account customer, you receive a VISA card and a checkbook. You can write checks and the money comes out of your money market fund. The checking and credit-card functions are carried out for Merrill Lynch by Banc One of Columbus, Ohio.

The response to the CMA account was overwhelming. Money flowed in from all over the country. Out of the banks and thrifts? Not all of it, but some of it, to be sure.

Other brokers established similar accounts. Merrill Lynch had copyrighted its CMA account, and it tried to make the others pay a fee for copying it. But the CMA-type account spread.

There wasn't much the bankers could do to compete. They couldn't offer money market rates (Reg Q, remember?) and they couldn't offer stockbroker services (Glass-Steagall, remember?). But then that all changed.

The October 21, 1983, *Wall Street Journal* carried a half-page Citibank ad which said: "Once it was smart to have a CMA. Now it's smarter to be in FOCUS.'' The ad compared the Citibank FOCUS account with the Merrill Lynch CMA account. A lot of things must have happened to let Citibank—a bank!—offer brokerage services and money market fund rates! That's right. You already know that the MMDAs were authorized in the Garn–St. Germain Act of 1982. You'll be reading about the banker–broker breakthrough in another chapter.

But before going on, think about this: Are Merrill Lynch and all those other brokers in the interstate banking business? Is Citibank FOCUS an example of interstate banking? You can argue about it if you want to. But it sure comes close. Right?

The Explosive Growth of Nonbank Banks

What's a nonbank bank? It's an ''almost bank'' that has something missing so that it doesn't meet the legal definition of ''bank.'' As of January 1984, the law says you're a bank if you're doing these two things: (1) making commercial loans, and (2) taking deposits. Suppose you aren't making commercial loans. Or suppose you make commercial loans but you don't take deposits. Either way, under the law, you are not a bank! You don't fit the legal definition.

Who can own a nonbank bank? Anybody who wants to. Since it isn't a bank, it doesn't fall under the banking laws. So, presumably, you could own one in each state if you wanted to!

Who owns nonbank banks? Lots of companies. Sears. Parker Pen. General Electric. Dreyfus Corporation and other mutual fund companies. Stockbrokers. Several bank holding companies. Some S&Ls. In 1983, Dimension Financial Corporation submitted an application to the Comptroller of the Currency to establish 31 of these nonbank banks, to be located in 25 different states.

Fed Chairman Paul Volcker was not in favor of approving any nonbank banks. He proposed legislation changing the definition of a bank to bring these nonbank banks under the banking laws. And he called for a moratorium on new nonbank banks until Congress had time to act on this issue.

Volcker's proposed new definition of ''bank'' was included in the omnibus banking bill introduced by Senator Garn in November 1983. And the Comptroller of the Currency agreed not to accept any new nonbank bank applications until after Congress had a chance to act on the legislation. But meanwhile the Comptroller will act on those applications received before the moratorium. It will be interesting to see what happens with Dimension Financial Corporation's application for 31 banks in 25 states! An interstate banking breakthrough? Maybe.

Not everyone wants to see the demise of the nonbank bank. In September 1983 the American Financial Services Association (formerly the National Consumer Finance Association) commented negatively on the proposed legislation. The Association referred to nonbank banks as "consumer banks" and argued that these banks have an important role to play in the nation's financial services industry.

Interstate Competition from Other Firms

You know that the brokers have moved into the banking business and that the bankers are moving into brokerage, cash management, and other financial services. And almost all of this is on a complete nationwide basis—no state boundary restrictions.

But did you know that much of the same is going on with Sears? And GE? And with the insurance companies? And J.C. Penny? And Exxon? And it was going on with Baldwin Piano Company, which became Baldwin United, went into the financial services business, and then went broke.

The list could go on and on. But that's enough for now. In some of the chapters coming up, you'll be reading about nonbank competition in the financial services industry. There you'll find out a lot more about what these nonbankers are doing in the banking business. And you'll see it has turned into a real *jungle* out there!

EFTS and Interstate ATM Networks

Is it possible for barriers to interstate banking to survive for long in the modern world of electronic funds transfer systems (EFTS) and nationwide Automated Teller Machine (ATM) networks? Not likely.

During 1982–84 the financial system of the entire nation was being meshed together in a sophisticated computer-telecommunications network. New interconnections and new functions were coming on line almost daily. And interstate barriers were dissolving.

Before you can understand the interstate implications of EFTS and ATM networks, you need to know something about what's happening in EFTS and how it has been developing over the years. That's what you'll be reading about in the next chapter.

Suggested Readings

Fraust, Bart. "Regional Pacts To Get Blessing in New Garn Bill," *American Banker* (October 27, 1983), 1.

Hector, Gary. "Citicorp Goes West," *Fortune* (November 29, 1982), 83–87.

"More Cracks in Banking's Interstate Barriers," *Business Week* (October 17, 1983), 173–175.

"More Nonbank Banks Appear on the Scene," *Banking Expansion Reporter,* Vol. 2, no. 14 (July 18, 1983), 4.

"Nonbank Banks Continue To Appear," *Banking Expansion Reporter,* Vol. 2, no. 16 (August 15, 1983), 10–11.

"Ohio Added to Regional Bank Group: 5 States, D.C. To Meet in Delaware Nov. 28," *American Banker* (November 4, 1983), 1.

Ringer, Richard. "11 States Weigh Interstate Banking," *American Banker* (October 25, 1983), 1.

"Suit Challenges Regional Reciprocity," *Banking Expansion Reporter,* Vol. 2 no. 16 (August 15, 1983), 15.

Weberman, Ben. "States Rights," *Forbes* (May 23, 1983), 36.

Part VI
Electronic Banking Booms in the 1980s

The Long-Awaited Electronic Banking Revolution Finally Begins, with Significant Impact throughout the Financial Services Industry

Chapter 18

Electronic Banking: What It Is and How It Works

As computer and communications technology expanded rapidly during the 1960s and on into the 1970s, it seemed to many observers that a nationwide electronic funds transfer (EFT) system was just around the corner. People were talking about the coming rapid expansion of EFT systems as both highly desirable and inevitable. Such terms as the coming of the "cashless society" and even the "checkless society" were frequently heard. A nationwide system that would operate mostly on magnetically coded plastic cards would transfer funds from one person to another and from one place to another across the nation, in seconds. This was soon to eliminate the time and cost required to process checks.

It was expected that point of sale (POS) terminals would be located in every store and even in some homes and offices, so that payments could be made without writing checks and without going to a bank to undertake transactions. The plastic "debit cards" would be used for purchases, deposits, withdrawals, bill-payment—in fact, for all kinds of financial transactions.

What Happened to the "Cashless Society"?

The "cashless and checkless society" did not come as rapidly as many had expected. For one thing there has been a lot of consumer resistance. People like the record-keeping that their cancelled checks provide them and they have not rushed to give it up. Also, there have been several legal problems in connection with electronic fund transfers. And sometimes the cost of the new electronic equipment has been prohibitive for some banks and other financial institutions.

There have been several obstacles that have retarded the progress in the use of EFT systems. But in general, technology has not been one of the impediments. The basic technology needed for a nationwide EFT network has existed for some time, and the unit cost of performing many basic functions has fallen sharply over the last few decades. The technology and the incentive to introduce it have existed, but customer resistance and legal obstacles have been the major problems. These problems are being overcome only slowly.

By the late 1970s, some bankers were changing their minds about EFT—suggesting that a nationwide electronic funds transfer system is something that really is not necessary and is too expensive. So the "cashless and checkless society by 1980" certainly did not arrive. But the move toward electronic banking was not dead, either. There has been a continual expansion in the use of electronic fund transfers, and that expansion is certain to continue.

The August 4, 1975, issue of *Business Week* ran an article entitled, "Bank Cards Take Over the Country." This article emphasized the revolutionary possibilities of electronic banking, saying:

> . . . electronic banking is sweeping the country—overwhelming the laws that govern banks and other financial institutions, changing dramatically the banking and savings habits of millions of Americans. Ultimately, electronic banking will revolutionize the very concept of money itself. . . . Certainly it will touch off a flurry of competition for the nation's financial businesses unlike anything seen before.

Less than two years later, *Business Week* ran another article in its April 18, 1977, issue entitled, "Electronic Banking: A Retreat from the Cashless Society." This article begins with the statement:

> Suddenly it appears that the great electronic banking revolution that has been 'just around the corner' for a decade may never arrive at all.

This article goes on to describe the consumer resistance and the various kinds of legal entanglements that have slowed the development of electronic funds transfer systems (EFTS).

It is easy to look back and see the enthusiasm and optimism with which some bankers and others were looking forward to the rapid introduction of EFT systems during the early and mid 1970s. Clearly, the strength of the impediments that would have to be overcome was underestimated.

The 1977 *Business Week* article did not mean to imply that electronic fund transfer systems had not already made important progress in this country, or that all future progress in electronic banking had been stopped dead in its tracks. What the article does illustrate, however, is that the previous and generally held forecast regarding the rapid introduction of a nationwide EFT system did not materialize. The expanded use of EFT systems had been continuing all along. But certainly not at the explosive rate which many observers had predicted.

It was not until the early 1980s that EFTS began to be widely accepted and to spread rapidly. That's when the revolutionary effects that had been predicted as far back as the 1960s began to materialize. You'll be reading about that soon. But first, what does EFTS mean? And what does it do?

There are many kinds of operations which can be included under the term "electronic banking" or EFTS. Several electronic functions are already in widespread use, while with others the available electronic techniques have hardly been introduced. The following sections of this chapter explain and evaluate several of these different kinds of electronic banking functions.

Kinds of EFTS Functions

When we talk about electronic funds transfer systems, we include several different kinds of functions, and in fact, several different "systems." But all of these systems are alike in that they transfer funds electronically rather than by the use of paper instruments, such as checks, drafts, certificates, etc. Each EFT system replaces manual processes, and transfers funds instantly. So an EFT system of any kind speeds up the transaction and reduces the amount of manual labor involved. The obvious advantage of any kind of EFT system results from the reduced labor cost and the increased speed.

The following sub-sections briefly describe eight different kinds of EFT arrangements. The first five of these involve EFT arrangements in which no direct "customer contact" is required. The electronic fund transfers are handled in "batches" by the interbank EFT networks. These are: wire transfers of funds, check truncation, automated clearing house arrangements, pre-authorized credit arrangements such as automatic payroll deposits, and pre-authorized debit arrangements such as bill-paying services. The last three of the EFT arrangements discussed in this chapter involve direct customer contact. These are: the automated teller machines (ATMs), point-of-sale (POS) terminals, and on-line telephone connections between the customer's telephone and the bank's computer.

Wire Transfers of Funds. Banks have been using "wire transfers" for the instantaneous transmission of funds from one bank to another since the 1950s, on the "interbank wire." Wire transfers amount to sending electronic messages (rather than paper documents) in order to move funds from one bank (or one account) to another.

The Federal Reserve System operates a major wire transfer network. This Federal Reserve Communications System network transfers large volumes of funds for member banks, for their correspondent banks, and for bank customers. The dollar volume of funds transferred through this system is several times as large as the amount of money handled by the Fed's check-clearing system. It is now possible to transfer funds to any place in the country, instantaneously. These transfers are going on in large volume, every day.

Check Truncation. The purpose of a check truncation system is to reduce the flow of checks through the banking system. The data from the check is entered into a computer, then sent back by electronic signals. With the usual design of a "check truncation" system, the customer who wrote the check never gets back the cancelled check. Once the data from the check is entered into the electronic system, the checks are stored for awhile and ultimately destroyed. All the customer gets is an accounting statement.

Technology now makes it possible to transmit the *image* of the check, not just the data. Perhaps this will speed the introduction of check truncation systems. There are also possibilities that non-personal checks—perhaps Federal Government checks—will someday be handled by check truncation.

Automated Clearing House (ACH) Systems. Automated clearing houses are arrangements for electronically settling debits and credits among banks. When checks are written on one bank and deposited in other banks, funds must be transferred from the banks on which the checks are written to the banks in which the checks are deposited. ACH systems permit the debit and credit items to be transmitted electronically, usually through a computer-generated magnetic tape.

Several ACH systems are now operating, handling a large volume of debit and credit items at various places throughout the country. For example, the California Automated Clearing House Association is called "CACHA," the North Carolina Automated Clearing House Association is called "NORCACHA," and other clearing house associations around the country have similar acronyms.

During the early 1980s, there were more than 10,000 financial institutions participating in these regional ACH systems. Since 1978 these regional systems have been linked together by the National Automated Clearing House Association. The Federal Government is the largest user of the ACH systems, through direct deposit of social security payments and other federal disbursements. These ACH systems are now playing a very important role in facilitating the flow of interbank settlements.

Preauthorized Credits: Automatic Payroll and Other Deposits. Preauthorized credit arrangements include such things as automatic payroll deposits by employers to the employees' bank accounts, automatic deposits of government social security and pension payments, and other kinds of recurring payments such as dividend and annuity payments.

Preauthorized payments are deposited automatically to the accounts of the recipients, and are distributed to the various banks through the ACH system. The employee (or other recipient of regular preauthorized payments) authorizes the employer (or other payor) to make direct payments, and then the payor prepares the data on a computer tape and sends it to the bank. Then the funds are automatically withdrawn from the payor's account and distributed to all of the payees through the ACH system. These preauthorized credit plans are now playing a significant and increasing role in the nation's payments system, and are significantly increasing the speed and reducing the cost of making these payments.

Preauthorized Debits: Automatic Bill-Paying. Preauthorized debit arrangements work very much like preauthorized credits except that the funds are being deducted from the individual customer's account and deposited into the company's account. Preauthorized debits are also cleared through the ACH systems.

Preauthorized debits are well suited for any case of regularly recurring bills, such as mortgage payments, insurance payments, and other payments of a definite amount. Bills which recur but which have varying amounts (such as utility bills) also can be handled through a preauthorized debit arrangement. But most customers have been unwilling to give their utility companies and others the authorization to automatically deduct bills from their accounts. So it isn't likely that all bills will ever be paid in this way. But preauthorized debits already are playing an important and increasing role in the payments system.

Customer-Contact EFT Systems

Automated Teller Machines (ATMs). The most important and most rapidly expanding EFT arrangement involving direct customer contact is the ATM. Automated teller machines provide a broad range of banking services to the customer and provide 24-hour access to the bank's services. They are playing an increasing role in reducing the "direct customer-teller contact."

ATMs often are located at the bank itself. But many are located in remote locations such as shopping centers, airports, etc. Customer resistance to the use of ATMs was difficult to overcome at first. But customer resistance now seems to be a problem of the past.

There have been some legal problems with the use of the ATMs concerning such questions as *where* the machines can be located and *who* will be provided access to the machines, and questions about customer *safety* and *privacy*. These issues will be discussed later.

Point-of-Sale (POS) Systems. As the name implies, point-of-sale systems involve terminals located in places of business—usually retail stores—which permit the customer to pay the store by EFT. The amount of the purchase is automatically deducted from the customer's account and simultaneously added to the seller's account.

It works like this: The customer's card is inserted in the POS terminal, the amount is entered either manually or through an electronic cash register or "products code reader," and the transfer of funds is made instantaneously. If the customer's bank is different than the store's bank, a "switching and processing center" (SPC) connects the computers of the two banks and completes the transfer.

Both the customer and the store receive a printed statement from the POS terminal at the time of the transaction. Then the customer's regular bank statement lists each one of the POS purchases individually.

POS systems have been introduced in a few cities, but there have been impediments to their expanded use. There has been customer resistance, and the cost of installing all of the POS terminals required is high. One clear advantage of such a system from the point of view of the seller is that the problem of bad checks is eliminated. These issues and the latest developments on POS will be further discussed later.

Telephone Bill-Paying Services. The technology now exists for customers with touch-tone telephones to use their own home phone to contact the bank's or thrift's computer to pay bills and perform other services automatically. A system like this was introduced in Seattle in 1973 by Seattle First National Bank, but the number of customers attracted to this service was so small that the service was withdrawn after only a few months.

Washington Mutual Savings Bank also introduced a telephone bill-paying service, with the belief that there will be a dramatic increase in acceptance of this service once people understand how it works. It appears likely that in the future these telephone bill-paying services will become an important kind of electronic banking in many places throughout the country.

Telephone Home Banking Services. During the early 1980s, as telecommunication technology continued its rapid development, "home banking" systems were introduced experimentally in several places in the country. These systems use either the TV cable or telephone line and are linked into the TV set. By 1984 this was beginning to look like "an idea whose time has come." You'll be reading more about that in a subsequent chapter.

CBCTs and RSUs. The ATMs and POS terminals and other terminals that serve as remote connections between customers and their bank or thrift institution are referred to in general as "CBCTs" and "RSUs." They are called "customer-bank communications terminals" (CBCTs) by the Office of the Comptroller of the Currency, which supervises National Banks. They are called "remote service units" (RSUs) by the Federal Home Loan Bank Board, which supervises most of the thrift institutions. Some CBCTs and RSUs are full-service ATMs. But others are less sophisticated terminals that do not provide the full range of services—such as receiving deposits, dispensing funds, transferring funds between accounts, making credit card advances, and receiving payments—that are provided by a full-service EFT terminal.

With such an array of impressive technology available, why didn't the financial services institutions rush to provide more EFT services in the 1970s? What was happening on this in the early 1980s? And what's the outlook? That's the subject of the chapters coming up.

Suggested Readings

Berry, Alexander B. III. "Branch Strategies for the 80s," *Journal of Retail Banking,* vol. 4, no. 2 (June 1982), 37–44.

Carter, Michael G. "An Integrated Approach to EFT and Retail Service Delivery," *Journal of Retail Banking,* vol. 4, no. 2 (June 1982), 1–13.

"Electronic Banking," *Business Week* (January 18, 1982), 70–80.

"Electronic Networks Springing Up All Over," *American Banker* (March 19, 1982), 2.

''Key Banks Program Allows Customers To Pay Phone Bills Using EFT,'' *American Banker* (October 19, 1983), 8.

Long, Donald G. ''The Business Case for Electronic Banking,'' *Journal of Retail Banking* (June 1982), 14–21.

Lordan, James F. ''A Fresh Approach to the Potential of ACH,'' *ABA Banking Journal* (March 1982), 123.

Padilla, Maria T. ''Home-Banking Tests Begin, But New Systems May Be Slow To Spread,'' *Wall Street Journal* (January 17, 1983), 25.

Chapter 19

Electronic Banking: Impediments and Slow Development in the 1970s

Customer-contact EFT systems have been introduced much more rapidly in some parts of the country than in others. The laws of some states have been highly restrictive, and in some states the banks and thrift institutions have been much more aggressive in introducing and experimenting with these systems.

Legal Impediments

One of the greatest impediments to the introduction of EFT systems for customer use has to do with location restrictions. The McFadden Act prevents banks from establishing branches in other states, and it requires them to abide by their own state's branching laws. More than half of the states now limit or entirely prohibit bank branching.

The legal question is this: Can a bank which is legally prohibited from establishing a branch in some place, establish an ATM or some other kind of CBCT there?

In 1974 the Comptroller of the Currency ruled that CBCTs were not branches, and that ATMs and POS terminals could qualify as CBCTs. But in a number of states the courts have reversed this decision. So banks in those states have been prohibited from establishing remote terminals in places in which they are prohibited from branching. This is one of the reasons why some states have ATMs and other CBCTs and RSUs located all over the state, and others do not. These anti-branching restrictions have curtailed the expansion of EFT systems in Illinois, Colorado, Michigan, Minnesota, Missouri, and in other states.

In some states where the law prevents banks from establishing EFT terminals in remote locations, the thrifts are not restricted by the same laws. So in some states the S&Ls have had an advantage in introducing remote EFT terminals.

The anti-branching restrictions in some states have caused many banks to install ATMs at the location of the bank office itself, rather than in other locations. When the machine is placed at the location of the bank (or the branch), this does not require the cooperation of third parties, such as merchants, to provide space for the terminals. Some businesses have been reluctant to accept EFT terminals that are hooked up to only one bank, in the belief that this might cause them to lose customers who deal with other banks. This problem could be solved by arrangements among the banks to share the use of each other's terminals. But these sharing arrangements have not been easy to work out, either. But more and more it is happening.

The Development of Shared EFT Systems

In the state of Iowa, the "Iowa Funds Transfer System" was set up as the nation's first statewide electronic banking network, in 1977. The system was started with 69 EFT terminals, including ATMs and POS terminals, located in 20 cities and towns. The banks worked together and shared the system. But it was not clear what the legal status of this arrangement was, because such cooperation among the banks might be challenged as "illegal collusive behavior" under the antitrust laws.

One reason why banks in several states are reluctant to enter into statewide EFT networks such as the one in Iowa is because of the fear of dominance of the system by big banks. In Iowa, that wasn't a problem because there aren't any giant banks in the state. But some people fear that smaller banks and thrift institutions will be pushed out of the running by the development of statewide and nationwide EFT systems. In Illinois, for example, there has been strong resistance by the rural independent banks against permitting the giant Chicago banks to reach into their territory by installing electronic terminals there.

If all banks are permitted to join a statewide (or ultimately, nationwide) EFT system, then this will require the sharing of EFT terminals by all banks that choose to participate in the system. Many states have already passed laws that require financial institutions to make their terminals available to other financial institutions on a "fair and equitable" basis. But again, the antitrust implications and legality of such arrangements have not as yet been made clear. And the McFadden Act prohibiting interstate banking continues to be an impediment.

One bank that has succeeded in establishing a nationwide electronic funds transfer system is Banc One (formerly City National Bank) of Columbus, Ohio. This bank claims to have "the first functioning nationwide electronic funds transfer system." This is the bank that is working in cooperation with Merrill Lynch with its nationwide "cash management account" program that was described in a previous chapter. Banc One of Columbus offers electronic funds transfers to several users, including retailers, repair services, and credit unions—some as far away as Alaska.

The Legal Environment Is Hazy

Major impediments to the introduction of EFT systems have been imposed by the legal systems of the states, the national laws prohibiting interstate banking, and the antitrust laws. Some EFT activities are definitely prohibited. But for the most part the legal environment is hazy and unclear. Clarification of the legal situation—making it clear what is legal and what is not—will come only slowly. And legal impediments will be removed slowly because there is a lot of resistance, especially from smaller banks and from vocal advocates of the dual banking system.

There are other legal questions having to do with EFT systems, concerning customer security and privacy. The Federal Government and the Federal Reserve Board have been working to clarify this situation, and to establish adequate rules to insure that consumer protection is guaranteed. These new rules and regulations will be explained in a subsequent section of this chapter.

Customer Resistance

Perhaps the single most important factor in the slow-down of the introduction of EFT systems was the lack of widespread customer acceptance of the EFT terminals. Early in the 1970s, the extent of customer resistance to these new banking machines was not foreseen. In fact, some banks and thrifts that introduced remote terminals seemed to assume that customers would be attracted to the use of the terminals automatically. But it soon became clear that this was not going to happen, and that only through concerted and effective marketing efforts could the banks and thrifts achieve the widespread use of the EFT terminals required to justify the costs.

Consumers have been reluctant to use the electronic banking machines for several reasons. For one thing, people were already satisfied with the present banking system. They had no objection to making purchases by check, paying their bills by check, and then receiving their cancelled checks as proof of their expenditures. Bank customers have become accustomed to being in complete charge of their deposits and withdrawals—deciding their own timing and writing their checks accordingly. Most customers did not rush to break this habitual pattern.

Apparently, customers in general are not eager to give up any of the control over their money. And they may also be concerned about questions of security and privacy. The executive director of the National Commission of Electronic Fund Transfers, John P. Benton, raised the question of whether EFT data banks might not in time work out ways to include information on all of an individual's habits, activities, and attitudes. This Commission was set up in the mid-1970s to study and report on various aspects of electronic fund transfer systems.

Perhaps another impediment to customer use of EFT services resulted from customer apprehensiveness about using these "strange new devices" which in the beginning were totally unfamiliar. But regardless of the reasons, the fact is that customer acceptance came only slowly, and at first, only in those places in which these services were aggressively promoted.

During the 1970s there was a significant shift in promotional techniques by the banks and thrifts. There was greatly increased use of retail merchandising techniques—newspaper ads, radio and TV commercials, etc.—to promote the use of EFT terminals. In some places these advertising and promotional programs had considerable success in increasing customer acceptance.

I Want My Float!

Another problem from the point of view of the customer is the fact that the use of a POS terminal eliminates "float." When a customer buys groceries on Friday afternoon and pays with a check, that customer knows that there is no way that the money can be taken out of his or her bank account until some time on Monday. So that customer's "average balance" over the weekend is higher. This extra money in the account over the weekend is called "float."

With a check-writing system, most customers have some float in their bank accounts most of the time. But the use of POS terminals eliminates float. The money is deducted immediately from the buyer's account and deposited immediately into the seller's account. So when POS terminals are in widespread use, this will reduce the average balances in the accounts of the buyers and increase the average balances in the accounts of the sellers. Some buyers are likely to be reluctant to give up this float.

If EFT terminals are going to come into widespread use by bank and thrift customers, then the following questions must be answered: "What's in it for the customer? How can the customer benefit?" With the ATMs, there is the advantage of 24-hour service, and perhaps time savings, because it isn't necessary to stand in line at the teller's window. But for many customers it may take more incentive than that to overcome the resistance. Perhaps some cost advantage may also be necessary—and that's what's coming.

Under new banking laws, soon interest will be paid on all bank deposits. This will eliminate the "free source of funds" that the banks have been receiving in their demand deposits. With the elimination of Reg Q, the banks and thrifts will be unable to fall back on their "partly free" sources of funds through their interest-limited savings accounts. As this occurs, and as the thrifts get involved in a broader variety of banking services, both the banks and the thrifts will be required to charge prices for their services. These prices will be forced, by competition, to approximately reflect the costs of providing those services.

The cost required to process a check is considerably higher than the cost associated with an electronic funds transfer. So the prices charged for these two different kinds of funds transfers must reflect the cost differential between them, with the check-using customer paying significantly more. So the customer has a real incentive to use fewer checks and more EFT transfers. And this is the incentive required to ensure the rapidly increasing use of EFT systems.

Regulation E: Customer Safety and Privacy

During the 1970s there was much concern about safeguards for the consumer in the EFT system. Sylvia Porter in her column warned of the risks and of the lack of adequate safeguards. She advised her readers: "Alert your Congressman." Many concerned people did write to Washington to advise that something be done about EFT safety and privacy. And something was done.

In early 1980, the Federal Reserve Board was just working out the final rules of their "Regulation E" (concerning electronic fund transfers) to implement the Electronic Funds Transfer Act of 1978. The Board had previously adopted rules for carrying out sections of the Act, and the first rules had become effective in February 1979. The rules deal with requirements for documentation of electronic fund transfers by financial institutions; notification requirements in connection with preauthorized electronic receipt of funds; requirements for prompt crediting of funds received electronically; procedures for resolving errors; and other matters.

The new rules in "Reg E" provide important rights and safeguards to consumers using EFT services. And the new Reg E rules will require major new responsibilities for financial institutions in providing protection and information to their EFT customers. These Reg E rules apply to ATMs, POS systems, and pay-by-phone plans, as well as to preauthorized credit (direct deposit) and preauthorized debit (automatic bill-payment) arrangements.

The EFT Act and Regulation E can be enforced by both civil liabilites and, in the case of knowing or willful noncompliance, criminal liabilities. Also, consumers may sue for actual damages, statutory damages, court costs, and attorneys' fees. The Federal Regulatory Agencies which are charged with administrative enforcement for the various financial services institutions will enforce the program, and institutions will be required to maintain records of compliance for a two-year period.

Will the EFT Act and the Reg E rules satisfy consumers that their safety and privacy will be protected? And are consumers in fact adequately protected? Perhaps so. But as technology continues to advance, new protection measures may be required.

The Outlook from FRB–Richmond as of January 1980

The expansion of EFT services in the 1970s did not occur as rapidly as many observers had expected. But in fact, much expansion did occur. And much was learned about how to deal with the problems that were impeding EFT development.

The following excerpts from an article by Aubrey Snellings provide an excellent summary on this subject and on the outlook from the point of view of January 1980.*

> . . . experience over the past decade indicates that progress toward realization of the full potential of EFTS may be slow. For while there are strong pressures toward development of EFTS capabilities, there are also important barriers to the adoption of certain aspects of the system. . . .
>
> The most important obstacle to the more rapid development of an EFTS has been the reluctance of the public to accept the new services. Most of the EFT systems that have been developed have certain features that are undesirable to the consumer. . . .
>
> Thus far, consumers have had little economic incentive to give

*Aubrey N. Snellings, "The Financial Services Industry: Recent Trends and Future Prospects," *Economic Review,* January/February 1980, pp. 6–8. Federal Reserve Bank of Richmond. Reprinted by permission of the author and publisher.

up checks in favor of an EFTS. For one thing, they are not presently required to pay the full costs of operating the payments system. Both the Federal Reserve and, perhaps to a lesser degree the commercial banks, subsidize the check processing system. It appears likely that the Federal Reserve System will soon begin to charge commercial banks the full costs of services provided, including check collection services. It will probably be necessary for the banks to pass these costs along to consumers together with that portion of such costs presently being absorbed by the banks. So the cost to consumers of using checks in the payment process is likely to rise in the not too distant future.

The unit costs of EFT transactions are fairly high at present, but there are at least two reasons to believe that these unit costs will fall quite rapidly as the EFTS becomes more widely used. First, an EFT system involves large fixed costs in the form of investment in capital equipment, but relatively small variable costs. Thus, as volume rises, unit cost per transaction should fall quite rapidly. In contrast, a check-based payments system is quite labor intensive, so that variable costs are a large part of total costs. As volume increases, therefore, marginal costs tend to remain high.

Second, technological improvements have occurred at an extraordinary pace in recent years. As a result, the cost of processing a single piece of data through a computer, for example, has fallen dramatically in the past two decades. It is doubtful that the possibilities for improvment in these areas have been exhausted, so continued reductions in equipment costs can be anticipated.

The major argument in favor of an EFT system, therefore, is that it holds the potential for increasing the efficiency of the payments mechanism and thereby reducing the unit operating costs. If financial instituions, including the Federal Reserve System, adopt a full-cost pricing approach for payments services, the greater efficiency of the EFTS will be reflected directly in the customer's transactions costs. Such a financial incentive may be more than enough to offset some of the objections to EFTS noted earlier.

Suggested Readings

Greguras, Fred. "Legal Issues Affecting Bank Automation in 1982," *American Banker* (December 9, 1981), 13.

"Interstate Deposit-Taking Is A Reality," *Banking Expansion Reporter*, vol. 2, no. 8 (April 18, 1983), 13–15.

"Missouri Proposal May Limit ATM Networks," *Banking Expansion Reporter,* vol. 2, no. 18 (September 19, 1983), 17.
"More Shared Networks Approved," *Banking Expansion Reporter,* vol. 2, no. 15 (August 1, 1983), 11–12.
"Shared ATM Networks Are Proliferating," *Banking Expansion Reporter,* vol. 2, no. 20 (October 17, 1983), 8–9.

Chapter 20

Nationwide Electronic Banking in the 1980s

From the last chapter you already know that during the 1970s the expected rapid introduction of EFT systems failed to materialize. Then what happened? The following quote from the *Business Week* article, "Electronic Banking," tells the story:*

> . . . retail electronic banking has made greater strides in the past six months [last half of 1981] than it made throughout the 1970s.

The Electronic Banking Revolution Finally Arrives

In 1980 the use of EFTS began increasing at an accelerating rate. And the rate was still increasing when this book went to press in January 1984. So it seems that the long-awaited electronic banking revolution finally is arriving.

As John Fisher, Senior Vice President of Banc One of Columbus, Ohio, said in his presentation to the Conference Board's Financial Outlook Conference in New York in February 1982:

*January 18, 1982, p. 70

> The ATM is now in its 12th year in the country. Right now there are about 39,000 of them out there and the acceptance curve is standing *straight up!* It is being projected that in the next five years the number of ATMs in place will expand to 125,000.

The electronic banking boom wasn't confined to ATMs. The entire field of EFTS seems to have caught fire in the early 1980s. More banks, S&Ls, and credit unions rushed to join and use the services of the automated clearing house (ACH) networks. Telephone bill-paying and home-banking services were introduced in several places.

In 1983, electronic corporate payments were initiated through the National Automated Clearing House Association (NACHA). And, also in 1983, the U.S. Treasury's Bureau of Government Financial Operations (BGFO) announced that (1) in the immediate future, all payments to vendors in amounts exceeding $25,000 will be made electronically via the FEDWIRE system, and (2) long-term plans are being made to make all vendor payments via NACHA.

Shared ATM networks—both intrastate and interstate—were springing up all over the country. Several *nationwide ATM networks* were set up in 1981–82 and were in operation before the end of 1983. Truly, these were exciting times in electronic banking. And that's what the rest of this chapter will be talking about.

The Rapid Growth of ATMs

In 1979, about ten years after the first ATMs were installed, there were about 13,800 ATMs in use. Before the end of 1983 the number exceeded 40,000.

According to statistics from the Federal Reserve Bank of Dallas, by the end of 1982, transactions (excluding balance inquiries) at ATMs nationwide were running at the rate of 3.1 billion per year. In 1982, withdrawals made up about 75% and deposits about 20% of total transactions. The average deposit size was $267, and the average withdrawal was $37. So the dollar value of deposits ($154.7 billion) exceeded that of withdrawals ($86.7 billion). The nationwide average use rate for an ATM was 7,200 transactions per month. The June 1983 issue of *Dallas Fed Roundup* says:

The widespread use of ATMs is a major step toward implementation of other electronic banking innovations such as point-of-sale (POS) terminals, telephone bill paying, and home banking. Each of these is designed to provide convenience to consumers and an efficient network of payment for business and financial institutions. Although ATMs are the most widely accepted of the new electronic banking innovations, there is a growing interest in the others because of their potential efficiencies in the payments mechanism.

Originally conceived as a means of reducing teller labor costs and offering extended service hours to customers, ATMs have also evolved as a marketing tool for financial institutions. Establishing an ATM network, or being linked to one, allows financial institutions to offer a customer service that provides 24-hour access to cash and account information.

Why the Rapid Growth of ATMs?

One explanation for the rapid growth in ATMs since December of 1982 was to attract funds to the new MMDAs and Super NOW accounts. Banks with ATMs could offer money market interest rates and instant access 24 hours a day.

Commercial banks and S&Ls were rapidly updating their ATM networks in December 1982 and early 1983 to put the new MMDA accounts on machine. This made it possible for the banks to advertise this "major advantage" over money market funds: the convenience of 24-hour access to MMDA money. Money fund customers, in contrast, operate mainly by mail. They have neither face-to-face contact with tellers or officers, nor immediate access by automated teller machines.

First Pennsylvania Bank, in ads for money market accounts, was promising "access to your money 24 hours a day." Many other banks were doing the same.

In early 1983 there were many banks that had only very few ATM machines—and some of them, none. But as you know, this was changing fast.

Other factors contributing to the rapid growth of ATMs were: (1) increasing cost of human teller transactions relative to ATM transactions, (2) the desire to attract and hold customers in the face of increasing financial services competition from American Express, Merrill Lunch, Sears, and several others, and (3) rapidly increasing customer acceptance. Why customer acceptance? Perhaps partly because of the increasing "computer acceptance psychology" of the public, which was ushered in by the explosive use of personal computers and video games. Also, perhaps partly because of the years of advertising and growing public familiarity with ATMs. But for whatever reasons, by 1982 ATM growth was rapid and increasing.

Will Human Tellers Be Replaced?

In 1983 it didn't seem that the impact of ATMs on the number of human tellers was going to be drastic. Most bankers agreed that human tellers would continue to be used throughout the foreseeable future. But everyone seemed to recognize that as banking grows, the number of human tellers is likely to decline.

A survey of bankers in mid-1983 indicated that, on the average, bankers expected ATMs to replace about 17 of every 100 tellers during the next three years.

One change in banking service distribution systems in the coming years is certain to be a reduced number of human-operated branches. For example, in New York, Citibank in 1983 closed three branches. That caused some reduced demand for personnel as the functions of those branches were consolidated and/or taken over by ATMs. Other large banks were announcing plans to close as many as 20 branches. It is probably through the reduction in the number of branches (not reduction in the number of teller windows in each banking office) that the reduction in the number of tellers will be seen.

Rapid Growth of Shared ATM Networks

During the early 1980s there was explosive growth in intrastate and interstate shared ATM networks. By the end of 1983 there were more than 100 of these networks scattered all over the country, and some of these networks were beginning to consolidate into larger regional networks.

What is a shared ATM network? It's an arrangement whereby several banks get together and agree to let each other's customers share each other's ATMs. So if your bank joins one of these networks, you can use the ATMs of all of the other banks that are members of that network—whether or not that bank is located in your home town or your home state.

How does it work? When you use your own bank's ATM, that's called an "on-us" transaction, and it works just as though your bank wasn't part of the network. But when you use some other bank's ATM, that's called a "non-on-us" transaction, and this goes through a central transmission interchange (a "switch") that connects the transaction to your bank. The bank that owns the ATM you used gets a service fee, and the central transmission unit (the "switch") does too.

Some Large Networks Are Merging

An example of the joining of two shared EFT networks occurred in October 1983. Two separate networks—the EFT group of Washington, D.C., and the Mid-Atlantic Exchange, Raleigh, North Carolina—agreed to a merger. The resulting shared network includes about 1,200 ATMs and spreads over an area including the two Carolinas, Virginia, Maryland, and the District of Columbia. The network includes 86 financial institutions and a card-holder base of more than four million. It is administered by a holding company called Mid-Atlantic Systems, Inc.

Other large shared networks in the United States include Detroit-based Magic Line, which has more than 1,300 ATMs. In Texas there are two large interstate networks: MPACT and PULSE. The MPACT network joins over 300 banks in Texas, Oklahoma, Arkansas, and Louisiana, has about 1.5 million card holders, and in 1983 was handling about three million transactions a month. MPACT is Dallas-based. PULSE is Houston-based. PULSE joins about 500 financial institutions in Texas and Louisiana, has about 600 ATMs, and serves more than four million card holders.

At the end of 1983, these four networks—Mid-Atlantic Systems, Magic Line, MPACT, and PULSE—were the largest in the country in terms of numbers of ATMs included. But the ground was shifting fast. Additional mergers were being discussed. By the time you're reading this, there's no telling which shared systems will have turned out to be the largest.

Joining Banks and Thrifts, Interstate!

There are some interesting things about the shared ATM systems. One is that they include banks, savings and loans, mutual savings banks, and credit unions. Another is that they operate interstate. But the networks promise that their ATMs in other states won't do anything that is prohibited by the banking laws—such as, for example, taking deposits in another state.

Can a bank join two different networks? The regulatory authorities in 1983 approved of this. So even prior to the merger that created Mid-Atlantic Systems, Inc., a bank in Virginia that wished to could have joined the EFT group (called the "MOST" system) and also the Mid-Atlantic exchange (called the "Relay" system), and that bank's customers would have had access to both systems.

On August 4, 1983, the Justice Department's antitrust division announced that it would not challenge dual membership of a Texas savings and loan association in both the PULSE and the MPACT system. And in Philadelphia the Pennsylvania Credit Union League has signed agreements to use the MAC automated teller machines of Philadelphia National Bank in the eastern half of the state (MAC-east) and also an agreement to use the Tri-Net ATM network (MAC-west) based in Pittsburgh. These are but a few of the many moves by banks and thrifts to get into state-wide and/or regional ATM networks and provide their cardholding customers with wider geographic access to their accounts.

It was only a matter of time before somebody would decide to put together a nationwide ATM network. And the fact is that several such systems had been created and were operating before the end of 1983.

Nationwide ATM Networks

By the end of 1981 there were more than a dozen different groups trying to put together nationwide ATM networks. Each group was out trying to get banks to join with them and not with someone else.

By mid-1982 there had been a shakeout in the "national ATM

network-building competition," and by the end of 1983 there were seven national networks either in operation or nearly so. These were: Visa International, Plus System, CIRRUS System, The Exchange, NATIONET, MasterTeller, and Express Cash (by American Express). Each of these national networks provided the same kinds of services nationwide that had been previously provided by the regional shared systems.

You can see the advantages that the customers of one of the regional systems would gain if that regional system decided to join one of the national networks. For example, if the MPACT System decided to join the Plus System or the CIRRUS System or Visa or one of the others, their customers would have access to ATMs in all of the major cities in the country.

What is the effect of all this on interstate banking? And how does it fit under the McFadden Act? There's no question that this is interstate banking. Even the "no-no taboo" of interstate deposit taking is being breached in some instances. But in 1980 the Comptroller of the Currency issued the opinion that ATM sharing arrangements with out-of-state banks do not violate the McFadden Act.

What About the Small Banks?

One important factor in this situation is that the small banks are not as likely to challenge these regional and nationwide ATM networks as they would be to challenge any attempt to repeal the interstate prohibitions of the McFadden Act. The following quote from David O'Connor, formerly Senior Vice President of Virginia National Bank and now President and Chief Executive of the EFT group of Washington, D.C., explains why:*

> For a while we (smaller banks) thought that the big national banks would be able to do everything and that we couldn't compete. But now we are seeing the beginning of national (nationwide) banking, and we are more comfortable about our ability to be a part of it.

*"Making National Banking Palatable to Washington," *Business Week,* January 18, 1982, p. 74.

One National System? Or Competing Systems?

Suppose you're a banker in Texas and you're trying to decide which regional system to join, PULSE or MPACT. And suppose your major competitors have already joined PULSE. If you join that system, you're going to give your competitors' customers access to your own network of ATMs. Do you want to do that? Many banks don't.

The same issue applies to the nationwide networks. The 34 banks that came together to create the Plus System, and now own the system, invested up to $150,000 each for the purpose of setting up the system and of insuring that some "exclusivity" could be maintained. In North Carolina, for example, the two largest banks are Wachovia and NCNB. NCNB is part owner and is on the board of directors of the Plus System. Wachovia is part owner and on the board of directors of the CIRRUS System. Neither bank is giving its major competitor's customers access to its own system.

What About the Exclusivity Issue?

There's a lot of disagreement in the industry on this exclusivity issue. The leader in the fight against exclusivity is Dee Ward Hock, President and Chief Executive of Visa International. Hock is outspoken in his criticism of bankers who insist on maintaining different regional and national ATM networks. Hock's point is that this kind of competition among the banks will open the door for other, nonbank businesses to set up ATMs accepting all cards. And the banks will lose a major share of the business. In his speech before the annual bankcard convention of the American Bankers Association in September 1983 (as reported in the *American Banker,* October 19, 1983, p. 6), Hock says: "The immediate, critical battle is not between regulated banks for market share, but between traditional regulated banks and predatory unregulated banks." He goes on to explain:

> The economics of a merchant-owned ATM accepting all cards in a secure, attended, lighted environment to which people custom-

arily and regularly go for daily purchases will be infinitely superior to an ATM accepting limited cards in the wall of a bank, unattended, on the sidewalk, in the rain. One reads every day of a major retailer or financial conglomerate buying a bank, stripping it of its commercial loan activity, and then engaging free of regulation in the retail banking business.

Many have nationwide customer bases superior to that of any single bank. They have only to provide the customer with an attractive market rate for surplus funds and appropriate access to it.

That such competition will exist is not debatable. It is a fact of life. The only unanswered question is whether banking will act together to provide superior service or engage in fragmented, internal fights which only insure the success of competitive nonbank systems.

Hock's Vision of a Worldwide Visa ATM System

Throughout 1983, Hock was moving ahead with plans to establish a worldwide network of ATMs that would let Visa card holders obtain cash at locations all over the world. But some of the Visa member banks are not thrilled with this proposal. They aren't worried so much about the international aspect as they are of the fact that their competitors' customers would have access to all of their ATMs—in which they have invested heavily, and about which they feel quite proprietary.

But Hock maintains that unless a unified card system can be developed, the bankers will be playing into the hands of their natural enemies: the large, diversified, unregulated institutions such as American Express, Merrill Lynch, Sears, etc.

Visa set up its nationwide ATM network in 1983 and hopes to build it into a global network with at least 8,000 machines in many countries throughout the world by the end of 1986. The Visa network will use ATMs of Visa member banks, as well as new machines to be located in airports and other places frequented by travelers. As an inducement to join the network, participating banks are scheduled to receive 75¢ for each interbank transaction processed on their machines.

The new nationwide ATM network associations (Plus, CIRRUS, NATIONET, etc.) don't take kindly to Visa's (Hock's) approach.

Visa was forced to compromise by permitting a bank that joins the system to block out the customers of all competing banks (a) within its own state, and (b) within two other states of its choice. But Hock is not in favor of this exclusivity feature. He says that in the long run, exclusive ATM systems will not survive. Eventually Mr. Hock hopes to get such networks as CIRRUS and Plus (each of which now links only one big bank in each state) to join the Visa system.

MasterCard has argued that Visa's scheme is too grandiose. The approach MasterCard is using is to arrange for card holders to be permitted to use two or three specially designated ATMs in each city. MasterCard holders can dial a MasterTeller telephone number for directions to the nearest machine that will take their card. Some banks belonging to Plus, CIRRUS, and other nationwide systems have agreed to also join the MasterCard plan.

As of early 1984, several nationwide systems did exist and were strong. For example, the Plus System, Inc., based in Denver, is owned by 34 major banks (all Visa members), and it had about 950 other financial institutions tied into the system. It started operations in mid-1983 with about 10,000 ATM machines connected.

The Chicago-based CIRRUS system was founded by 13 major banks. It started operations in January 1983, a few months before Plus began functioning. The CIRRUS network included over 5,000 ATMs and over 20 million card holders. CIRRUS was projecting, by 1986, over 8,500 ATMs in place. In advertisements they were saying:

> Enhance your image as an innovator by becoming a part of a powerful, national network, while offering your customers the widest scope of ATM convenience. CIRRUS. It's the future of banking, within your reach today.

In addition to Plus and CIRRUS, the other nationwide ATM networks were competing actively to try to sign up more banks. What will happen on this? Will there be a shakeout, leaving only one or a few nationwide systems? That's what happened with bank credit cards in the 1960s. Now most of the bank cards you see are Visa and MasterCard. Will that pattern be repeated in nationwide ATM networks? And is it true, as some are suggesting, that eventually all banking machines will be accessible to every customer, just as phone booths are today?

Only time will give the answers to these questions. But meanwhile, here's one thing of which you can be quite sure: Nationwide electronic banking is here to stay.

While all of this shared ATM activity is going on, the groundwork is being set to expand the functions of this sophisticated, interconnected, electronic funds transfer network. Point-of-sale terminals are expanding rapidly and being interconnected. Banks and thrifts are being tied in without distinction. And home-banking activities, which are coming on line in increasing numbers, also can benefit from these interconnections. Truly, the electronic banking revolution is finally arriving.

Is POS on the Threshold of an Explosion?

During the 1970s there were several experimental attempts to develop point-of-sale (POS) payment systems. But none of them worked out very well. The equipment was very expensive and not very efficient. But by mid-1983, pilot POS projects were showing positive results, and there was an increasing number of operational systems.

Des Moines, Iowa, was one of the nation's leaders in operational POS systems. Two supermarkets there, Dahl's and Hy-Vee, have been operating a total of 24 POS checkout terminals since mid-1981. Customers of some 205 Iowa banks, S&Ls, and credit unions can use their debit cards at these terminals. The terminals are connected directly to the customers' accounts in the 205 different depository institutions through a computer-switching arrangement. The computer "switch" that makes this multibank arrangement possible is operated by ITS, Inc., of Des Moines.

This system has become something of a model for others to follow, or to try to improve on. Representatives of BankAmerica, Barnett Banks, Barclays Bank, Security Pacific, Kroger Co., and several other U.S. and foreign banks and businesses have studied the ITS system. Several of these companies (and many others) are considering introducing POS systems.

An ambitious POS project sponsored by Rocky Mountain Bank Card began operations in 1982, with POS terminals projected for some 500 retailers in the Denver area. This system links POS terminals into the already existing shared-ATM network.

By mid-1983, NCR was considering POS system installations in 20 states. Barnett Banks announced plans to establish a POS system including some 500 supermarkets in Florida. California's top five banks are joined through their "Interlink" system, which permits some six million cardholders to use debit cards to buy groceries, gasoline, and other items from POS terminals.

Publix Super Markets, Inc., in Florida says it will be able to accept debit card payments in all 263 of its supermarkets in 1984. In 1983 Montgomery Ward was accepting debit cards at 32 of its stores in several states. In the fall of 1983, Exxon, Atlantic Richfield, and Mobil all began pilot projects accepting debit cards for gasoline purchases.

Perhaps Robert Hand, President of Dahl's Supermarkets in Des Moines, where POS terminals have been operating successfully since 1981, was right when he said, "One day this thing is going to explode."* There's a lot of preparatory activity going on that would seem to support Hand's projection. And new technology—including the current rapid development of more sophisticated credit/debit cards—will help to speed the process.

Home Banking: The Operational Phase Begins

For several years experimental pilot projects on home banking have been going on at several places throughout the country. By 1982 these experiments had been undertaken in Ohio, Florida, New Jersey, New York, North Dakota, California, Washington, Tennessee, Nebraska, Massachusetts, Connecticut, Minnesota, and other states.

By the end of 1982, some 25 banks in the country were testing and/or using some form of home banking system. During 1983 the number of banks involved in home banking experiments and/

*"Iowa, the Debit Card State," *Forbes,* August 29, 1983, p. 46.

or operations more than doubled. But even with this much attention and growth, home banking by 1984 was still in its infancy.

The first commercial home-banking and information system was put into operation by Chemical Bank of New York in September 1982. The system, called "Pronto," allows customers to use home computers to obtain account information and to perform banking transactions. In 1983 Chemical Bank began licensing other banks to use the system. And many other large banks were working out their own systems, as were several nonbank financial institutions and nonfinancial businesses. There was a race to develop the best home-banking system.

In November of 1983 a home-banking and information system was introduced in the three-county Miami, Florida, area. This system, called Viewtron, is offered by Viewdata Corporation, which is a joint venture of Knight-Ridder Newspapers, Inc., and American Bell.

The home banking part of the Miami area Videotex system is provided by four banks: Banc One (Ohio), Southeast Banking (Miami), Wachovia (North Carolina), and Security Pacific (Los Angeles).

Viewdata is the first company in the nation to offer a Videotex (also spelled Videotext) system. Chemical Bank's Pronto system requires a home computer. Videotex is a home information system that links the home TV set to the telephone line or TV cable and uses an adapter (cost, about $600 in 1983) to convert the electronic data signals into images on the TV screen. A keyboard or keypad is used by the viewer to give instructions and to respond to data presented on the screen.

Several other banks and nonbank companies (including CBS) were pushing to get a head start in this electronic home information and banking field. Beginning in September 1983, the big stockbroker firm, E. F. Hutton, began offering "Huttonline," which lets customers with personal computers retrieve their account information. The Huttonline information is also available through the Viewtron Videotex system to those customers who live in the Miami area.

So what's the future for home banking? Bright. Other forms of EFTS will grow faster for a few years. But home banking is coming—by the end of the 1980s it will be in a period of rapid growth, and by the mid-1990s it will be playing a major role in the financial services industry.

Future Outlook for EFTS

By 1984 it seemed clear that EFTS was an idea whose time had come. Rapid expansion of installation and use of ATMs, POS terminals, and home-banking activities seemed destined to continue. And rapid expansion of automated clearing house (ACH) transactions seemed certain to occur, especially with the addition of corporate payments by ACH and the movement of the federal government in the direction of making all vendor payments electronically.

In 1981, there were about two billion electronic payment transactions nationwide during the year. By 1986 that number is predicted to increase to 16 billion.*

But does all this mean that traditional banking offices, transactions, activities, etc., will quickly disappear? Are we finally approaching the "cashless and checkless society" that so many people were talking about following the introduction of the first ATM in Valdosta, Georgia, in 1970? Don't count on it.

The Atlanta Fed's Projections on "The Checkless Society"

The Federal Reserve Bank of Atlanta, in its August 1983 issue of *Economic Review,* presents some information on this issue. This publication reports a study done by the Atlanta Fed on the outlook for future transactions by personal check. The study predicts that transfers by personal checks out of household checking accounts will decline from 97% of transactions in 1979 to 51% by 1994. In terms of personal checks written, the study predicts a decline from about 18 billion per year in 1984 to about 16 billion in 1994.

The study distinguishes between the three main reasons why people write checks: (1) to acquire cash, (2) to make retail purchases, and (3) to pay bills. Checks are already being displaced by ATMs when people want to acquire cash. As the use of POS terminals expands, this will reduce the dependence on checks in making retail purchases. In the payment of bills, checks will be

*"The Growth of Electronic Payments," *Business Week,* 1/18/82, p. 74.

displaced more slowly by home banking and bill-paying by telephone, by preauthorized ACH payments, and by the establishment in convenient locations of electronic terminals (like telephone booths) that can be used for paying bills.

How accurate are the predictions of the Atlanta Fed's study? Will the total volume of checks actually decline? Probably so.

You can see that, even if the study's projections are far from the mark, when we get into the 1990s there will still be a lot of checks used in the payments system. And, to be sure, you will be able to go into a bank and talk to a teller in person. But there's no question that a much larger percentage of transactions will be handled electronically, and the cost of our banking services will be lower and the efficiency of our banking system greater because of it.

Suggested Readings

"Armchair Shoppers," *The Economist* (June 11, 1983), 32.

"Atlanta Fed Quantifies Check Demise," *Banking Expansion Reporter*, vol. 2, no. 19 (October 3, 1983), 2.

Fisher, John F. "In-Home Banking Today and Tomorrow," *Journal of Retail Banking* (June 1982), 23–30.

Garsson, Robert M. "EFT-Mid Atlantic Merger to Create Big ATM Network," *American Banker* (October 19, 1983), 3.

Garsson, Robert M. "Mobil Will Offer Point-of-Sale Services," *American Banker* (October 25, 1983), 1.

Louis, Arthur M. "Visa Stirs Up the Big Banks Again," *Fortune* (October 3, 1983).

"Microcomputer-Based Services Gaining Fast at Banks," *American Banker* (October 18, 1983), 31.

Trigaux, Robert. "Visa Planning National Network of Shared ATMs," *American Banker* (April 5, 1982), 1.

Part VII
Impact of Revolutionary Change on Fed Policy and on the Financial Marketplace

The Fed Needs New Monetary Targets and Policies, and in the Financial Markets, Unbridled Competition Is the Name of the Game

Chapter 21

New Money Supply Definitions and Fed Policy Targets

The revolutionary changes are bringing a "new world" in the financial services industry. The changes are having a profound impact on the financial institutions and markets. Think of it: New laws. Crumbling barriers. No more Reg Q. New deposit instruments. New functions for banks and thrifts. New competition from nonbank financial firms and from nonfinancial firms. And now, explosive growth in EFTS—intrastate, interstate, nationwide, international. A profound impact? Unbelievable.

The Impact on Fed Policy

What about the impact on the Fed? And on monetary policy? Think back. It was the Fed's money-supply-growth-targeting policy (plus rapid inflation) that led to such high and volatile (nominal) interest rates. And it was that high-interest-rate environment that led to falling Fed membership, to disintermediation, the explosion of the MMMFs, the crisis of the thrifts, the intolerability of Reg Q, and ultimately *new legislation* aimed toward deregulation: the DIDMCA of 1980, the Garn–St. Germain Act of 1982, and, in 1984, new legislative initiatives in the Congress designed to take additional steps in the same direction.

What has been happening to the Fed's monetary policy? And monetary targeting? What has been the effect of all this on these questions: "What is money?" and "How do we measure it?" and "How do we—and how *should* we—control it?"

With the rapid growth of EFTS and the new kinds of "money" deposit instruments, the entire payments mechanism of the economy has been undergoing rapid change. So the definition of money must change.

How does the Fed target the money supply when we're not quite sure what that is? Or how to measure it? It isn't easy. How is the Fed adjusting to meet the needs of this new monetary/financial environment? That's what you'll be reading about in this chapter.

The Effects of the New Transactions Accounts

As the savings and loan and other thrift institutions began to offer transactions accounts, and as brokerage firms set up "money market funds" such as the Merrill Lynch "cash management accounts" (CMAs) against which checks can be written, this had a significant impact on the competitive environment among the financial institutions. But another important effect has been the effect on the question: "Exactly *what is* the nation's money supply?"

The money supply has traditionally been defined (in its narrowest sense) as currency, plus checking accounts at commercial banks. This definition has made sense in the past because almost all actual payments have been made either with currency (cash) or by checks written on checking accounts (demand deposits) at commercial banks. But what happens to the old definition of the money supply (defined as M1) when the thrift institutions and brokerage houses and others begin offering accounts against which checks can be written? Are the "money balances" in these new transaction accounts a part of the nation's "immediately spendable money supply" or not?

Also, in the days of high interest rates no one likes to leave much money in a checking account where it earns no interest. So people and businesses have figured out ways of reducing the amount of money in their checking accounts, while still having that money available the moment it is needed for spending. One obvious instance of this is the case of the automatic-transfer-from-savings (ATS) accounts where the depositor keeps a zero checking account balance and all of the money is deposited in a savings account. Then when checks are written the funds are automatically transferred from the savings account into the checking account, and the check is paid—again leaving the checking account balance at zero. Is the money in the ATS savings account a part of the nation's "immediately spendable money supply" or not?

Repurchase Agreements

Another technique—one that corporations have discovered to keep from holding large idle balances in their demand deposit accounts drawing no interest—is called "repurchase agreements" (RPs or "repos"). Repos work like this: Suppose a corporation has $100,000 in its checking account, needed to cover payroll checks four days from now. The corporation can buy securities from the bank (or from any other investor, for that matter) with the agreement that the bank (or other investor) will buy back the securities in four days. That way the corporation earns interest on its money for four days and then gets the money back in its checking account just at the moment it is needed to cover the payroll checks. You may think that earning interest for only four days is not worth the trouble. But in a high-interest-rate environment, a corporation using these repurchase agreements on a regular basis can earn a lot of interest income!

The banks benefit from these repos also. When the corporation takes its money out of its checking account to buy the "repo" securities, that reduces the total amount of demand deposits held by the bank. So the bank can hold less non-interest-bearing reserves in its account at the Fed. At the same time, the bank can use the money borrowed from the corporation to increase its reserve deposits at the Fed.

Banks can sell securities to corporations on Friday afternoon and then buy them back on Monday morning and that increases the bank's reserves and reduces the bank's total demand deposit balance over the weekend. That reduces the amount of reserves the bank must hold for the remainder of that week. When banks are paying 15% or 18% or 20% in the "Fed funds" market to borrow money to maintain their required reserves at the Fed (or when they have the opportunity to lend their excess reserves to other banks at these high interest rates) you can see why they would be interested in using repo agreements!

But what about the effect of all this on the size of the money supply? When the Fed is trying to figure out how much money exists at any moment in the American economy, it looks at the total amounts in checking account balances at that moment. But it doesn't see the money that has been temporarily removed from checking accounts by RPs.

Why Is the Money Supply Definition Important?

Why does the Fed need to know how large the money supply is at any moment and whether it is expanding or contracting, and by how much? What difference does it make anyway?

It's *vitally* important, for this reason: The Fed is trying to control inflation by limiting the size—the rate of growth—in the money supply. To succeed in doing this, it is absolutely essential that the Fed know what the money supply is. Otherwise it can't know how large it is or if it's increasing, and by how much.

The Fed's definition of the money supply needs to include all of the immediately spendable purchasing power balances held by the public—individuals, businesses, other organizations, etc. That's why the question is not just academic. It has extremely practical importance.

The problem is that today there are so many things that can be considered to be money, or not—depending on how you choose to look at it. There are many highly liquid assets that are "almost money," which have not been included in the Fed's narrow definition of the money supply (M1).

Parthemos' Comments on the Money Supply Definition*

With the changes that are now occurring, there is an increasingly broad spectrum of highly liquid assets that the public can hold. There are now being created many close substitutes for money, such as NOW accounts, and all of these are tempting individuals to take them and to use them to make payments. When individuals have more of these highly liquid assets, they don't need to hold as much in the form of demand deposits. So the traditional type of demand deposits that we include in our money supply, M1, gets smaller.

There are several ways we could handle the situation. We might go ahead with our traditional definition of M1 (currency plus demand deposits) and consider that the increase in these other "money substitutes" actually amounts to an increase in the *velocity of circulation* of money itself (M1).

The route that we in the Federal Reserve feel that we ought to take is a little different one. From the practical standpoint (as opposed to the purely theoretical), it's extremely difficult to deal with this concept of the "velocity of money." What we are really talking about is the *demand function for money balances.* We in the economics profession have had a lot of difficulty in specifying an empirical demand curve for anything. So it's very difficult to work *empirically* with the velocity concept, because of the impossibility of specifying an empirical demand curve for money.

We feel that it is more practical now to have another hard look at some combination of liquid assets—those assets which bear a very close relationship to total spending. So right now there is some sentiment to redefine M1 to include such things as NOW accounts, plus some fraction of automatic transfer accounts, some money market funds, and my own feeling is that we should include the repurchase agreements that banks make with their corporate customers. I think we should *not* include *all* transaction balances—not where the volume of transactions is very low.

*Statement, made on December 3, 1979 by James Parthemos, Senior Vice President and Director of Research at the Federal Reserve Bank of Richmond and Associate Economist for the Federal Open Market Committee.

In any case, it appears that early in 1980 we will come out with a new definition of M1 which will include some of these new, highly liquid assets that the various financial institutions now are generating.

A Quote from the Richmond Fed's *Economic Review*

On this issue, the *Economic Review* of the Federal Reserve Bank of Richmond had this to say:*

> There are some important causes and consequences of the rapid pace of financial innovation of recent years, especially as it relates to the nation's payments system. First, high market interest rates, different reserve requirements on various types of deposits, and legal restrictions on the payment of interest on demand deposits have together provided increased incentive for the market to create and use new kinds of deposit liabilities. Second, rapid development of computer and communications technology has contributed to this outcome. Third, regulators have allowed greater competition among financial institutions, thereby promoting more rapid innovation.
>
> Because financial innovation involves creation of money substitutes, it causes problems for monetary control. . . . since data on demand deposit substitutes are limited, it is hard to know the extent of their use, and consequently, it is hard to estimate the total stock of money.
>
> Fortunately, reforms can ease this monetary control problem. The most important of these include extending the coverage of legal reserve requirements to all deposits used as payments balances and removing restrictions on interest payable on deposits. The recent adoption of these reforms should go a long way toward improving monetary control.

*Marvin Goodfriend, James Panthemos, and Bruce Summers, "Recent Financial Innovations: Causes, Consequences for the Payments System, and Implications for Monetary Control," *Economic Review*, March/April 1980, pp. 26–27, Federal Reserve Bank of Richmond. Reprinted by permission of the authors and previous publisher.

The Fed's New Definitions of the Money Supply: February 1980*

During the late 1970s economists at the Fed and many economists outside the Fed were concerned about the declining validity of the traditional definitions of the money supply. Many studies were undertaken, most of which concluded that new definitions of the money supply were needed. But there was disagreement as to the specific form that the redefinitions should take. Then in 1979 and early 1980 it became imperative that the money supply be redefined to more accurately reflect the new conditions in the rapidly changing money and financial markets.

In February of 1980 the Fed announced its new definitions of the money supply. The new definitions were designed to include (1) the new kinds of transaction accounts, (2) money "temporarily removed from checking accounts" by RPs, and (3) some other kinds of highly liquid (almost money) assets which are being generated by ingenious profit-seeking finance experts in response to the high-interest environment and other special circumstances in the money and financial markets.

When the new money supply definitions were announced by the Fed in February 1980, the most basic change was the inclusion of the new "checkable accounts" as a part of the M1 money supply. Temporarily, the former M1 was renamed M1A, and the new M1 was called M1B. Then a few months later M1A was dropped and M1B (including NOW accounts, ATS accounts, and credit union share draft accounts) became the new M1.

In the period 1980 through 1983 there were adjustments in the money supply definitions—minor additions or subtractions from one or another of the "M aggregates." For example, in February 1983, M2 was redefined to *include* tax-exempt MMMFs and to *exclude* IRA/Keough retirement fund balances. But the definitions of the monetary aggregates remained basically the same up until early 1984, when this book went to press.

*A complete explanation of the new money supply definitions, together with a comparison of the new definitions with the old definitions, is reported in the *Federal Reserve Bulletin,* Feb. 1980 (Vol. 66, No. 2) pp. 97–114.

Definitions of the Monetary Aggregates

The important items included in each of the Fed's "aggregate definitions" of the money supply are:

M1 Currency and travelers checks outstanding, plus all bank and thrift deposits with unlimited check-writing privileges.

M2 M1, plus all MMDAs and MMMFs, savings deposits and small denomination time deposits at banks and thrifts, overnight RPs at commercial banks, and overnight Eurodollars held by U.S. residents.

M3 The third definition of the money supply, M3, consists of M2 plus large-denomination time deposits at all depository institutions, including negotiable certificates of deposit (CDs) plus repos that run for a longer term than overnight issued by commercial banks and savings and loan associations.

L Finally, the Fed defined a very broad measure of liquid assets, (called L) which includes M3, plus the following additional assets: other Eurodollar holdings of U.S. residents other than banks, banker's acceptances, commercial paper, savings bonds, and marketable liquid Treasury obligations (T-Bills, e.g.) with less than 18 months remaining to maturity, and U.S. savings bonds.

What a lot of definitions! You may wonder why the Fed can't just decide what is money and what isn't, include everything that is and exclude everything that isn't, and let it go at that. But it isn't as simple as that.

Total spending in the economy, which supports employment and production and keeps the economy going (and also, by the way, pushes up prices), is influenced not only by the amount of money held by people and businesses. It is also influenced by how much in highly liquid assets the public holds—assets that can easily be transferred into money when people want to spend more.

In order to understand what's going on and what's likely to happen in the economy it is necessary not only to "keep a watchful eye on the money supply." It is also necessary to keep an eye on what's happening with the other highly liquid "near money" assets held by the public. These various definitions of the money supply permit the Fed to do this. And as the many economists and financial experts outside the Fed—whose business it is to make decisions based on what's likely to happen in the economy—are making their decisions, the Fed's published figures on each of these five "money supply aggregates" can be very helpful.

Not everyone was in complete agreement with the Fed's decisions about exactly what should be included in each of the new money supply figures. For example, there could be some argument in favor of including overnight RPs in the M1 measure. But there are also some good arguments for including it in M2 as was done. Although not perfect, these money supply definitions seemed to serve adequately—but less adequately as time went on.

Declining Confidence in "Monetary Aggregate Targeting"

During the early 1980s the nature of money in the U.S. economy was changing fast. And the velocity of circulation was behaving in unaccustomed ways. Historical trends weren't being followed. The Federal Reserve Bank of Dallas *Voice* of June 1981 carried the following quotes from Fed Board Member Lyle E. Gramley:

> I am willing to grant that shifts in money demand over the past seven or eight years have not totally destroyed the usefulness of monetary aggregates as a policy target or guide. But they have certainly made the task of running monetary policy more difficult, and that of explaining what is going on to a skeptical public nearly impossible.
>
> The problems of interpreting the monetary aggregates will get much worse if, as I suspect, we are on the verge of an explosion in the use of EFT [electronic fund transfers]. In a world of mature EFT systems, where transactions costs will be much smaller than they are at present, very few large economic entities will have identifiable transactions balances at the end of a business day.

> The internationalization of banking and financial markets creates further measurement and interpretational problems of monetary policy. Changes in onshore deposits and domestic private credit flows no longer measure very precisely the amount of money and credit available to finance domestic economic activity."
>
> Developments such as these greatly complicate the life of a central banker. It is not easy to develop new rules of thumb that are robust in a world of rapid innovation, or to estimate new large-scale econometric models that capture the new ways financial variables affect economic activity. Monetary policymakers will, I am afraid, be operating by the seat of their pants for a long time to come.

During 1982 and 1983 Fed Chairman Paul Volcker made several statements to the Congress concerning the lack of reliability of the monetary aggregates as policy targets. And in the June 22, 1982, *Wall Street Journal* (p. 34) Boston Fed Chairman Frank E. Morris said:

> I have concluded, most reluctantly, that we can no longer measure the money supply with any precision. The consequences are obviously far-reaching.

In October of 1982 the Fed announced its policy shift away from strict "monetary aggregate" targeting, partly because of some loss of confidence in the reliability of this approach. Then in December 1982 and early 1983 the new MMDAs and Super Now accounts caused the monetary aggregates to behave less reliably as depositors shifted their assets into the new accounts.

Benjamin Friedman's Suggested Target: Total Debt

Professor Benjamin Friedman of Harvard has been trying to convince the Fed to take a broader look, not just at some aggregate measure of the money supply, but at the *total quantity of credit (debt) outstanding* in the economy. Friedman's investigations indicate that the size of total debt bears a reasonably close and stable relationship to the level of nonfinancial economic activity.

So why not monitor total debt? If it's increasing too fast, that tells the Fed it's time to tighten up. One problem is that it takes a while to get the needed data to compute a total debt figure. Another is that the Fed's "control handle" works a lot more directly and visibly on M1 and M2 (etc.) than on total debt.

But in February of 1983, Volcker announced that the Fed will begin to keep an eye on total debt. In his statement to Congress on February 16, 1983, he explained the action on this issue taken by the Federal Open Market Committee (FOMC, the Fed's unit that decides on monetary policy objectives and actions). Volcker said:*

> The Committee set forth for the first time its expectations with respect to growth of total domestic nonfinancial debt, and felt that a range of 8½ to 11½ percent would be appropriate. Data for such a broad credit aggregate are not yet available monthly, nor are the tools available to influence closely total flows of credit. While the credit range during this experimental period does not have the status of a "target," the Committee does intend to monitor developments with respect to credit closely for what assistance it can provide in judging appropriate responses to developments in the other aggregates.

What about the "total debt" measure as a target in the future? Who knows? It might become an important indicator to help to guide monetary policy.**

Barnett's Weighted Monetary Aggregate: The Divisia Aggregates

Are all of the assets listed in the definition of M1 identical? Or M2, etc.? Do they all have the same degree of "money-ness?" Of course not. So, eureka! Why not put together a monetary aggre-

Monetary Policy Objectives for 1983, Federal Reserve Board, Washington, D.C. (1983), p. 20.

**Total debt, more precisely, is: Total Domestic Nonfinancial Sector Debt. It is outstanding debt of all domestic governmental units (federal, state and local), all households, and all nonfinancial businesses. For an easily understandable explanation of Professor Friedman's argument, see: Benjamin M. Friedman, "A Two-Target Strategy for Monetary Policy," *Wall Street Journal*, Jan. 27, 1983, p. 26. References to other articles by Professor Friedman are listed at the end of this chapter.

gate that assigns a weight to each asset in the group? People hold some assets because—and *only* because—those assets serve as a medium of exchange—cash in your pocket, for example. You don't earn any interest on cash. When you hold cash, you lose the opportunity to earn interest.

What about your NOW account? That's M1 money, too. But its "money-ness" is less than that of cash. People hold NOW accounts for two reasons: (1) as a highly liquid form of interest-earning savings, and also (2) as a medium of exchange. So the money-ness (medium of exchange function) of the NOW account is a little less than that of cash. So in the weighted (Divisia, named for an Italian mathematician) monetary aggregate, cash gets a higher weight than NOW accounts.

How do you assign the weights to different assets in the mix? By looking at the interest rates you can earn on each—the less interest, the more money-ness. Or you could look at how frequently the asset turns over—that is, its velocity—how frequently it is used in making payments.

The Results of the Divisia Aggregates

Professor William A. Barnett of the University of Texas at Austin and Fed economist Paul A. Spindt have assigned weights to the monetary aggregate components. Both researchers conclude that money growth since 1979 has not been nearly as rapid as the unweighted monetary aggregates indicate. During the first quarter of 1983 (a confusing time for monetary statistics to be sure!) according to the Fed's estimates, M1 rose at a 14% rate and M2 rose at a 20% rate. But Barnett's Divisia estimates were: for M1, 10.6%; for M2, only 3.6%!

So what does the Fed choose as "appropriate monetary policy?" It depends a lot on which estimates they choose to believe! And with this much disagreement, is there any wonder that they have backed off from their reliance on the M1 and M2 figures as their sole guide to monetary policy?*

*For more information on the Divisia approach, see: William A. Barnett and Paul A. Spindt, "Divisia Monetary Aggregates: Their Compilation, Data, and Historical Behavior," Staff Studies Paper 116, Board of Governors of the Federal Reserve System, Washington, D.C., May 1982.

A Revolution in Monetary Policy?

Back in October of 1979, the Fed announced that it was going to target and control the size of the money supply. The Fed was sure, as were most of the financial community and most of the economics profession, that this was the appropriate policy.

How different the situation is as we enter 1984! The Fed, the financial community, the economics profession, all are split on what to do—what to target to try to achieve stabilization objectives. Almost everyone agrees that the Fed should be "tight enough" to hold inflation in check. But how tight is that? And what do you look at to see if more (or less) tightening is needed?

Monetary policy in the 1980s is a difficult (and risky!) business. But it's critical to the health of the economy—and of the financial markets and institutions. We can all hope that the Fed chooses the right indicators. And we can hope that it reads them accurately and responds appropriately. Failing that, we can hope that it lucks out! A lot is depending on it.

Suggested Readings

Barnett, William A. "Economic Monetary Aggregates: An Application of Index Number and Aggregation Theory," *Journal of Econometrics,* vol. 14, no. 1 (September 1980), 11–48.

Barnett, William A., Spindt, Paul A., and Offenbacher, Edward K. "The New Divisia Aggregates," University of Texas at Austin and Board of Governors of the Federal Reserve System, 1981.

Friedman, Benjamin. "Monetary Policy with a Credit Aggregate Target," National Bureau of Economic Research Working Paper No. 980, September 1982.

——. "The Roles of Money and Credit in Macroeconomic Analysis," National Bureau of Economic Research Working Paper No. 831, December 1981.

Jaroslovsky, Rich. "Reagan Calls Fed's Money-Supply Figure 'The Wrong Signal' for Markets to Heed," *Wall Street Journal* (January 20, 1982), 3.

Kopcke, Richard W. "Must the Ideal 'Money Stock' Be Controllable?" *New England Economic Review* (March-April 1983), 10–23.

"Monetary Policy Report to the Congress," *Federal Reserve Bulletin* (August 1983), 579–590.

Solomon, Anthony M. "Waves of Banking Innovations and Financial Deregulation Compel the Fed To Think Twice About Monetary Targets," *Challenge* (March-April 1982), 19–24.

Chapter 22

The Financial Services Marketplace: An Overview

The changes that occurred in the financial services markets in this country in the period between 1980 and 1984 are difficult to conceptualize. And if you look at it carefully enough to see the whole picture, it's difficult to believe. Here are some examples:

- The cover story of the June 8, 1981, *Time* is: "The Savings Revolution." On page 2 of that issue, the publisher says: " 'Revolution' is not a word that *Time* uses lightly, but this week's cover story on the dramatic change in the way Americans are saving their inflation-pinched dollars fully deserves that billing."
- The May 16, 1983, issue of *U.S. News and World Report* (p. 69) carries the story "Revolution in Banking: Has It Gone Too Far?" The subtitle of the article is "The Headlong Rush by Banks, Brokers and Others To Be All Things to All Customers Is Causing Worry in Washington."
- The July 18, 1983, issue of *Newsweek* (p. 61) carries the story "The Brave New World of Superbanks." The introductory paragraph of that article says:

  > Today it is the Main Street Savings & Loan. Tomorrow: Superbank. . . . You will be able to shop for stocks and bonds, insurance and real estate—even for a package deal for the family vacation. You may bank at home by personal computer, borrowing money, say,

to buy a refrigerator from the bank's department-store subsidiary next door. Superbank will be big, powerful and more convenient than the neighborhood supermarket; keeping money there will seem easier than you could have dreamed.

- The April 23, 1983 issue of *The Economist,* in its article "Financial Supermarkets," begins:

  Thaws have a way of bringing floods. That has clearly been the case with the deregulation of American financial institutions. Hardly a day goes by without some formerly unheard-of development. . . .

- Economist Irving Leveson at the Hudson Institute looks at the financial services revolution and coins "Leveson's Law": "Everything happens in one-third the time!" ("The Fight for Financial Turf," *Fortune,* December 28, 1981, p. 54.)

The New Industry Called "Financial Services"

James Robinson III, Chairman and CEO of Shearson/American Express, is quoted in the January 3, 1983, issue of *Forbes* (p. 71), saying:

> The industry that was once known as *banking,* the industry known as *insurance,* the industry known as *brokerage*—and a host of additional businesses—are all now evolving into a new industry called *financial services.*

Exactly what is going on in this new industry called financial services? What does this "financial services" market look like? And who is in that market? Buying and selling what? And what are the motives of the buyers? And of the sellers? Those are the things you'll be reading about in the remainder of this chapter.

The Nature of the Financial Services Marketplace

At a recent banking conference at Appalachian State University, North Carolina National Bank Senior Vice President, Winton Poole said:

> The president of our bank is fond of saying: 'When things appear to get so complex and complicated in our business, what you need to remember is that the banking business is really nothing more or less than buying and selling money. Everything we do, in one way or another, is related to those two activities and we shouldn't lose sight of that.'

The banks and all of the other financial services institutions are "buying money" from somewhere. In past years when the "time value" of money wasn't very high, the depository institutions "bought" much of their money from savers in the form of savings and checking deposits. People and businesses didn't care much that they weren't earning much on their savings. Interest rates in the market were so low it wasn't worth the bother to try to earn more. But those times have gone. So what does this market look like today, this market in which financial institutions "buy money"?

The Market Where Institutions "Buy Money"

People who own dollars these days do not automatically deposit those dollars in banks or thrifts. There are many alternatives, and the financial firms have advertised and educated the public about them. A person would have to be deaf and blind to be unaware that there are better alternatives for placing dollars than to leave them in a non-interest-bearing checking account!

What do the savers (the dollar-asset owners) seek? What are their motives? It's all very simple: They would like to have a high return, safety, liquidity, convenience, and a desirable personal relationship if possible. Probably most people realize that there are some trade-offs among these objectives—you can get a better return if you're willing to give up some safety, or give up immediate access to your money.

Giving Dollar-Asset Owners What They Want

Each financial institution hopes to attract (buy) money from these savers (dollar-asset owners). So each institution needs to offer various combinations of financial (deposit) instruments, providing just the right mix of tradeoffs between earnings, liquidity, safety, convenience, friendly personal service, and whatever else the individual saver might desire. Those financial institutions that succeed in putting together the most attractive alternatives (financial instruments with high return, safety, immediate access, ease of shifting from one form of asset to another, maximum convenience, minimum hassle, etc.) will pull in the dollars. Competition in this "buying dollars" market has been fierce in recent years. It promises to stay that way.

Financial institutions are devising all kinds of new accounts to provide a better return and maximum convenience for the dollar-asset owners: All kinds of CDs. Money market deposit accounts. Super NOWs. Sweep accounts that automatically move money from low-interest accounts into higher paying alternatives. Automatic investment of dividends and interest. Automatic transfers from high-income-earning accounts to cover checks. All these and many more recent innovations are designed to attract more depositors—to give the institution a competitive edge in "buying more money."

The Market in which the Financial Institutions "Sell Money"

Financial institutions sell money to people who want to borrow and spend. They "sell money" as consumer loans, commercial loans, and home mortgage loans. Within each of these categories are many different kinds of financial instruments by which financial institutions "sell money." To the home buyer, the banks and thrifts "sell money" in exchange for a financial instrument called a home mortgage. What are the features of that financial instrument? How long is the term? What's the interest rate? Is it variable? And if so, how frequently and under what circumstances? Can it be paid off early? Can the term be extended?

It hasn't been many years since the home mortgage was a fairly standard financial instrument. Not anymore. And the same is true of the instruments used in business and consumer finance. Different lenders (sellers of money) are designing a great variety of instruments with different arrangements and terms.

During 1983, interest rates on various kinds of consumer loans differed by several percentage points between one lender and another. And the "newly sophisticated financial services consumer of the 1980s" was responding intelligently to the variety of loans available in the marketplace.

If the financial institutions are going to be successful in selling their funds to borrowers, they must offer what the borrowers want. And what is that?

What Kinds of Loans Do the Borrowers Want?

Consumer borrowers want to be able to get their loan conveniently, quickly, and with minimum hassle. They want terms that fit their circumstances, repayment flexibility, and the best rate they can get.

Consumers like easily or immediately available credit, such as the line of credit attached to their credit card, or overdraft privileges that provide for an automatic loan by the bank whenever there isn't enough money to cover checks. Convenience of location and pleasant relationships are also important. But in the days of the 1980s, with high interest rates and more "financially aware" consumers, these characteristics are not so important in attracting borrowers as was true in the past.

What do the business borrowers want? It isn't too different from what the consumers want. Low rates. Flexible terms. Minimum time and trouble in arranging and repaying the loan. But sometimes businesses want something more: they would like the bank to buy an asset for them and then lease them the asset. This doesn't show up as debt on the balance sheet.

In short, each business wants a banking relationship that serves its specific needs—one that is (1) dependable, (2) as low-cost as is available in the market, and (3) sufficiently flexible to meet its own special circumstances. Whatever financial service institution does the best job of offering that to a business is likely to be successful in "selling money" to that business. And it doesn't have to be a bank or a thrift—it could be an insurance company, a brokerage firm, or General Electric, General Motors, or Ford. You'll be reading about some of the competitors in this market in a few minutes.

The Focus of the Revolution: The Financial Services Marketplace

You can see that the financial services market is really two markets: the market in which the financial intermediaries buy money from the dollar-asset owners, and the market in which the financial intermediaries sell money to the consumer, business, and residential housing borrowers.

Some financial institutions focus their efforts primarily on one side or the other side of this market. Then they depend on other financial institutions to "complete the circle." But many institutions that in the past focused on one or the other side of the market are beginning to move more into both the buying and selling of money—and to get involved in selling a lot of other financial services as well.

As interest rates have gone up and the time value of money has increased rapidly, both the saver-depositors on one side and the borrower-spenders on the other have sought ways to get a better deal in the financial services marketplace. The banks and thrifts have been limited by law (Reg Q) from offering market rates to their depositors. So their depositors "disintermediated" and went to other "money buyers" who were paying market rates.

Lenders in some states were restricted by usury laws from charging market rates. Somehow money seemed to flow from those states and those institutions and wind up in loans somewhere else where market rates on loans were permissible. Banks and thrifts are restricted in what they can do on an interstate basis. But the power of the marketplace has largely overcome the effects of this, too.

The Power of the Marketplace: The Reflex Principle

Anyone who understands the power of the marketplace and the powerful way in which prices cause things to happen will not be too surprised by what has been happening in the financial services industry. Here's a quote from Dr. Bowden's *Principles of Economics* that states the general principle:*

> Market forces exercise great power in directing the economic activities and choices of the society. Prices and wages can be administered. Markets can be regulated or "rigged" in various ways. But the "rigging" will set off a chain reaction which will immediately begin to bring everything back into balance. This indirect "balancing effect" is what I call the reflex effect of real-world markets.
>
> What is this "reflex effect"? *It's the irresistible power of prices as they work in the real world to bring everything into balance—to move every market toward equilibrium.*

The Market Attracts Everybody

The experience in the financial services market in the early 1980s is an excellent illustration of the *reflex principle.* The financial services market is in the center—like the boxing ring at Madison Square Garden. And all around this focal center are the financial services enterprises: banks and thrifts, brokers, insurance companies, credit card companies, mutual funds, real estate companies, consumer credit and commercial credit companies, mortgage banking companies, investment banking companies, and so on.

And there are a lot of *nonfinancial businesses* out there looking to see what they can get into, provide successfully, and make a profit. Nonfinancial firms that have entered the "boxing ring" include Sears Roebuck, National Steel, American Can, Parker Pen, Kroger Supermarkets, Control Data, J.C. Penney, Gulf and Western Industries, and a lot of others.

What are all these financial and nonfinancial firms doing in the financial services market? Responding to the demands of the marketplace. Those services that banks and thrifts were prohibited from providing (or didn't provide quickly enough or well enough

*Elbert V. Bowden, *Principles of Economics, 4th edition,* South-Western Publishing Company, Cincinnati, 1983, p. 494.

or cheaply enough), others with entrepreneurial bent and talent were quick to provide. So our orderly, structured financial services boxing match has turned into a free-for-all!

What Banks Don't Provide, Someone Else Will

A great variety of financial and nonfinancial businesses are out there "buying money"—offering dollar-asset owners various combinations of high return, safety, liquidity, ease of shifting assets, convenience, etc. And the monopoly on checking accounts that such a short time ago belonged to the banks now seems a distant memory. Now many nonbank companies are offering unlimited checking privileges on their nationwide accounts.

Also, the "selling money" side of the market is busy with intense competitive activity. This great variety of bank and nonbank and nonfinancial firms are all trying to sell money—making loans to consumers and businesses and homebuyers, offering rates and other terms that are competitive in that marketplace—terms designed to meet the special needs of the various borrowers.

The forces of the marketplace have almost completely pushed aside the remaining restrictions of Glass-Steagall and of McFadden, at least so far as many enterprising and loophole-seeking institutions are concerned. For example, Citicorp has a nationwide network of offices (in 40 states!) doing "95 percent of what we want to do," according to Senior Vice President Wilford Farnsworth.* And Stephen McLin, Senior Vice President for Strategic Planning at Bank of America, says, "We decide what business we want to be in, and then get around the laws."**

The next chapter continues the story. In that chapter you'll read about this "Madison Square Garden boxing ring"—about these financial markets where money is being aggressively bought and sold. You'll be reading about who is in there and what they're doing. Meanwhile here's a quote you may enjoy from *The Economist* of June 18, 1983:***

*"The Brave New World of Superbanks," *Newsweek*, July 18, 1983, p. 61

**Ibid.

***"American Bankers Strain at the Regulatory Bit," *The Economist*, June 18, 1983, pp. 87–88.

> Last month, Sears Roebuck's chief executive, Mr. Edward Telling, told shareholders that by 1986 their chain will have more than 600 in-store financial centers across the country. In all but name, these will be commercial banks, investment banks and insurance companies rolled into one. This makes commercial bankers—from Citicorp's chairman, Mr. Walter Wriston, downwards—livid. They still cannot own investment banks, insurance companies or department stores. The day will come when they can.

Suggested Readings

"A Look at All the Players," *American Banker* (October 24, 1983), 13.

Eisenberg, Richard. "Checking Out the Financial Supermarkets," *Money* (May 1983), 141–147.

Ford, William F. "Banking's New Competition: Myths and Realities," *Economic Review,* Federal Reserve Bank of Atlanta (January 1982), 4–11.

Greene, Richard. "S&Ls in the Candy Store: The Commercial Loan Market," *Forbes* (June 6, 1983), 44–45.

Hector, Gary. "How Dreyfus Plans To Beat the Banks," *Fortune* (March 21, 1983), 64–72.

Hill, G. Christian. "Group of Large S&Ls Plans a Major Move into the Lucrative Corporate Loan Market," *Wall Street Journal* (March 9, 1983), 3.

"Sears, Roebuck: Half a Pound of Home Loans, Please," *The Economist* (January 15, 1983), 81–82.

Smith, Lee. "Merrill Lynch's Latest Bombshell for Bankers," *Fortune* (April 19, 1982), 67–70.

Chapter 23

Battleground of the Revolution: Everybody into Banking and Banks into Everything

The previous chapter gave you a look at the financial services market—the place where the buying and selling of money takes place. This chapter tells you who is in there buying and selling money and how they're doing it—trying to hold on to a share and maybe get a little more.

The Broker Invasion: Merrill Lynch and the CMA

As long ago as August 8, 1977, *Business Week* carried an article entitled: "Merrill Lynch: The Bull in Banking's Shop." This article reported the creation by the Merrill Lynch stock brokerage firm of its new kind of consumer account called the "cash management account," or CMA. These CMAs were introduced by Merrill Lynch in cooperation with City National Bank (now renamed Banc One) of Columbus, Ohio. Under the CMA program, customers of Merrill Lynch can borrow, write checks, and make Visa card purchases against their CMA accounts. And the idle money in the accounts earns interest. These accounts were made available to Merrill Lynch customers nationwide.

The banks considered this to be unfair competition. Both David Rockefeller, Chairman of Chase Manhattan, and William Spencer, at that time President of Citicorp, complained of this unprecedented intrusion into the banking business by a brokerage firm. But in July of 1977 the Fed stated that the Merrill Lynch CMA program doesn't violate Fed regulations.

The Merrill Lynch CMAs were carefully designed to make their way around the Glass-Steagall restrictions. And because of the convenience and other customer advantages of the CMA program, Merrill Lynch soon became a successful competitor—a "quasi-banker" in the nation's financial services markets.

This is a case where a brokerage firm (Merrill Lynch), operating in cooperation with a bank, offers what amounts to both demand deposit and savings deposit accounts, funds transfers, automatic bill paying and record-keeping services, loans to depositors, and, in effect, a broad range of financial services for which most customers go to their banks. And these services are actively marketed nationwide.

What kind of reserves should be held behind these CMAs, if any? And if not, how can we justify requiring reserves behind the deposits of the commercial banks? What does this new competition do to the concept of prohibiting interstate banking? What does it do to the effectiveness of the Glass-Steagall Act, which prohibits brokers from engaging in commercial banking (and vice versa)? Is it really legal for non-depository organizations to offer checking account services to their customers, and to pay interest on deposits which can be transferred by check?

Were these questions about the CMA account ever resolved? Of course not. The market forces just continued to exert their pressure in the financial markets, and an increasing array of institutions and financial instruments and products continued to pour into the market. While Congress deliberated on some of the issues, the speed of change accelerated.

The Booming Success of the CMA

As you might guess, the Merrill Lynch CMA turned out to be a very effective way to "buy money." The January 24, 1983, issue of *Fortune* (p. 107) carries the article, "Rival Managers for Your Cash." The first paragraph of the article says:

> The hottest new product on Wall Street is the one-stop berthing and tending of affluent folks' money. Other brokerage firms yawned when Merrill Lynch first unveiled its Cash Management Account in 1977. But a stampede of customers, starting in 1981, has swelled Merrill Lynch's roster of CMA clients to 900,000, who have parked an estimated $50 billion with the Bull.*

The article goes on to point out that the other major brokers have rushed in with similar "asset management account" services. By mid-1983 there wasn't a major brokerage firm in the country that was not offering some such account. And it wasn't just the brokerage companies. The banks were in, too. Crocker National Bank with its "Working Capital Account" and Citibank with its "FOCUS" were the first to get in. But many others were working rapidly to begin asset management programs.

Crocker National Bank in California began marketing its Working Capital Account in May 1982. This new account attracted over $200 million in deposits in the first nine months.

Citibank launched its FOCUS program in mid-April 1983. By the end of July (three months later) it already had $20 million in deposits. That doesn't sound like much, compared with the estimated more than $50 billion in Merrill Lynch CMA accounts at the end of 1982. But there is no question that it indicates a strong demand for this kind of financial product.

You can see that the banks got a slow start when you compare these figures with the mid-year 1983 estimates for CMA type accounts: $75 billion for Merrill Lynch, $9 billion for Dean Witter, $4.3 billion for Shearson/American Express, $3.6 billion for Prudential-Bache, and $2.4 billion for Paine Webber.** All of these other brokers started their asset management accounts in early 1982, except for Paine Webber, which began in March 1983.

What Does the CMA-Type Account Offer?

All of these asset management accounts offer a checking account, a brokerage account, money funds, a debit or charge card,

*John J. Curran, *Fortune,* January 24, 1983, p. 107. © Time Inc. All rights reserved.

**"A Buyers Guide to the Financial Supermarkets," *Forbes,* August 1, 1983, p. 144–152.

and some sort of comprehensive statement to the depositor. You can have your money in a regular money market fund, in a government securities fund, or a tax-exempt securities fund. Or you can have your money invested directly in the stocks or bonds of your choice.

All dividends and interest earned on your stocks and bonds go automatically into your account and are swept into the money fund of your choice. You can call any time and buy or sell stocks or bonds, and shift the money out of or into your money fund. The checks you write are drawn out of your money fund. You can send more money for deposit or withdraw money from the funds at any time. In most accounts you can also get low-interest loans against your portfolio of stocks and bonds. And you can call in your instructions to your service representative *toll free*!

By the end of 1983, Merrill Lynch still had not given up on its attempt to get other brokers and banks to pay royalties for using its patented CMA account. The response of James Howard of Dean Witter's Active Assets Account was: "You can't patent oxygen!" In 1983 Paine Webber filed a motion in U.S. District Court in Wilmington, Delaware, asking the court to declare the Merrill Lynch CMA patent invalid. So, as of January 1984, the issue wasn't settled yet.

How do stockbrokers offer banking services? And how do bankers offer stockbroker services? It's easy. The brokers make arrangements to work through a bank (or to acquire one), and the bankers make arrangements to work through a broker (or to acquire one).

The Banks Invade the Brokerage Business

At the beginning of 1982, no major bank in the United States offered discount brokerage services to its customers. But by the end of 1982, almost 600 commercial banks and thrifts had announced plans to enter the business. And some observers were expecting as many as 3000 banks and thrifts to begin offering discount brokerage services. How did this happen? And why didn't it start until 1982?

You already know that the Glass-Steagall Act of 1933 says that a bank may not underwrite securities offerings (except for general obligation municipal bonds) and may not buy and sell securities from its own portfolio. But does that mean that banks cannot offer brokerage services? It had generally been assumed that the banks could not. But in 1982 it turned out that they could!

It was April of 1982 that San Francisco's Crocker National Bank, the twelfth largest in the United States, announced its plan to establish a "Working Capital Account," run by Boston's Massachusetts Financial Services. Customers of this account would be able to buy and sell stocks and bonds and other securities through Bradford Broker Settlement, Inc., a New York brokerage firm. So Crocker was the first bank to offer a CMA-type account and to become (in a sense) a banker-broker.

In May of 1982, the Federal Home Loan Bank Board allowed the establishment of a joint arrangement between three S&Ls to establish an investment services program called "Invest," based in Tampa. Invest plans to provide wholesale services to hundreds of subscribing thrift institutions. Invest brokers located in participating S&Ls can trade stocks and bonds, offer mutual funds, and provide portfolio analyses and other investment advisory services.

By May of 1983, the Invest brokers were located in 23 S&Ls and savings banks nationwide. Plans were to have as many as 300 thrifts join this program by the end of 1984.

In November of 1981, BankAmerica Corporation signed an agreement to acquire Charles Schwab and Company, a large discount stock brokerage firm. This was the first bid by a bank to actually acquire a brokerage firm. BankAmerica was soon involved in a bitter dispute with the Securities Industry Association, which contended that the merger would violate the Glass-Steagall Act. Approval of the proposed acquisition was entangled and delayed.

Banks Acquire Brokerage Companies

By August 1982, Crocker National and a few other banks were already providing discount brokerage services by working through an affiliated brokerage company. But, except for the BankAmerica bid to acquire Charles Schwab, no bank had attempted either to create its own brokerage unit or to acquire a brokerage firm.

Then, in August 1982, Security Pacific Bank became the first bank cleared by the Comptroller of the Currency to create its own discount brokerage unit. Security Pacific established a subsidiary, Security Pacific Discount Brokerage Services, Inc., with plans to expand its discount brokerage service outside its home state of California. This amounted to a new interpretation of the Glass-Steagall Act and paved the way for other banks to follow suit.

Security Pacific had been providing discount brokerage services in conjunction with Fidelity Brokerage Services Inc. of Boston. But, following the Comptroller's approval, the bank proceeded to set up its own brokerage operation, register it as a broker with the SEC, and apply for membership in the National Association of Securities Dealers.

In mid-January of 1983 (more than one year after its initial proposal), BankAmerica received federal permission to acquire Charles Schwab. This was another precedent-setting decision. The Securities Industry Association immediately announced plans to appeal the merger, but their attempts to block the merger were unsuccessful.

In mid-February 1983, Chase Manhattan began discussing plans to acquire Rose and Company, a Chicago-based discount brokerage firm. It appears almost certain that many more banks will be acquiring or establishing their own brokerage units during the next few years. A brokerage subsidiary certainly makes sense for any bank that decides to enter the booming competition in CMA-type asset management accounts.

Is it legal for banks to be in the brokerage business? For a long time the question was clouded. But on August 10, 1983, the Fed issued a decision that bank holding companies can freely seek permission to provide discount brokerage services. So, unless the Congress or the courts do something to change that, that's the way it is.

Brokers (and Others) Acquire Nonbank Banks

You already know a good bit about nonbank banks from the discussion in previous chapters. You know that they have been used a lot to circumvent the legal barriers to interstate banking. So you won't be surprised to find out that many firms outside the banking industry that wanted to get into banking have acquired nonbank banks.

So, at the same time that some banks were acquiring brokerage firms, some brokerage, mutual fund, and other companies were acquiring banks—and then turning them into "nonbank banks," which fall outside the legal definition of and restrictions on banks.

The leader in this move was the Dreyfus mutual fund company, which in 1982 was controlling about $20 billion in money market fund assets. In 1982 Dreyfus made an offer to buy Lincoln State Bank in New Jersey. It also applied to the federal government (Comptroller of the Currency) for permission to establish a national bank in New York. Both of these bids were opposed by Fed Chairman Volcker. But in early 1983 they were approved by C. T. Conover, Comptroller of the Currency.

You probably remember that under the Bank Holding Company Act, a "bank" must (1) take deposits and (2) make commercial loans. Neither of the Dreyfus "banks" will make commercial loans, and that's why the acquisitions are legal. As you can see, this "nonbank loophole" is opening the doors to more competition in the financial services marketplace. It's letting a lot of nonbankers get into banking, and it's speeding the development of the "everything and everywhere financial service business of the 1980s."

What financial services can a nonbank bank engage in? It can do anything any other bank can do except make commercial loans. Or if it makes commercial loans, it can't take deposits. And one company can own several nonbank banks, scattered all over the country—that is, unless this loophole gets plugged before the company can scurry through it.

In 1983 Paul Volcker and some members of Congress were pushing hard to plug the nonbank loophole. In mid-1983, Comptroller of the Currency Conover declared a temporary moratorium on new nonbank bank applications. What will happen? We'll just have to wait and see.

Other Financial Institutions Enter the Fray

The insurance companies gather up billions of dollars every year from their policyholders. Then they invest that money for a return and they make payments under their policies as required. But is that all?

In 1981, Prudential Insurance acquired the Bache (pronounced Baysh) brokerage firm. And it has been expanding its role in the financial services field ever since. The September 26, 1983, issue of *Business Week* (p. 50) announced that Prudential has hired a banker to run its "nonbank"—the name is "Prudential Bank and Trust Company"—which will provide home equity loans and federally insured CDs. Prudential has also bought a major real estate firm.

Insurance? Brokerage? Banking? Real estate? Yes. And Prudential isn't alone in this. Other insurance companies, including Aetna, Metropolitan Life, Cigna, Travellers, and a number of others have been diversifying into all of these financial services—including CMA-type asset management accounts and financial planning services.

The same pattern is developing among the mutual funds. You already know about the Dreyfus expansion into banking. Dreyfus and other mutual funds are broadening in the direction of "full financial services businesses." Billions of dollars of their assets have been draining off into the new money market deposit accounts at the banks and thrifts. So the mutual funds are fighting back by entering into new activities.

The credit card companies are expanding their financial services, too. The American Express Company has leapt into this competitive arena we call the "nonfinancial services marketplace." By mid-1983 it was already involved in stock brokerage, banking, asset management, and a broad range of financial services in this country, and in 1983 it was adding to its string of banks overseas.

Where are the lines of demarcation that tell you whether a company is an insurance company or a brokerage house? Or a commercial bank? Or a real estate firm? Or a personal investment advisory service? Or a depository institution? All of these "financial conglomerate" firms are involved in checking accounts and various kinds of savings accounts, real estate, financial planning, consumer and commercial loans, and a broad spectrum of financial services. So it really doesn't make much sense to try to draw clear lines between the different firms. All of them are responding to the demands of the marketplace.

Here's how it has been going: Each financial institution decides what functional and geographic segments of the market it wants to serve. Then it figures out how to do it—and how to make it legal. Then it proceeds to carry out its plans. That's what has been happening. As of early 1984, there's no change in sight.

The Invasion by Nonfinancial Businesses

The number of nonfinancial firms entering the financial services industry is growing all the time. You've already seen a list of these, ranging from National Steel to Parker Pen to Sears Roebuck. And the list of financial services that they offer is growing all the time. What services? Just about anything you can think of—real estate, insurance, mutual funds, annuities, savings accounts, checking accounts, consumer loans, commercial loans, home mortgage loans, asset management accounts, stock and bond brokerage, financial planning, credit card services, income tax preparation, and more.

Not all of these firms offer the full range of financial services, but most of them offer several. And in 1983 many of them either owned or were considering acquiring nonbank banks in order to complete their range of financial services and/or to expand their geographic coverage.

The Banks Broaden Their Range of Activities

You can see that the banks and thrifts are faced with intense competition in every segment of their marketplace. Who is competing with them in the buying and selling of money? Almost everybody!

So what can the banks do to fight back? First, they try to compete as effectively as they can in their traditional markets. And you already know that they're going into the brokerage business and setting up asset management accounts. But that isn't all. They're spreading out into other fields. As John W. Morrison, Chairman of Northwest Bancorporation (the nation's eighteenth-largest bank holding company) said: "If banks want to survive, we have to become more aggressive in nonbanking fields."* In 1981, Northwest acquired Dial Corporation, a consumer finance organization with 520 offices covering 38 states.

In July of 1982, Citicorp received Fed approval to enter the data processing industry. The decision limits Citicorp's activities to computing services that involve the processing of banking, financial, and economic data. Some industry observers were projecting that by 1990 Citicorp might be earning as much as $250 million annually from its data processing activities.

In 1983, Citicorp was also establishing a banking unit in South Dakota, which will permit Citicorp to go into insurance. South Dakota's laws do not prohibit insurance activities by banks. Several other banks around the country have been getting into insurance, and also into real estate.

Banks have been moving into mutual funds, some in connection with the new asset management accounts. Some funds are referred to not as "mutual funds," but as "common trust funds for the collective investment of assets." A "non-mutual-fund mutual fund?" Why not?

New Competition in "Selling Money"

Most of what you have been reading so far in this chapter has dealt with competition in the financial services markets in "buying" money—about how the banks and the brokers and the insurance companies and Sears and the mutual funds and Shearson/American Express and all of the others have been trying to pull in dollars from the public.

What's going on in the other market—the market where the financial intermediary sells that money to the borrower-spenders? The businesses? The consumers? The home buyers? The competition in that market is tough, too.

Before the end of 1983, both Shearson/American Express and Merrill Lynch were operating in more than 25 states, lending money to home owners. Their advertisements invite home owners to use the equity in their homes as collateral for loans. This

**Fortune*, October 19, 1981, p. 16.

promises to be a major new market for loans. It's a market that both Shearson/Amex and Merrill Lynch were going after quickly. And in 1983 they were pricing their loans lower than current bank rates on fixed-interest mortgages.

What about in consumer lending? The banks haven't fared so well. In the early 1980s, General Motors, through its credit subsidiary General Motors Acceptance Corporation (GMAC), had more consumer installment credit outstanding than the three biggest banks in the nation. Ford Motor Company had more consumer installment credit outstanding than either Bank of America or Citicorp. So did Sears. In automobile loans, auto finance companies were taking an increasing share of the business, leaving banks a smaller percentage of the take.

Who do you think is the largest consumer lender in the United States? Probably in the world? It's GMAC. For the past several years banks have been getting a declining share of the consumer lending market. But note this: Several of the consumer-lending companies are owned by bank holding companies. So the situation for the banks may not be as bad as it might seem.

What about business lending? Here the banks are under pressure of increased competition, too. But as of the early 1980s, they still had the lion's share of the pie. In the early 1980s, almost ¾ of the short-term commercial and industrial (C and I) loans in the United States were made by commercial banks. But this does not mean that the nonbank commercial lenders aren't making an important dent in the bankers' business. There are a dozen or so major industrial-communications-transportation firms in the country with a major presence in the commercial lending field. And in commercial mortgage lending, the major insurance companies have the lion's share.*

Important commercial lending competition comes from GMAC and Ford, both of which have expanded their lending activities into commercial lending. In recent years, General Electric Credit Corporation has become a major entity in this market. The August 30, 1982, issue of *Business Week* (pp. 54–58) carried the article "General Electric Credit: From Financing Home Appliances to an Aggressive Source of Funds for Industry." That article begins:

*For statistics on the relative market shares of banks and various nonbank competitors, see Harvey Rosenblum, Diane Siegel, and Christine Pavel, "Banks and Nonbanks: A Run for the Money," *Economic Perspectives*, Federal Reserve Bank of Chicago, May/June 1983, pp. 3–12.

> To raise $850 million for a new mill and a coke oven battery, U.S. Steel Corp. might ordinarily tap either banks or the securities markets almost anywhere in the world. So might Scott Paper Co., which wanted $91.5 million for a new boiler at one of its paper mills; Eastern Air Lines Inc., which needed financing for new planes; and the management of Standard-Coosa Thatcher Co., which wanted $40 million to take the company private. Instead, these companies recently turned to General Electric Credit Corp.
>
> The *Business Week* article goes on to explain that GECC is one of the largest, most aggressive—and, among competitors, sometimes resented—sources of capital for business.
>
> With $12.3 billion in outstanding loan and lease receivables, the offspring of the industrial giant is the nation's third biggest finance company in lending volume, ranking just behind the far more consumer-oriented captives of General Motors Corp. and Ford Motor Co.

Clearly, there is strong competition on both sides of "the banker's business"—the business of buying and selling money. Each firm in the financial services industry is spreading out more and more, several going all the way across the industry. And some nonfinancial firms are doing the same. The lines between firms are getting more blurred all the time.

What about the lines between banks and thrifts? For all practical purposes, those lines have already dissolved. Those thrifts that want to act like commercial banks are already doing so. Thrifts now have the power to compete in the marketplace. Except for a few special circumstances (and except for some 700 that didn't survive the trauma of the early 1980s), the thrifts should be able to hold their own in the financial marketplace. Those with outstanding management can be expected to excel.

A Summary Comment

This chapter could touch only a small fraction of what's been happening in the financial services marketplace. But even that small fraction tells enough to be somewhat mind-boggling. Revolution? No question about it.

The banking business is really only buying and selling money. But there are a lot of ways of buying money and a lot of ways of selling money. And everybody is out there trying to figure out better ways to buy it and sell it. The ones that succeed will take your customers. So *alertness* and *innovation* are necessary to survive.

The banking business (now the financial services industry) is a new world. Just about anybody who wants in can get in. And once you're in, you can do just about anything you please—and do it just about anywhere you please. How do banks and thrifts respond to this new environment? How can they survive in this new competitive jungle? That's what you'll be reading about in the next (and final) part of this book.

Suggested Readings

"American Express Expands Its Supermarket," *Business Week* (July 25, 1983), 72–74.

"Bankers as Brokers," *Business Week* (April 11, 1983), 70–74.

"Credit Unions Take on Banking's Goliaths," *U.S. News & World Report* (January 18, 1982), 73–74.

"E. F. Hutton To Establish a State Bank in Delaware," *American Banker* (October 14, 1983), 3.

Hector, Gary. "The Banks Invade Wall Street," *Fortune* (February 7, 1983), 44–48.

McMurray, Scott. "Citicorp Wins Approval To Start Discount Broker," *American Banker* (November 4, 1983), 1.

"Mutual Funds: Trying to Lure Back 'Lost' Billions," *Business Week* (March 7, 1983), 88–89.

"The Cornerstone of G&W's New Financial Empire," *Business Week* (October 24, 1983), 169.

"Travelers To Join Scramble by Big Insurers To Create a Financial-Planning Network," *Wall Street Journal* (September 29, 1983), 16.

Part VIII Challenges, Opportunities, Success Strategies, and Outlook for the Industry

The New Environment Requires Strategic Planning, Innovation, Better Management of Resources, Funds, and People—and the Kind of Competitive, Entrepreneurial Spirit That Seeks Out Challenges and Greets Them Head On

Chapter 24

The Banking Environment and Survival Strategies for the 1980s

During the decade of the 1980s, the name of the game for the financial services industry is "competition." By 1984 the barriers that had insulated the financial services institutions from competition from each other and from other kinds of businesses were virtually gone. There was much more spatial (geographic) competition, competition from other financial firms performing more kinds of services, and competition from businesses outside the financial services industry.

Any financial institution that was unable to meet these new kinds of competition could not survive. Some 700 thrifts and several banks disappeared between 1980 and 1984.

The final part of this book presents statements by several members of the financial services industry, each giving an assessment of the conditions which can be expected to exist in the coming years, and suggestions as to how financial institutions can rise to meet the new challenges. Then the final chapter of the book gives an overview assessment and outlook for the banking and financial services industry for the 1980s.

The first four comments are by North Carolina bank and thrift officers who were speaking at the November 1981 Banking Conference at Appalachian State University. The final comments are statements by three other outstanding members of the profession from North Carolina, Oklahoma, and the State of Washington.

Adams' Suggestions: Increase Productivity*

Banking in general has done a very poor job in terms of productivity and efficiency. We will have to do much better during this decade than in the last. It will be interesting for you as a consumer to see how those changes affect you. Likely you will wait in line a little longer if you choose to use a teller. We will price our services to encourage you to eliminate, as the telephone company does, the utilization of a person in that banking transaction. We don't have the luxury any more of assuring that when you walk into the bank you'll have a loan officer or a teller to immediately handle your transaction.

We also will reevaluate our existing and prospective branching locations. We will close some branches, we will relocate some, and we will staff differently. We will try to determine the needs of each individual market. For example, we gather deposits and we make loans in almost all of our retail locations. In the past we have not studied the market enough to determine the degree to which we should emphasize the loan effort or the deposit effort. We will determine those markets in which we expect branches to be deposit gatherers (acquirers of funds) and we will emphasize the deposit-gathering function.

Everyone is familiar with the function of loan officers. An attractive career path historically in banking is to have been on the loan side of the organization—commercial lending in particular. How many people have you ever heard about who become CEOs who were deposit officers? Many banking institutions are looking more closely at upgrading—in terms of ability, training and compensation—the skills necessary to attract and maintain deposits in certain markets.

There's one advantage that I think we as commercial bankers have over our nonbank competitors, and I think the degree to which we take advantage of this perception in the short term and intermediate term will be a prime determinant of how successful we are. And that is, the commercial banker is seen as the person who has the knowledge of financial products or services that the banking customer needs. More specifically, today's consumer or

*Austin A. Adams, Group Executive Vice President, Northwestern Bank, North Wilkesboro, North Carolina.

small businessman—with all the problems that he faces in today's economy and the myriad of investment opportunities that are available—needs a single source to which he can go for objective, knowledgeable counseling and financial products.

I think we commercial bankers have the advantage in this regard, at least in the short term. Our organization is trying to make sure we have those financial counselors—those financial experts who can intelligently discuss with our customers the financial alternatives that are available to them.

A key question is: "Can banks continue to be quasi-public utilities?" I have heard bankers respond: "Well, we have an obligation to provide banking services to everybody in the community." In the past that may have been a desirable objective, but in the future I don't think we're going to be able to afford that attitude anymore—not if we're going to meet the demands of the marketplace, and survive.

It will be difficult for financial organizations to provide better customer service while maintaining satisfactory levels of profitability in this new environment. It will require substantially better planning and management than most banking organizations historically have had.

Bodenheimer's Suggestions: Reassessment and Imaginative Banking*

In the past two or three years we have nearly killed the banking industry as we have known it. We have had a tremendous increase in our cost of funds and in our operational costs. So what are we going to have to do to survive? We're going to have to (1) charge more for the money we lend, (2) double or triple the cost of our services, and (3) reduce our cost of operations.

The total services of the bank must be reviewed—the trust department, different kinds of deposits, international payments—all of these. We're going to have to change the pricing of all our services if we're going to be able to provide them. And we must

*Furman P. Bodenheimer, Jr., Senior Vice President, First Citizens Bank & Trust Company, Durham, North Carolina.

look for unique ways of being different. Otherwise, some of us are not going to survive.

We're going to have to identify those few things that we do well, and seize on those opportunities that offer the greatest profit potential. We each need to build our own competitive edge. But we must understand that what we do today is not something that we can cut into stone—to stay with forever. Things are changing too fast for that. Also, we need to remove the barriers to imaginative banking. And in the absence of our own imagination, I think we can look forward to having more and more regulations to tell us what we can do.

But the picture isn't all bad. All of us who are bankers have chosen this profession. Nobody roped us into it, and nobody's keeping us in it. We've served this profession well and the profession has served us well.

Woody's Suggestions on Markets, Branches, Pricing, and Management*

I think there are four major areas we need to talk about: markets, branches, pricing, and management.

Markets. We've learned in the last three or four years that money is very liquid. It's going to move to the highest point of return. Modern communications and almost perfect product knowledge in this country have proven that money's going to flow out of Boone and into Boston if Boston is offering a higher rate. So markets are *nationwide.*

Branches. Everything we're doing in banking is to keep people out of the bank. We have credit cards, check overdraft lines, ATMs, and direct deposits—everything to keep people out of branches. So we're not going to need as many branches. A lot of banks, mine included, have actively started closing marginal branches, and you won't see many new branches being built. The bank's assets will be redeployed into different, more efficient delivery systems.

*Stephen W. Woody, Senior Vice President, First Union National Bank, Charlotte, N.C.

Pricing. We're going to start charging fees for everything. But *pricing* implies that you know what your *costs* are. Good cost accounting is going to be crucial if we're going to price right and remain competitive.

Management. We've got to be better managers. More and more it is being recognized that the key to *successful banking* is *successful management.* It has been said that there are more than a hundred banks in the billion dollar category, but only a couple of dozen people capable of running them! That's a heavy indictment of bank managers. But in the past we didn't have to be good managers. Banking was an easy business to run. We had cheap money—just put a price on the cheap money and lend it out! Everybody made money. Success was easy. Now we're going to have to reorient our thinking. We're going to have to get tougher. And smarter. We're no longer living in the nice, protected, structured environment of the past. Banking in the future is going to be a challenging environment, and for the winners, *very* rewarding.

Blaine's Ideas on Credit Unions: Role, Strategy, Outlook*

A credit union is a nonprofit, cooperative financial institution. It is a private corporation. It operates just like a bank except that it is owned cooperatively. The organization is run solely for the benefit of the members.

The State Employees' Credit Union (SECU) in North Carolina is a $450 billion credit union, one of the largest in the country. We are a full-service consumer financial institution. We offer home mortgages, personal loans, credit cards, both interest and non-interest checking accounts, and consumer finance for automobiles, washing machines, whatever you want. But we do not deal in the commercial sector. I understand that the federal government wants to give us the power to do that. If so, that's fine. But we are not asking for it.

We already have our market segment—the teachers and state

*James C. Blaine, President, North Carolina State Employees' Credit Union.

employees in North Carolina. We know who they are, what they are like, what their salaries are, where they work, where they live, and we have a pretty good idea of what kinds of financial services they need. We are ahead of the game in understanding our market segment.

On what does success depend? I have three points—three 'requirements for success'': (1) You must offer quality financial services—*quality;* (2) You must price your services reasonably—not necessarily the lowest prices, but reasonable prices; (3) You must be able to deliver those services in a convenient manner.

How important is *convenience?* We have found out that, even though it takes four days to get your money back from a money market fund in New York, when the interest they are paying is 18%, people are willing to wait! Convenience is important, but not convenience at any price. But in the convenience area, we must provide ATMs, direct deposit, POS (point of sale) terminals, pay by phone, a state-wide computer network for a state-wide institution, with state-wide availability of services, and eventually it will be nationwide. Soon every financial institution is going to have to be able to tell you that, even if you go to Juarez, Mexico, you'll be able to cash your bank or credit union check there.

What about *reasonable price?* How can we achieve that? Through efficiency. Productivity. If we keep our costs down, we can keep our prices down. One way we can keep costs down is by check truncation. That just means you don't get your checks back. Our credit union already does that. Use of electronic funds transfers and electronic delivery of services will increase productivity and keep costs down, too.

What about the *quality* of financial services? The quality of financial services, just like 1, 2, 3, means: People! People! People! That's what financial organizations are all about. Quality services depend upon the people. You can put in ATMs, you can put in drive-in teller windows and all kinds of things. But if you don't have the people in your organization who are capable of and interested in providing quality services to your customers, then you're in trouble. We need people who are interested in dealing with other people. We need people who can meet the challenges required to run the financial organizations of the future.

The current environment is presenting some problems to all financial institutions and all managers. But it's extremely exciting.

It really is a revolution. But we don't view it as a problem. We want to get in there and deal with it!

Baker's Survival Strategy for the Thrifts.*

Fewer than half of today's thrifts will be around to celebrate New Years Day, 1990. The survivors will be those that act quickly to take advantage of Congress' liberation of the financial services industry from outmoded and damaging regulatory constraints.

As the thrift industry enters the 1980s, it is confronted with (1) the passing of the thrift ethic generation; (2) capture of the "baby boom" generation and others by commerical banking; (3) increasingly deep market penetration by nonbanks, i.e., money market funds, huge retailers such as Sears, and credit unions; (4) the devastation of double-digit inflation, and (5) a new pattern of consumer savings that will reduce whatever deposits the industry is able to attract, to average balances more akin to the $2,000 level of the commercial banks rather than the $5,000 thrift balances of the past.

Today's thrift CEO would appear to have three options, and time is extremely short in which to initiate the strategic planning needed for implementation.

- The first, simplest and perhaps most profitable option initially would be an aggressive move into mortgage banking. One can expect that field will become crowded as the 1980s advance, however, raising reasonable questions about adequacy and cost of lendable funds later in the decade.
- The second, and probably the most evident move during the next ten years, will be merger of the thrifts into other financial institutions. The rules will change to permit marriages between thrifts and commercial banks.
- The third option is to move aggressively toward full-service banking. It is a more demanding business than running a

*Bruce F. Baker, Senior Vice President, Washington Mutual Savings Bank, Seattle, Washington. These are excerpts from an article that was previously published in the *Business Journal* of the School of Business, Eastern Washington University, and is included here by permission of the author and previous publisher.

> traditional thrift, with more functions to administer, more people to manage, and a lower return on average assets. But it is a more exciting, challenging business than mortgage banking, and a more satisfactory climax to a career than submerging one's identity and management prerogatives through a merger.

The CEO will be well advised to join ranks with the cadre of thrifts that have awakened to the new banking world of the 1980s and are fighting for competitive parity in the unforgiving marketplace. Unfortunately and ironically, time is running out for the very institutions that have sponsored and promoted thrift and affordable home ownership for hundreds of millions of Americans. Those institutions whose managements fail to heed the warning will struggle to survive, while the others, employing the new business strategies available for the 1980s, will move on into the future with strength and vitality.

Craig's Comments on Bankers' Responses to the New Competition*

As we all know, the financial services industry is in the midst of the most sweeping period of change since the great depression. The major forces at work in the industry today include the following:

1. Old restrictions on financial intermediaries are rapidly breaking down, primarily due to technological innovations, mushrooming communications networks, and the high interest rates of recent years.
2. Depository institutions are being buffeted by ever-increasing competition from "near banks" like Sears, American Express, Merrill Lynch, and Prudential.

*Ben T. Craig, Chairman, Northwestern Financial Corporation, North Wilkesboro, North Carolina. Excerpts from Craig's "Opportunities And Problems In Bank Structure And New Bank Funding Instruments," a paper presented to the North Carolina Commissioner of Banks' Conference, Raleigh, North Carolina. Included here by permission of the author.

3. But instead of uniting against these "near banks," the depository institutions have tended to fight each other and ignore this ominous new competition.
4. Until recently, the banking and thrift industries have been reluctant to innovate or test new products and services, preferring instead to sit back and wait for government and regulators to tell them what they can do.

As Richard Rosenburg, Vice Chairman of Wells Fargo, pointed out recently, the banking industry helped American Express create the gold card in 1966. And yet, it took the commercial bankers who run the MasterCard and Visa organizations until 1981 to recognize that the affluent customer is not only willing and able, but eager, to pay a premium for a service like this.

In short, Rosenburg concludes, "It was not regulation or legislation that handed American Express this attractive product, it was the commercial banks' lack of innovation and their failure to recognize changing consumer attitudes.

Who was the biggest U.S. money manager at the end of 1982? Merrill Lynch asset management! At the end of 1981, Merrill Lynch was managing customer assets of $41 billion, almost $39 billion of which was money market "deposits." Only a year earlier, Merrill Lynch had $17 billion. (Now we know why they are bullish on America!)

It is incredible that banks, savings and loans, and credit unions continue to regard each other as their primary competitive threat! This is a classic case of carefully examining individual trees—and missing not only the whole forest, but all the hungry predators lurking there as well.

One of the most explosive U.S. markets is going to be the liquification of personal assets (including homes) for affluent and middle class individuals and families. This is what people want, and what Merrill Lynch, American Express, Sears and others are giving them.

Where does this put bank managements? As one observer has put it, "the changes in banking are being driven not by economic or regulatory forces, but by technology. The economist finds the rationale after the barn door has been open for a while—and then sometime after that, the politician/regulator looks for ways to try and close it."

Bank and thrift managements are quickly learning that they can no longer afford the luxury of sitting back and casually waiting for the regulators to tell them what is and what isn't permissible. The competitive forces are simply too massive and are moving too quickly. So these managements are increasingly venturing into new, relatively untried financial service waters.

Swearingen's Ideas on the New Environment and Personnel Needs*

From the point of view of day-to-day operations, banks are going to see *more* regulations, not less. Bank examiners today are looking into *every facet* of bank operations and management. The consumer protection laws are requiring increasing administration time and effort and cost on the part of the banks.

Bank examiners are required even to evaluate the quality of management in the bank. And many of the examiners who appear at the bank are recently out of college, often in their early twenties and have no idea what "good bank management" is. Yet the law requires them to do that.

During the decade of the 1980s we are going to see more *intensive competition,* and more *price* competition than ever before. Competition is going to come from other banks in the same state, from banks in other states, from savings and loan associations, from the enormous credit unions which have grown rapidly in recent years, and from such organizations as GMAC, and also from Merrill Lynch, E. F. Hutton, and other brokerage firms that have introduced new tough competition in this market and are succeeding in drawing funds out of the banks.

Also foreign banks are going to be tough competitors. It has been estimated that foreign banks are now making about 11% of all commercial and industrial loans in this country. The foreign banks have a leverage advantage. For example, the banks in Oklahoma maintain an equity capital ratio of about 8%.

*Eugene Swearingen, Ph.D., Chairman of the Executive Committee, Bank of Oklahoma, Tulsa. Excerpts from his presentation at the American Bankers Association "Education and Training Forum" in Chicago on April 10, 1980, presented here with Dr. Swearingen's permission.

[*Explanatory note:* This means that the actual *ownership value*—the *investment of the stockholders*—amounts to about 8% of the bank's assets. The remainder of the assets are made up mostly of loans which borrowers owe to the bank, and other debt instruments such as government bonds and other securities which represent amounts owed to the bank. All of these debt instruments bring income to the bank. The lower the equity capital ratio, the more loans and other investments the bank holds for each dollar of its equity capital. So the lower the equity capital ratio the higher the "leverage"—that is, the higher the bank's potential earnings on its equity capital. The higher the *leverage* permitted, the more loans the bank can make on a given amount of equity capital, so the more *income* it can earn on its equity capital and the more aggressively it can afford to compete with other banks in making loans.]

The big Eastern banks maintain capital in the range of 3% or 4%, while the Japanese banks operate on less than 2%—operating on something like a 60-to-1 leverage on equity capital. And these banks are growing faster than U.S. banks.

Manufacturers Hanover some years ago was the fourth largest bank in the world. It is still the fourth largest bank in the United States, but it is now twenty-seventh in size in the world. This indicates something about the relative growth of foreign banks. There are now about 325 foreign bank institutions operating in the United States. These kinds of competition, from outside the country, from outside of the state, and from various kinds of nonbank entities, are going to be intense during the decade of the 1980s.

The increased competition and rapidly changing conditions in the 1980s are going to require new approaches and more cost effective methods in training and upgrading bank personnel. There will be more college graduates and more bright new MBAs. These people are going to need to be promoted to vice president positions fairly quickly—the banking industry is going to have to move them up, or lose them.

The training program must be redesigned to allow more *selectivity* in courses, and to allow more *specialized* training to accommodate people for changing careers in banking, or who are entering banking from the outside. There needs to be more *study modules* so people can take what they need; arrangements need to be made to provide more credit for self-study; and there needs to be more emphasis on *self-development* and *attitude development.* But training needs to be concerned not only with "IQ," but also with "I will!"

In summary, banking is going to see more change in the 1980s than in the 1970s, and the rate of change is going to be faster. There will be a new competitive environment that will challenge the very best abilities of bank managers and personnel. Under such circumstances, the personnel and training functions take on new and greater importance. The banks that succeed in the new environment of the 1980s will be the ones that successfully rise to this challenge.

Suggested Readings

Baldwin, Earl. "For Mortgage Lenders, Control of Risk Is a Must," *American Banker* (October 18, 1983), 21.

Gross, Laura. "Marketing Convention Highlights Niche-Picking, Changing Industry, and New Financial Environment," *American Banker* (October 26, 1983), 1.

Hawke, John D. Jr., Sweet, William J. Jr. and Mierzewski, Michael B. "Revised BHC Act Offers Banks New Opportunities," *Legal Times* (December 20, 1982), 17–22.

Helyar, John. "Regional Banks Search for a Niche in Face of New Rules, Competition," *Wall Street Journal* (February 4, 1982), 4.

"Matching Assets and Liabilities in a Thrift Portfolio," *Federal Home Loan Bank Board Journal,* Vol. 16, No. 8 (September 1983), 3–7.

Rose, Sanford. "How Bankers Can Shake the Interest-Rate Willies," *Fortune* (May 3, 1982), 200–210.

Wallich, Henry C., and Varvel, Walter A. "Evolution in Banking Competition," *The Bankers Magazine* (November-December 1980).

Chapter 25

Joss' Suggestions for Successful Banking in the 1980s*

Thoroughly understanding your business is an absolute competitive necessity for survival and superior performance. Just because all of our institutions call themselves banks does not mean that we are all in the same business. Far from it. And even though another institution does not call itself a bank, it may still be actively engaged in one of the same businesses that you are in.

The most important job of executive bank management is to *choose* their businesses—carefully, logically, and in a concentrated way that permits the bank to succeed at its chosen ventures without wasting or diverting energy to less attractive alternatives. It is equally important to thoroughly review those choices on a periodic basis. It is the product of these periodic choices that defines the business of banking for each institution.

*This chapter consists entirely of excerpts from Robert L. Joss, "People in Banking in the 80s," an address presented at the American Bankers Association "Bankers Education and Training Forum" in Chicago, April 10, 1980. Mr. Joss is Senior Vice President and head of the Asia-Pacific Division of the International Banking Group of Wells Fargo Bank in San Francisco. Printed by permission of the author.

What Is the Business of Banking?

Nearly all the business we see being pursued within banks today can be covered under one of five major business headings:

1. *Originating Credit Contracts* (finding the borrower, assessing the risk, setting the price, doing the paperwork, and readying the asset for booking or sale).
2. *Inventorying Credit Contracts* (holding the financial asset in the bank's own portfolio).
3. *Financing the Bank* (selling debt and equity instruments to raise funds sufficient to finance the assets the bank has decided to inventory).
4. *Originating and Processing Non-Credit Financial Transactions* (providing payment and other financial transfer services for a price).
5. *Selling Financial Advisory and/or Management Services* (providing non-credit, non-transactional services for a fee).

These five activities make up my general answer to the question: What is banking?

All of these businesses that fall under the heading of "banking" are *simple in concept* but very *complex in implementation.* This is because implementation is of, by, and through *people* and *people organizations.* Implementation of personal services through human beings and human organizations and institutions is inherently a complex chore. *People* are the principal competitive weapon a bank has, and they represent the largest and most expensive resource of the bank.

Key Trends in Banking

What do we expect to unfold in the coming decade? This is a difficult but not impossible question. It is not impossible because some of the trends for the 1980s are already in motion and do not require any "futuristic" skill to see.

I have given you my own framework for defining the broad businesses that constitute banking today. I would like to use that framework now in analyzing business trends for the decade ahead:

1. *Originating Credit Contracts.* One business we are in is that of originating credit contracts. Sometimes these are originated for sale to others, but most often they are originated for the bank's own inventory. Competition in this business is substantial and always growing, but banks continue and should continue to be strong competitors here. We have a substantial reach of facilities and skilled people—which are the principal competitive weapons in the origination business. Looking ahead to the next decade I see:

   a. a major opportunity to originate for placement with other institutions who are better able to inventory certain credit contracts than are banks;

   b. a critical need to be aware of market prices for various credit contracts, since failure to originate at market rates will make placement or sale impossible, and;

   c. a critical need for each bank not only to develop expertise in originations but also to build specialized expertise in the particular categories of credits that make sense for the bank in its market. Without this specialized expertise the bank risks losing out to more expert competitors who understand a particular credit segment extremely well.

   Bankers have not viewed the origination function as a necessarily distinct or critical one. Furthermore, since many bank credit contracts have been originated at below market rates for the bank's own portfolio, it is not clear just how good bank personnel will be when it comes to originating at market rates.

2. *Inventorying Credit Contracts.* A second business we are in is that of inventorying credit contracts. Most of these we originate for ourselves and place in the inventory. Looking ahead, it seems to me that banks will become increasingly

less able to perform this inventory role effectively. This loss of competitiveness will be due principally to the fact that the largest cost of playing this role is the cost of debt and equity to fund the inventory.

Banks are now and will continue to lose out here to competitors who have much lower equity requirements—pension funds, commercial paper market, mutual funds, money market funds, new funds and markets that develop, and foreign banks. These competitors are now able to inventory credit at a lower cost than a bank, and will therefore tend to win out more often than not in the bidding for the assets to place in inventory. I would expect this trend to become more powerful and evident in the 1980s. Unless the United States government decides to reduce bank capital requirements (an unlikely event) there seems little to stop the trend away from banks as inventory holders.

Holding inventory is not a particularly high value-added service, and compensation will be directly related to the riskiness of the assets held, as well as to the financing risk undertaken to fund the inventory.

3. *Financing the Bank.* A third business we are in is that of selling financial instruments to savers as a means of raising funds to carry assets. The past year has most dramatically highlighted the clear inferiority of bank instruments in the competition for savings. This will get worse in the 1980s unless government rules change drastically. I don't expect them to change enough and therefore banks will have to purchase more and more money at market rates through wholesale instruments, as their retail instruments lose competitive effectiveness in terms of price.

4. *Originating and Processing Non-Credit Transactions.* A fourth business is that of originating and processing non-credit transactions. The significant role here is the provision of payments (or funds transfer) services. This is perhaps the most important area to watch in the 1980s because:

   a. Banks have historically had an exclusive franchise on the funds transfer business. This is now breaking down as NOWs, share drafts, money funds, and other institutional arrangements gain momentum.

b. With the exclusive franchise broken, the key to success for commercial banking as an industry—the fact that nearly everyone *needs* a checking account—is now threatened. Banks will not be able to rely on customers coming *to* them. Bank marketing will have to adjust quickly to an environment where the whole customer relationship is up for grabs from several sources, and banks must go *to* the customer.

c. The new funds transfer technology—a marriage of telecommunication and information processing—is one with which bank management is neither experienced nor comfortable. Instead, a whole new set of competitors is possible—and these competitors are very large, sophisticated, and technologically advanced—people like AT&T, IBM, ITT, RCA, GE, TRW, and Dun & Bradstreet. They have the capital and people to dominate any bank. It is by no means assured that the next generation in funds transfer technology will be managed and controlled by banks. After all, the buggy manufacturers did not continue to be responsible for basic transportation after the technology switched to automobiles.

d. The emerging technology is quite capable of bringing funds transfer service right into the home or office—the ultimate in convenience and very threatening to branch overhead structures. In sum, the transactions processing business promises to be full of excitement over the next 10 years.

5. *Selling Financial Advisory and Management Services.* The last business area I mentioned was that of selling advisory and management services. For years banks have been doing this in very selected areas such as trust services. More recently, growing activity in areas like corporate finance, merchant banking, investment counsel, and financial consulting has been noted. Banks will be tempted to enter more and more of this activity in an effort to build non-asset intensive revenues. The principal competitive weapon in this business area is people quality, as these are often highly personalized services. Competition in this business is extremely tough and varied.

The Implications of this Analysis for Banking in the 1980s

What should bank management be doing in the 1980s to ensure superior performance? This is the tough part of the assignment, but let me complete my task by offering you the following prescriptions for successful banking in the decade ahead.

First, it is critical that the bank *perform well.* Long-term return on assets and return on equity must be adequate and sustainable. Capital must be sufficient to permit growth in tandem with business growth, and the principal, most reliable source of capital is internal—from profit generation. Management must set tough financial performance standards and insist on high-quality employee effort. Good performance is essential for many reasons:

- Competitive demands are going to be substantial, and the better capitalized and more profitable firms have all the better chance of survival and success.
- Good performing companies attract good people.
- Good performers have more margin for error, in a decade where this margin in general will be shrinking for the industry.

The 1970s witnessed the beginning of substantial differentiation among bank performers. Indeed, a few large banks even failed. The 1980s will see much more differentiation, with the industry becoming more clearly divided between the excellent and the mediocre. No one wants to be in the latter category. But many will.

Second, to perform well, the bank needs a sound *business plan*—a strategy which:

- is soundly based on a thorough understanding of market demands, costs, and trends;
- takes account of competitors' strengths and weaknesses;
- builds on the bank's own inherent advantages;
- positions the bank so that it is stronger or smarter or with services superior to any competitor in its chosen businesses.

Executive management of any organization has two principal roles. If they perform these roles well, then good performance is highly probable. If they perform them poorly or not at all, then poor performance is nearly inevitable. The two roles are:

1. To define and continually refine a good business concept and strategy for each business they choose to have the bank enter.
2. To implement these strategies by installing good people as managers of key organizational units and to provide direction and control to see that those people perform and generate good performance from the people below them.

Therefore, my *third* conclusion is that good performance through good planning can only be implemented through a *good personnel and good organizational* climate. A bank is only as good as its people—and its leadership of those people. The quality of effort spent on finding, employing, paying, training, and developing people is particularly critical. This personnel effort will become much more demanding. It will be essential to have your business strategies and personnel plans in concert. You cannot accomplish what your people are incapable or unwilling to accomplish.

Fourth, banks are going to have to recruit and hire different kinds of people in the 1980s than they may have been doing in the past. Just as "banking" is a poor description of the various businesses we are in, so too is "banker" a poor description of the people we need. The trend toward specialization of work effort will continue in the 1980s. Banks need good sales people, analysts, programmers, teleprocessing experts, financial staff, systems specialists, loan originators, managers, and many more.

Sharper interviewing and testing will be necessary. New recruiting sources will need to be found. You will have to go out to find the right people—they won't just walk in saying, "I want to be a banker."

Fifth, banks will have to establish different forms of compensation in the 1980s to meet the needs of the different people and business trends. I think sales and other incentive programs will become more important and more widespread—potentially applied wherever good measurement is possible. Salary structures will have to allow for the integration of "non-traditional" hires at more senior levels, as you bring in technical expertise in areas like telecommunications, systems engineering, marketing research, treasury and funding, and sales management, just to name a few disciplines.

Perhaps most important, salaries are going to have to be competitive with the better organizations involved in your mix of businesses. It will not be satisfactory to compare yourself only to "banks" in salary surveys. You must compete with other credit contract originators (mortgage companies, life insurance companies, brokers, commercial credit companies, underwriting firms) or other financial service companies (investment counsellors, securities dealers, etc.). In businesses where people *are* the service, you cannot afford to attract less than the best. If managed properly, "high-priced" people need not be "high-cost" people.

Sixth, the bank's training and development activities will be severely tested in the 1980s. For example:

- A more diverse group of entry hires (in terms of age, race, sex, handicapped, education level) makes "packaged" training almost impossible. Ways to economically provide effective individualized training are necessary.
- It is much less clear today than ever before exactly what training and experience one needs to become a "good banker." There will be opportunity and need for your more talented people to have more diverse experiences—moving in and out from sales to operations to credit to treasury to staff support to management.
- It is not at all clear what is the best "route to the top." I believe strongly it will not be through the more traditional credit areas. More likely it will be considered essential by the end of this decade for the Bank CEO to have solid background in operations and personnel.
- It will become increasingly common for the bank to "outgrow" some of its managers in terms of complexity and competitive pressure. Training and placement need to be prepared for supporting solutions.
- More banks will begin in the 1980s to recognize that people—like plant and equipment—need a certain regular "maintenance and refurbishing." So a regular investment in training and development will need to be made.

Seventh, banks will have to dedicate considerable management time toward building a positive work environment. This requires a whole combination of sound policies, well-trained supervisors, good company communications, good corporate performance, sensitivity to employee attitudes, integrity, and high standards. Those banks that can create and maintain this kind of atmosphere have an intangible asset of rare value in this competitive race for people and business.

Eighth, and most important of all, I see the personnel function in banks assuming greater importance in the 1980s—provided the people responsible for leadership of that function bring their organization to realize the potential for personnel excellence to drive corporate performance.

The challenge is yours. If you fail, either your organizations will suffer or others will be put in to take your places. But if you succeed, as some of you will, the rewards will be that incredibly unique sense of satisfaction that comes from being part of and partly responsible for a human organization that is realizing its potential for excellence. I wish all of you that success.

Suggested Readings

"BankAmerica and Citicorp: The New Banking Forces New Strategies," *Business Week* (July 13, 1981), 56–66.

Banking's Squeeze: High-Interest-Rate Gridlock," *Business Week* (April 12, 1982), 67–85.

Gross, Laura. "Banks Should Focus on Generating Earning Assets, Loans, Say Analysts," *American Banker* (October 25, 1983), 22.

Hanweck, Gerald, A., and Kilcollin, Thomas E. "A Note on Bank Profitability and Interest Rate Risk," Working Paper No. 51, Board of Governors of the Federal Reserve System (July 1981).

Morrissey, Thomas F. "Options, Commitments, and Risk Adjustment," *Federal Home Loan Bank Board Journal,* Vol. 16, No. 7 (August 1983), 15–17.

Nicholas, Arthur. "How a Winning Bank Manages Its Investments," *Bottom Line/Personal* (July 15, 1983), 5.

Tyson, David O. "Response to Each Community's Needs Is Called the Key to Bank Success: Key Banks Chief Stresses Attention to Changing Economies," *American Banker* (October 26, 1983), 3.

Chapter 26

Summary Highlights, Unresolved Issues, and the Outlook

This final chapter takes a look at the expected "end results" of all of the issues and conflict and change that have been explained throughout this book. Each section in this chapter focuses on one aspect of the financial services industry and describes the conditions and changes that are expected to appear during the coming years.

This chapter discusses future legal changes, the future expansion and effects of EFTS, the new situation for bank customers, and the outlook for the institutions in the financial services industry. Then the final section of the chapter presents some concluding comments.

Further Changes in the Regulatory Environment

Sweeping, revolutionary legislation influencing the financial services industry was passed in March 1980 and in October 1982. But there will be other significant legislative and regulatory changes during the 1980s.

New legislation at the national level and in many states will permit wider use of EFT systems. Barriers to both intrastate and interstate branching will continue to be removed, as will legal limitations on the kinds of businesses banks can engage in. In general, these changes will open new opportunities—and more competition—for financial services institutions.

Current practices are rapidly eroding several of the legal restrictions. As time passes, the pressure to remove restrictions will continue to mount. But there is some strong and dedicated opposition to legal changes that would open the financial services institutions to more kinds of business activities, more locations, and increased competitive pressures. So Congress will move slowly.

It is likely that some of the banking laws among the various states will be brought more into line with each other. But these adjustments sometimes will be difficult to achieve as each state legislature responds to the political pressures within its own borders. Strong proponents of "states' rights" and of the "dual banking system" will fight long and hard against those changes that they consider to be encroachments. But reciprocal interstate banking laws will be passed by more states.

The regulators and lawmakers will continue to be concerned about everybody getting into everybody else's business—about the homogenization (or de-heterogenization?) of the financial services industry. The banks, thrifts, securities firms, insurance companies, mutual funds, real estate and credit card companies—all are making aggressive moves to get into each other's businesses. And Sears, J.C. Penney, National Steel, American Can, General Electric and so many others are pushing for a piece of the financial services action. Several of these firms have acquired nonbank banks.

In September of 1983, Fed Chairman Paul Volcker in testimony before the Senate Banking Committee warned that if this situation is left unattended: ". . . you're going to have a mess." Some observers might comment that we already have a mess.

Bank Regulators Can't Turn Back the Clock

The conditions that now exist in the financial services markets are as they are, like it or not. The market is demanding and the institutions are responding—serving the market and making profits in the process. Maybe it looks like "a mess" out there. But we can't turn back the clock.

How nice if we could go back to the early or mid-1970s and begin from there. We could work out a logical, consistent, efficient (etc.) legal and regulatory framework to guide the growing, changing financial services industry. We could provide for a safe, flexible, and efficient system—one that would meet the financial demands of the economy, make monetary policy more manageable, and forestall many of the crisis conditions that occurred in the early 1980s. How great that would be! But it's too late for that. We're here now.

What functions can a financial intermediary perform? What financial functions can Sears perform? The answers to both questions are the same: They both can do just about anything they want to. The barriers between the functions that can be performed and between the financial and nonfinancial companies are just about gone. Anyone who wants to take the initiative can work out a way to do just about anything they wish.

Where—in what geographic locations—can these financial services be offered? Just about anywhere you want to offer them. Those barriers are gone too, effectively. Many have crossed over these barriers. There's no way to turn back that clock, either. All regulatory and legislative decisions from here on are going to have to recognize these new facts of life in the financial services marketplace.

It is very likely that the legal definition of "bank" will be changed to try to deal with the proliferation of nonbank banks. But by the time the legislative barn door is closed, the horse will be long gone. It was already too late even before the Comptroller of the Currency in 1983 announced a moratorium on new applications for nonbank banks.

In October of 1983, the Securities and Exchange Commission (SEC) announced that it was considering overseeing the brokerage activities of the banks and thrifts. Enter another regulator.

We can expect to see increasing regulation imposed in the area of consumer protection. Regulation aimed toward ensuring equal access to credit, truth in lending, and other areas in which bank customers want to be insured a "fair and equitable deal," will become subject to more government scrutiny.

The problems and cost of complying with consumer protection laws and regulations will increase. And there will be continual arguments as to whether or not—or, at what point—the cost (to the consumer) of this maze of regulations equals or exceeds the value of the "consumer protection" gained.

It's likely that there will be regulatory changes regarding international banking and U.S. bank dealings in the Eurodollar market. It also seems likely that the several different federal supervisory/regulatory agencies now overseeing the banking and financial services industries will be consolidated so that the financial services industry will have to deal with only one federal regulatory body. In 1983 Senator Proxmire was pushing his bill, which called for the consolidation of the regulatory agencies.

Depository Insurance Changes

It's likely that there will be some changes in the FDIC and FSLIC insurance programs. There are legislators and regulators who would like to (a) combine the insurance agencies, (b) charge insurance premiums based on the safety (or riskiness) of the depository institution, and (c) reduce the maximum insurance from $100,000 to $50,000 and let the depositor suffer the loss of anything over $50,000. The argument is that this would cause shaky banks to lose their big customers, and this might induce the banks to be more careful to follow sound practices.

The Effects of Expanded EFT Systems

Electronic banking will be expanding more rapidly throughout the remainder of the 1980s. It will be spurred on by interest-bearing transaction accounts, the cost-based pricing of bank services, and increased competition.

Several other factors will help, including: the new consumer protection guarantees of Reg E; the increasing efficiency of EFT technology; the knowledge that has been gained from the EFT experiences of the 1970s and early 1980s; the removal of some of the legal impediments and uncertainties; the increasing cost of manual operations as compared with EFT operations; the increased cost-effectiveness of promotional programs in overcoming consumer resistance when many institutions are attacking the problem simultaneously; and the expanding general awareness that the efficiency of the nation's financial services system requires it.

As customers find that EFT transactions cost them less, they will switch to EFT. As the use of EFT systems expands, not only the financial services institutions but also the businesses, the consumers, and the productivity of the economy will reap significant benefits.

With more efficient electronic payments systems, bank officers and other personnel can shift their energies more toward effective contact with *people*—the customers who need personal contact—and away from the more routine clerical services. Banks can price their electronically performed routine clerical services more cheaply because the services will be performed more efficiently. And banks can price all of their services more accurately to reflect each customer's total relationship with the bank.

Businesses will benefit from point-of-sale (POS) terminals by receiving their money receipts from sales immediately, thus generating larger cash flow balances. And they will be relieved of most of their losses from bad checks.

The widespread use of EFT systems will be another element contributing to the increased competition in the banking environment. This will contribute to the demise of some financial institutions that cannot withstand the competitive pressure.

There appears to be no reason why well-managed small banks cannot survive and also profit from the expanded use of EFT systems. But it is clear that EFT systems will continue to contribute to changes in bank structure, competitive conditions, market shares, areas served, and services rendered by the financial services institutions.

A New Situation for Bank Customers

The most basic change for bank customers is that they are being paid market value for most of the money they leave on deposit and they are paying more for the financial services they require. As the financial institutions pay more for the funds they receive from depositors, they must also earn more to be able to cover their costs.

These higher earnings must come from the combination of (a) higher interest on loans and other investments, (b) charges for the services performed for bank customers, and (c) reduced costs resulting from increased efficiency. The higher interest payments to depositors may be covered by a combination of all three of these, but it is certain that one of the sources will be *higher costs for customer services.*

In this new financial services environment, those who save the most get the most benefit from the changes. Those who save least, who borrow more, and who use more bank services, find themselves in a worse position. The changes increase the rewards of saving and the penalties of borrowing and spending. Perhaps this will induce some people to save more and spend less.

Consumers are feeling the effect of increased competition among the financial services institutions. Customers are being wooed in various ways. They are being offered an increasing variety of more and better financial services, and at costs that are held low by the competitive pressures among the institutions. In general, the financial services markets are more accurately reflecting the true economic circumstances in those markets. The payments made and the charges levied are more accurately reflecting the market values of the deposits received, the loans made, and the services rendered.

Changes in the Financial Services Institutions

The different kinds of financial services institutions (banks, S&Ls, mutual savings banks, credit unions, etc.) are looking more alike. This will continue as the 1980s go by. More of the legal barriers will be removed in the coming years. But this is not to say that all financial services institutions will soon look alike. Far from it!

Many institutions may choose to specialize in one segment or another of the financial services market and will become specialized and highly efficient in their chosen segment. For some, this will help to ensure their success. Managements will recognize that within the new competitive environment they cannot hope to survive if they waste their energies trying to offer the kinds of financial services at which they cannot become highly efficient. Inefficient lines of services will be dropped, and the freed energies and funds will be shifted into segments of the market in which the institution can compete effectively.

Many of the thrifts will become full-service financial units. But it is also likely that many will not—depending on their chosen objectives and their assessments of the special circumstances existing in their own market areas and their own areas of expertise.

In general, the various financial services institutions probably will tend to specialize in areas in which they have been most intimately involved in past years. The larger commercial banks will be likely to continue emphasizing business loans; the S&Ls and mutual savings banks are likely to continue to play an important role in the mortgage loan field; and credit unions are likely to continue to emphasize consumer loans. But all of these institutions are not unlikely to be found providing kinds of financial services with which traditionally they have not been involved. Some institutions may do a complete turnabout—deserting some of their former areas of specialty and developing new specialities that they think will provide them greater opportunities for success in their own customer, market, and competitive environment.

Many Firms Will Disappear

It appears very likely that the number of firms in the financial services industry will continue to decline. In the new competitive environment, firms that are inefficient and that cannot overcome their inefficiencies will be squeezed out. Firms that make the wrong choices about what services to offer, what geographic areas to deal in, and what mixture of assets and liabilities to hold, will not be able to survive. And many firms will decide to merge with others.

The "orderly removal from the system" of the poorly managed and inefficient institutions by healthy competition from the more efficient, better managed firms will contribute to the overall efficiency of the system. This kind of healthy competitive shakeout will result in spillover benefits for consumers, businesses, and the entire economy. But it may be necessary to maintain safeguards to ensure that it is *efficiency* and not just *bigness* that wins out in the competitive struggle.

By the end of the 1980s it is likely that there will be a significantly smaller number of financial institutions in the United States than there is today. But the entire financial industry will be better managed and more efficient. All of us will benefit from that.

Asset/Liability Management Is Critical

The money market conditions of the 1980s are placing new and stringent requirements on the asset/liability managers of the financial institutions. No longer is it possible to assume that the cost of funds will be stable. Therefore, no longer is it possible to safely invest in "fixed rate assets" while holding mostly "variable rate liabilities." Financial institutions now find it absolutely necessary to balance the "interest rate sensitivity" of their asset structure with their liability structure. That is, if market rates go up, the cost of liabilities will go up. So the assets need to be structured so that the return on assets will also go up.

One way to successfully hedge against the threat of interest rate changes is to strive for "matched maturities" between assets and liabilities. If you're a banker and you have an asset that pays a set rate for three years, then try to get a liability that will pay a set rate for three years. And be sure there's a "profitable spread" between what you are paying on the liability and what you are earning on the asset. All financial institutions have moved in the direction of this goal. It is this goal that has resulted in the widespread use of variable-rate mortgages and floating-rate commercial and consumer loans.

We will see more of these variable-rate financial instruments in the coming years. We may even see the introduction of PLAMS (price-level-adjusted mortgages) and PLADS (price-level-adjusted deposits). The value of these would be adjusted to reflect inflation. Milton Friedman recommended this idea in his June 13, 1983, *Newsweek* article (p. 70), and some other economists are supporting it. Maybe this is coming, but it isn't likely that public acceptance of an idea like this will come any time soon.

The Need for Strategic Planning

In this era of open competition in the financial services market, each institution must have a *strategy* guiding its decisions about such things as which markets to serve and which services to offer. It must decide *exactly how* it's going to meet the challenges of the increasingly competitive environment.

It is no longer true that if each function or department in the bank is excellently managed, the total result will be a successful bank. An overall *strategic plan* is essential. Which departments will be expanded? Which cut back or eliminated? Which markets will receive the full effort required for success? Which will be abandoned? The same questions must be answered regarding specific "products" or services: Which to emphasize? Which to eliminate? The ultimate success of each financial services institution will hinge heavily on the wisdom with which these choices are made.

Another strategic question is this: Does this institution wish to be a survivor? Or do we want to be merged into some other institutions? And under what circumstances or conditions? There are few financial institutions that will be able to avoid these questions in the 1980s. So the sooner they begin to think about such things, the better.

Concluding Comments

The changes that are occurring in the banking and financial services industries are truly revolutionary. The financial services institutions have moved into an era of new and different competition. In this environment bank management is going to have to be outstanding. Banks that have mediocre management simply will not survive.

Banks are going to be required to price their services, and price them *realistically.* No longer will the "profitable 20 percent" of the customers carry the cost of providing services to the "unprofitable 80 percent." So the "unprofitable 80 percent" are going to have to pay more for their banking services.

The banks that try to compete by offering below-cost services are not likely to survive. We are now going through a period of trial and error as banks feel their way on this issue. Banks that price their services too high will lose customers and probably will not survive. All banks are hard-pressed to figure out the right prices for their services, caught between the squeeze of costs on the one side and competition on the other. In this process there will be a considerable shakeout of small banks—and perhaps some large ones, too.

No matter what happens during the remainder of the 1980s, and no matter what the ultimate pattern of the results may be, we can all be quite sure of one thing: banking and finance will be interesting and exciting in the coming years. People who enjoy working with challenges, with considerable uncertainty, and where the stakes are high, will enjoy working in banking and being a part of all this.

What happens on these issues is of much more far-reaching importance than just to the banking and financial services industry. The impact is going to be felt throughout the economy—on all businesses large and small, on such things as the rates of employment, income, inflation, and growth in the economy, and on the personal lives of all of us. You, as a thoughtful reader of this book, will be able to understand these changes as they are occurring throughout the decade of the 1980s and beyond.

Suggested Readings

Beck, Felix M. "Daring and Vigilance Are Musts in Today's Market," *American Banker* (October 18, 1983), 27.

"FDIC Enumerates Financial Industry Changes," *Banking Expansion Reporter* Vol. 2, No. 18 (September 19, 1983), 2–3.

Greenspan, Alan. "Onward the Revolution in Financial Services," *Wall Street Journal* (September 16, 1983), 32.

Helyar, John. "Banks Cut Costs, Change Strategies as Deregulation Alters the Industry," *Wall Street Journal* (March 29, 1983), 37.

Kaufman, George, Mote, Larry, and Rosenblum, Harvey. "Implications of Deregulation for Product Lines and Geographic Markets of Financial Institutions," Staff Memoranda 82–2, Federal Reserve Bank of Chicago (1982).

Parker, George G. C. ''Now Management Will Make or Break the Bank,'' *Harvard Business Review* (November-December 1981), 140–148.

''Statements to Congress'' by Preston Martin, Vice Chairman, Board of Governors, on the Regulatory Reform Act of 1983, *Federal Reserve Bulletin* (August 1983), 595–598.

Thygerson, Kenneth J. ''Thrifts and Deregulation: Freddie Mac's Role,'' *Federal Home Loan Bank Board Journal,* Vol. 16, No. 7 (August 1983), 2–6.

Index